CULTURE IN MANCHESTER

MANCHESTER
1824

Manchester University Press

Culture in Manchester

Institutions and urban change
since 1850

Edited by
Janet Wolff
with
Mike Savage

Manchester University Press

Published by Manchester University Press
Altrincham Street, Manchester M1 7JA, UK
www.manchesteruniversitypress.co.uk

British Library Cataloguing-in-Publication Data is available

Library of Congress Cataloging-in-Publication Data is available

ISBN 978 1 5261 0688 9 *paperback*

First published by Manchester University Press in hardback 2013

This edition first published 2016

Printed by Lightning Source

Contents

Figures and tables

Figures

Tables

Contributors

Angela Connelly is a researcher based at the School of Environment and Development at the University of Manchester. She completed her PhD at the Manchester Architecture Research Centre under the supervision of Professor Michael Hebbert and Dr Andrew Crompton. Working closely with the Methodist Church Property Office, her thesis traced the social and architectural history of Methodist Central Halls. She uncovered the key characteristics and significance of a previously undiscovered building type. She is interested in how building types and neighbourhoods adapt over time – both physically and in use – for which the city of Manchester offers an abundance of opportunities for research.

Viv Gardner is Professor Emerita at the University of Manchester. She is a theatre and performance historian, whose work has focused on gender and sexuality in performance at the *fin de siècle*, particularly the exchange between the radical and the popular. A monograph, *Staging the New Sex*, is in preparation. Her interest in Manchester theatre stems from work on Annie Horniman and the Gaiety Theatre, and she contributed a chapter on provincial repertory and touring theatre (1900-1934) for volume 3 of the *Cambridge History of the British Theatre* (2004). She is co-editor with Maggie B. Gale of the series, *Women, Theatre and Performance*, for Manchester University Press.

Andrew Miles is Reader in Sociology at the ESRC Centre for Research on Socio-cultural Change (CRESC), University of Manchester, where he leads a core theme of work on participation, inequality and engagement with the cultural sector. He has previously held posts at the Universities of Keele, Warwick, Cardiff and Birmingham and has published widely on issues of stratification and social mobility. His current research includes studies of everyday participation, cultural élites and cultural policy in the period since 1945 and he has a particular interest in interdisciplinary and mixed methods approaches to social and cultural research.

Stephen J. Milner is Serena Professor of Italian at the University of Manchester, having previously held posts at the University of Bristol and the University of Cambridge. A graduate of history from Cambridge, he undertook his PhD at the Warburg Institute, University of London. Amongst his recent publications are *The Erotics of Consolation: Distance and Desire in the Middle Ages* (2008) co-edited with Catherine Lèglu; *At the Margins: Minority Groups in Premodern Italy* (2005) and *Artistic Exchange and Cultural Translation in the Italian Renaissance City* (2004) co-edited with Stephen J. Campbell. He is currently co-editing *The Cambridge Companion to Boccaccio* for publication on the septcentenary of Boccaccio's birth in 2013.

Michael Powell is Librarian of Chetham's Library in Manchester and is Honorary Archivist of Manchester Cathedral. He has published widely on book history and on the history of the North West.

Mike Savage is Professor of Sociology at the London School of Economics, as well as Visiting Professor at the University of York and Visiting Research Fellow at the University of Manchester, where he was Director of the ESRC Centre for Research on Socio-Cultural Change (CRESC) between 2004 and 2010. His recent books include *Culture, Class, Distinction* (with Tony Bennett, Elizabeth Silva, Alan Warde, Modesto Gayo and David Wright, 2009) and *Identities and Social Change in Britain since 1940: the Politics of Method* (2010). He is also a past managing editor of *The Sociological Review*.

Selina Todd is a Lecturer in Modern British History at the University of Oxford and a Fellow of St Hilda's College, Oxford. She read history at the University of Warwick before studying for her MA and PhD at the University of Sussex. Her research interests lie in the modern history of women and the working class in Britain. Her first book, *Young Women, Work, and Family in England, 1918–1950* (2005), won the Women's History Network Book Prize. She is currently finishing her second book, *The People. A History of the British Working Class in the Twentieth Century*.

Bill Williams was born in Manchester and educated at Stonyhurst College and Trinity College, Cambridge. Following graduation, he spent seven years as an Education Officer in what was then Malaya. On his return to England he worked as a lecturer in history at a teacher-training college in Birmingham, before joining the Education Department at Manchester Polytechnic in 1967, the year of its creation. In 1973 he became director of the Polytechnic's Manchester Studies Unit, a research and archive retrieval centre of his own devising. In the early 1980s he joined the University of Manchester as a member of the Centre for Jewish Studies, where he remained until his retirement in 2006. His written works include *The Making of Manchester Jewry, 1740–1875* (1976) and *'Jews and Other Foreigners': Manchester and Refugees from European Fascism, 1933–1940* (2012), as well as articles and popular works related to Manchester Jewish history. He is currently working on a history of Manchester's black community.

Terry Wyke teaches social and economic history at Manchester Metropolitan University. His recent publications include *The Challenge of Cholera* (with Alan Kidd, 2011) and *Bridgewater 250: The Archaeology of the World's First Industrial Canal* (with Michael Nevell, 2012).

Janet Wolff is Professor Emerita of Cultural Sociology at the University of Manchester, where she directed the Centre for Interdisciplinary Research in the Arts from 2008 to 2010. She returned to Manchester, her home town, in 2006. Before that, she taught at the University of Leeds, the University of Rochester, NY, and Columbia University. Her books include *The Social Production of Art* (1981/1993), *Aesthetics and the Sociology of Art* (1983/1993), *Feminine Sentences* (1990), *Resident Alien* (1995), *AngloModern* (2003), *The Aesthetics of Uncertainty* (2008) and co-edited with Jackie Stacey *Writing Otherwise* (2013). She is currently working on a book combining memoir, family history, transatlantic reflections and visual imagery.

Manchester: city of culture

Mike Savage and Janet Wolff

This collection of essays is premised on the belief that Manchester, through a period of two hundred years and of enormous changes, has been – and remains – an impressive city of culture. The popular version of this view is likely to focus on the more visible moments of innovation – from the proliferation of pioneering cultural institutions associated with the rise of the industrial bourgeoisie in the mid-nineteenth century to the music scene in 'Madchester' in the 1980s – and these certainly are high points in Manchester's history. But this narrative is too easily woven into another story, that of a history of cultural 'decline', from a supposed heyday as a great Victorian city to a provincial cultural centre.

The writer W.G. Sebald, who taught at Manchester University for two years in the 1960s, participates in this story, in his semi-fictional account of the artist 'Max Ferber'. Ferber tells the narrator about his arrival in Manchester in 1945, descending on foot after walking across the moors from Buxton:

> From a last bluff he had had a bird's eye view of the city spread out before him, the city where he was to live ever after. Contained by hills on three sides, it lay there as if in the heart of a natural amphitheatre. Over the flatland to the west, a curiously shaped cloud extended to the horizon, and the last rays of sunlight were blazing past its edges ... Not until this illumination died ... did his eye roam, taking in the crammed and interlinked rows of houses, the textile mills and dying works, the gasometers, chemicals plants and factories of every kind, as far as what he took to be the centre of the city, where all seemed one solid mass of utter blackness, bereft of any further distinguishing features.[1]

The (unnamed) narrator himself, arriving in Manchester in 1966, wanders the city, remarking on the signs of decline and desolation:

> I would regularly be overcome by such a sense of aimlessness and futility that I would go out, purely in order to preserve an illusion of purpose, and walk about amidst the city's immense and time-blackened nineteenth-century buildings, with no particular destination in mind. On those wanderings, when winter light flooded the deserted streets and squares for the few rare hours of real daylight, I never ceased to be amazed by the completeness with which anthracite-coloured Manchester, the city from which industrialization had spread across the entire world, displayed the chronic process of its impoverishment and degradation to anyone who cared to see.[2]

The decline of industry, and notably the cotton manufacturing industry, in the city and region was real enough, but the reader may perceive Sebald's depressing view, as well as his chosen walking routes, as rather selective.[3] Still, Sebald is hardly alone in portraying a city in decline, its physical and cultural assets destroyed or fading into ruin. It is one of the main aims of this introductory essay, as well as of the volume as a whole, to counter this story.

In a well-known, and much cited, essay of 1957, the celebrated modern historian A.J.P. Taylor presents a stark version of this narrative of urban cultural decline, which we contest in this volume.[4] Taylor himself had Lancashire roots, and he moved to the city in 1930 as a lecturer in history at the University of Manchester, where he remained until he left for Oxford in 1938. His essay is generally read as an encomium to the city, praising it as a 'symbol of civilisation' and as the 'last and greatest of the Hanseatic towns', marked by its independent spirit and its energetic cultural life.[5] He names the Hallé Orchestra, the Free Trade Hall, the 'daily newspaper of international reputation' (presumably the *Manchester Guardian*), and the university, 'a rival version to Oxford and Cambridge or what a national University should be'.[6] And yet this praise is grudging, the condescension of a London-centric point of view quite apparent. Before we get to the compliments, Taylor insists on the total lack of aesthetic quality in the fabric of the city, the interiors of buildings, the city's art collection and even, in a rather disturbing aside, the female students in his lectures. ('I used to peer along the serried rows of note-takers in the hope of finding a pretty girl. The only one I ever spotted turned out to be an Italian visitor.'[7]) Against considerable counter-evidence and opinion, he finds Manchester's architecture ugly.[8] On returning to the city, nearly twenty years after living there in the 1930s, he discovers that 'Manchester is quite as ugly as people say. In fact it has got uglier.'[9] He finds that the city's once unique institutions have disappeared or declined – double-decker trams, the tripe shop, Lancashire cheese, a university now slipping to 'second rank', the John

Rylands Library – even the *Manchester Guardian*, on the verge of moving to London. Finally, in another part-reversal of his elegy for the city, and perhaps evidence of his conflicted relationship to his own region of origin, he reflects briefly on certain improvements another twenty years later, on the occasion of the reprint of his essay in 1976: 'The city is now clean and the people have brightened up. The Midland Hotel has emerged a glossy red.' But, he goes on, the Cotton Exchange has closed, the John Rylands Library has been absorbed by the university, the *Guardian* is now a London newspaper. He concludes: 'Manchester has become an agreeable provincial town. It is no longer one of the world's great cities.'[10]

Taylor's account may be perceived as a little idiosyncratic, and certainly by now it has been overtaken by the more serious, less impressionistic, accounts of other historians. Still, although the current volume is not presented as ammunition in a campaign to claim 'great-city' status for Manchester, it is motivated by the desire to make known some of the important, but less well-known, cultural institutions and activities of the city. In order to explore Manchester's cultural history, and its transformations over the decades, we need to work with a broad definition of 'culture', which includes high-art institutions (galleries, orchestras, museums) and at the same time considers other forms (societies and clubs, leisure activities, people's theatre). This volume, with its studies of the Dante Society, Belle Vue Zoological Gardens, the Methodist Mission, and the community theatre group MaD, is intended to provide such a perspective for re-thinking the city's social and cultural topography from the nineteenth century to the present day. Of considerable importance is the cosmopolitan reach of Manchester's cultural institutions, which would defy any simple reading of the city as 'provincial'. Although this aspect is not specifically addressed in many of the papers, an excellent example can be seen in Bill Williams's exploration of the remarkable Manchester International Club.

The question of Manchester's industrial and economic transformation is not the focus of this book; our objective is to demonstrate, and illustrate, the continuing and varied cultural vibrancy of the city throughout the decades. This is something which would remain invisible in a model of history intent on investigating only the major arts institutions and inattentive to the complexity of cultural forms in specific urban settings. Unsurprisingly, London would immediately appear far superior to Manchester on this criterion. (London itself, one could add, would appear impoverished too, if its own multiple cultural practices were excluded by this narrow focus.) But it is not just that alongside the Hallé Orchestra, the Literary and Philosophical Society, the City Art Gallery and the Manchester Museum there have thrived smaller musical societies and theatre groups, as well as local popular cultural practices and pursuits. A 'high culture' perspective also makes it impossible to explore the constant and complex interactions *between* these levels. Middle-class culture is always somehow in dialogue and exchange with working-class culture. This relationship is especially striking in Manchester, as is evident from several of the essays in this volume. In addition, the assumption of separate and distinct (class-based) audiences and participants distorts the reality of social engagement, as several of the essays in this collection make clear. Finally, a dynamic view of social and cultural change, rather than a static account of institutions in particular periods, depends on an open definition of 'culture'. It is with all of this in mind that we present the following essays.

We are therefore challenging any simple notion of the cultural superiority of the metropolitan centre, London. Even within the narrower category of 'high culture' and the arts, Manchester can stake a claim to considerable competition with the capital. Admittedly, the city's art gallery has a collection which cannot compare with the national collections – largely because Manchester's wealth post-dated the days of the Grand Tour and associated purchases of Old Master works (though there have long been many of these in local private collections of members of the gentry and aristocracy in the north-west of England).[11] Nevertheless, the strength of its collection, particularly in Victorian and Pre-Raphaelite art, reflects the moment of bourgeois ascendancy in the early years of the Royal Manchester Institution, and the consolidation of its collection in the formation of the gallery in 1882.[12] The architecture of nineteenth-century Manchester, as already noted, in particular the civic buildings and the warehouses, was in the forefront of building design at the time, and was greatly admired both nationally and internationally. Many of the buildings are still considered superlative works of art.[13] The Hallé Orchestra, the oldest permanent orchestra in Great Britain and a world-class orchestra today, was founded in 1858.[14] And the year before that – in fact the occasion for the first performances of Charles Hallé and his musicians – the 1857 exhibition of Great Treasures of the Nation took place in Manchester, organised by local artists and entrepreneurs and sponsored by Prince Albert and Queen Victoria.[15] This ambitious event, which included more than 16,000 exhibits and attracted more than 1.3 million visitors, is acknowledged to have been the first modern art exhibition in the world, with contemporary forms of hanging and display, and a focus solely on the visual arts (painting, photography, decorative arts), separate from manufacturing goods and machinery and museum objects. The Literary and Philosophical Society, founded in 1781, which survives to the present day, operated from the start as a lively and innovative forum for discussion, with many important philosophical and scientific papers delivered and immediately published in the society's *Memoirs*.[16] Many of these institutions have persisted through the twentieth and into the twenty-first centuries – of course in physical and material form in the case of the buildings, and also in the continuity of events and performances. In the decades since the mid-nineteenth century, other cultural institutions of national and international rank have been created or have found a home in Manchester: the Whitworth Art Gallery, the Royal Exchange Theatre, the Lowry performing arts centre, the BBC Philharmonic Orchestra (now based at Media City, Salford, in Greater Manchester), the Manchester Camerata, the Royal Northern College of Music (with its own wide-ranging and impressive concert and performance programmes), the Cornerhouse cinema and arts centre, and many others. In terms of 'mainstream' cultural activity, therefore, Manchester has certainly maintained a distinguished profile on the national scene.

However, of more interest to the contributors to this volume are the practices hidden from this official story. There has already been important work in this area by historians of Manchester and the region, especially focusing on the city's dynamic youth cultures.[17] But this is not simply an alternative history, of cultures apart from the mainstream, or of the cultures of distinct social groups. On the contrary – one thing that emerges from some of the studies that follow is the inseparability of forms of culture. Viv Gardner's essay on theatre architecture in the early twentieth century demonstrates the importance of looking at the range of theatrical ventures as they coincide – and compete – in physical space and in terms of audiences. The contemporary studies – by Andrew Miles and Selina Todd – take as their central question the complicated interplay between social position and cultural engagement, something never as clear-cut as some accounts have claimed. Both these studies show that the working classes have a much more complicated relationship with the city's cultural institutions than is implied in the common view that it is predominantly the middle classes who are culturally engaged. Janet Wolff's study of the role of the calico printers in the early years of art education shows, in line with other sociological accounts of the emergence of the field of fine art, that the idea of the purity of the aesthetic is always already compromised by its histories in social and political interests. Other essays present in-depth explorations of institutions and associations not previously studied, each with its own oblique relationship to the more visible – and more often recorded – cultural practices of the time: Michael Powell and Terry Wyke's account of the operations of the Belle Vue Zoological Gardens brings to light the role of commercial involvement in cultural provision at an early stage; Stephen Milner's analysis of the social origins of the Manchester Dante Society demonstrates the remarkable links to Italian culture which the city sustained; Angela Connelly's study of the Manchester and Salford Methodist Mission, and in particular one of its key buildings, complicates any simple ideas of religious decline in the early and mid-twentieth century; and Bill Williams's detailed narrative of the origins and early years of the Manchester International Club demonstrates the city's high-profile role in championing internationalist politics in this period. In a volume comprising only eight essays, this book clearly offers a necessarily selective account of Manchester's cultural history. But it is a collection indicative of some of the wider issues we wish to highlight. Each essay illuminates both a moment of cultural involvement and the historic links between past and present. Together, they provide an overview of the city's continuing, and changing, cultural landscape.

This book originated in a series of seminars held under the auspices of the Centre for Research on Socio-Cultural Change (CRESC) at the University of Manchester. This research centre, which is jointly managed with the Open University, was based in the School of Social Sciences in 2004 with large-scale core funding from the Economic and Social Research Council for ten years. This has been the largest ever social science investment with a brief to conduct rigorous research on cultural activities. It has produced the most extensive study of cultural tastes and participation ever conducted in the UK.[18] It has also had a strong interest in analysing the changing historical dynamics of cultural engagement.[19] Much of this work has been in association with organisations in the cultural sector, such as the Department of Culture, Media and Sport, and the Arts Councils, and CRESC has also collaborated with other centres at the University of Manchester with interests in this area.[20] CRESC has always emphasised the need to locate forms of cultural activity in specific local contexts, and since its inception has made a point of focusing on the city of Manchester as a key site for the analysis of the ways in which different forms of art, music and leisure activity are generated and appreciated by diverse audiences. In this context, Mike Savage, as one of the founders and directors of CRESC, invited Janet Wolff, a colleague at the university, to convene and co-ordinate a series of seminars on Manchester in 2008–9. Several of the essays included in this volume were initially papers presented at the seminar, and others are the result of subsequent invitation by the editors. We gratefully acknowledge the financial support of CRESC, through its 'Trajectories of Participation and Inequality' theme, in the editorial preparation of this volume.

As will be clear, the authors who have contributed to the volume represent a range of disciplines: sociology, literature, drama, town planning, history, library studies. The approaches and methods employed are accordingly quite diverse, ranging from archival research to broader historical overview to urban and architectural analysis to ethnographic studies of arts consumers. The essays are presented in more or less chronological order, covering a period of about two hundred years. We believe that this selection of essays across this time period will encourage readers to question simple ideas of urban cultural trajectories, particularly when these are couched in terms of 'rise' and 'fall'. Our hope is that the particular stories told will contribute both to an understanding of cultural practice in its broadest sense and to a recognition of the long-standing and continuing importance of Manchester as a centre of culture.

Many thanks to Rosemary Deller for excellent editorial assistance in the preparation of this volume. Thanks, too, to Michael Powell for suggesting – and providing – the image for the cover of the book.

Notes

1. W.G. Sebald, *The Emigrants*, p. 168
2. *Ibid.*, p. 156
3. Janet Wolff, 'Max Ferber and the persistence of pre-memory in Mancunian exile'.
4. A.J.P. Taylor, 'Manchester'.
5. *Ibid.*, pp. 307, 308.
6. *Ibid.*, pp. 316–18.
7. *Ibid.*, p. 310.
8. *Ibid.*, p. 309. See also John H.G. Archer (ed.), *Art and Architecture in Victorian Manchester*.
9. *Ibid.*, p. 319.
10. *Ibid.*, p. 307.
11. C.P. Darcy, *The Encouragement of the Fine Arts in Lancashire 1760–1860*; John Seed, '"Commerce and the liberal arts": the political economy of art in Manchester, 1775–1860'.
12. R.F. Bud, 'The Royal Manchester Institution'; Stuart Macdonald, 'The Royal Manchester Institution'.
13. Archer (ed.), *Art and Architecture*.
14. The Hallé's claim to be the oldest orchestra in Britain was successfully contested by the Liverpool Philharmonic in 2011. 'Manchester's Halle forced to hand claim of being oldest orchestra to Liverpool Philharmonic after complaint to ASA', *Manchester Evening News*, 19 October 2011: http://menmedia.co.uk/manchestereveningnews/news/s/1462385_manchesters-halle-forced-to-hand-claim-of-being-oldest-orchestra-to-liverpool-philharmonic-after-complaint-to-asa (accessed 21 August 2012).
15. Tristram Hunt and Victoria Whitfield, *Art Treasures in Manchester: 150 Years On*.
16. *Memoirs of the Manchester Literary and Philosophical Society*, Vols 1 and 2.
17. See, for example, Simon Gunn, *The Public Culture of the Victorian Middle Class: Ritual and Authority in the English Industrial City 1840–1914*; Claire Langhamer, *Women's Leisure in England 1920–60*, which includes a case study

of Manchester; and Andrew Davies, *Leisure, Gender and Poverty: Working-Class Culture in Salford and Manchester, 1900–39*.

18 Tony Bennett *et al.*, *Culture, Class, Distinction*.

19 Mike Savage, *Identities and Social Change in Britain since 1940*.

20 In particular, the Institute for Cultural Practices, in the School of Arts, Languages and Cultures.

Bibliography

Archer, John H.G. (ed.), *Art and Architecture in Victorian Manchester* (Manchester: Manchester University Press, 1985).

Bennett, Tony, Mike Savage, Elizabeth Silva, Alan Warde, Modesto Gayo-Cal and David Wright, *Culture, Class, Distinction* (London: Routledge, 2009).

Bud, R.F., 'The Royal Manchester Institution', in D.S.L. Cardwell (ed.), *Artisan to Graduate: Essays to Commemorate the Foundation in 1824 of the Manchester Mechanics' Institution, now in 1974 the University of Manchester Institute of Science and Technology* (Manchester: Manchester University Press, 1974).

Darcy, C.P., *The Encouragement of the Fine Arts in Lancashire 1760–1860* (Manchester: The Chetham Society, 1976).

Davies, Andrew, *Leisure, Gender and Poverty: Working-Class Culture in Salford and Manchester, 1900–39* (Buckingham: Open University Press, 1992).

Gunn, Simon, *The Public Culture of the Victorian Middle Class: Ritual and Authority in the English Industrial City 1840–1914* (Manchester: Manchester University Press, 2000).

Hunt, Tristram and Victoria Whitfield, *Art Treasures in Manchester: 150 Years On* (Manchester: Manchester Art Gallery/Philip Wilson Publishers, 2007).

Kennedy, Michael, *The Hallé 1858–1983: A History of the Orchestra* (Manchester: Manchester University Press, 1982).

Kidd, A.J. and K.W. Roberts (eds), *City, Class and Culture: Studies of Cultural Production and Social Policy in Victorian Manchester* (Manchester: Manchester University Press, 1985).

Langhamer, Claire, *Women's Leisure in England 1920–60* (Manchester: Manchester University Press, 2000).

Macdonald, Stuart, 'The Royal Manchester Institution', in Archer (ed.), *Art and Architecture in Victorian Manchester*.

Memoirs of the Manchester Literary and Philosophical Society, Vols 1 and 2 (Warrington: T. Cadel, 1785).

Savage, Mike, *Identities and Social Change in Britain since 1940: The Politics of Method* (Oxford: Oxford University Press, 2010).

Sebald, W.G., *The Emigrants* (London: The Harvill Press, 1997).

Seed, John, '"Commerce and the liberal arts": the political economy of art in Manchester, 1775–1860', in Janet Wolff and John Seed (eds), *The Culture of Capital: Art, Power and the Nineteenth-Century Middle Class* (Manchester: Manchester University Press, 1988).

Sutherland, W.G., *The RMI: Its Origin Its Character and Its Aims* (Manchester: RMI, 1945).

Taylor, A.J.P., 'Manchester', in *Essays in English History* (Harmondsworth: Penguin, 1976 [originally published in *Encounter*, 1957]).

Wolff, Janet, 'Max Ferber and the persistence of pre-memory in Mancunian exile', in Jean-Marc Dreyfus and Janet Wolff (eds), *Memory, Traces and the Holocaust in the Writings of W.G. Sebald, Melilah: Manchester Journal of Jewish Studies*, Suppl. Vol. 2 (Gorgias Press, 2012): www.mucjs.org/MELILAH/articles.htm#2012Sebald (accessed 6 September 2012).

Calico connections: science, manufacture and culture in mid-nineteenth-century Manchester

Janet Wolff

Indeed chemistry may be, not improperly, called the corner stone of the arts. (Thomas Henry, apothecary, 1781)[1]

Any branch of study ... should be regulated by the practical necessity for such instruction ... I should give them merely such exercises as were necessary for their future pursuits. (William Dyce, first Superintendent of Normal School of Design, London)[2]

I think that there is a good deal of irritation upon the subject; but my own feelings and that of others as largely interested as myself is [*sic*] this, that it is not by technical Art teaching or teaching design that you can improve the manufactures, but by the higher class of Art teaching. (Edmund Potter, calico printer)[3]

Edmund Potter's evidence to the Select Committee on Schools of Art (1864–65) is surprising at first glance. As a manufacturer, with a calico printing works in Glossop, Derbyshire, and a warehouse and office in Manchester, he might be expected to have had a clear interest in the development of an art education with practical goals. At the time of the original Select Committee, set up in 1835 to consider the establishment of art and design schools, it was clear that the primary – perhaps sole – intention was to improve design in industry. A good deal of the pressure had come from calico printers in the Manchester region, frustrated by copyright laws which prevented them from copying designs from abroad.[4] As Geoffrey Turnbull says, it was clearly understood at the time of the initiation of the schools 'that the specific object was the instruction of students in the distinctive principles of ornamental design and its application for the purposes of manufacture, with the object of producing a direct improvement in the designs of our manufacturers'.[5] One suggestion I will make in this essay is that that difference of thirty years – 1835 to 1865 – represented the transformation of art education from an immediate, pragmatic project to a more autonomous concern, in which art for art's sake could now be countenanced. My main interest, though, is in the early part of that process, and in exploring the close connections between manufacture and art education, and also between manufacture and scientific research, especially in chemistry. In both cases, the preliminary stages of consolidation of the two spheres, art education and science, involved a central role for calico printers. More than other manufacturers – for example, cotton spinners – their product depended on both: they needed design for the prints, and they needed scientific knowledge about dyeing. In the middle decades of the nineteenth century, they were instrumental both in advancing the case for art and design schools and in introducing chemists and dye experts to the north-west of England. By the later part of the century, art education and scientific inquiry were firmly institutionalised, their original links with industry superseded. Nowadays these links are barely recalled.

My study is microcosmic, in the sense that it does not make a claim about calico printers in general. The connections I hope to show are clear in the specific cases I consider. More particularly, I think they are there structurally – that is, in the social-historical account of the rise and development of these two areas of intellectual pursuit and their grounding in the economic, financial and political investments of certain key figures. In some ways, this is a rather modest claim. After all, the calico printers were not a particularly large group. For example, Anthony Howe shows 94 calico printing factories in Lancashire in 1841, compared with 1,105 cotton manufacturers.[6] Calico printing was centred on Manchester and its near neighbours, while cotton manufacture covered a much wider area of the north-west.[7] The average size of a calico printing firm in 1841 was 292 employees, though some firms employed more than 500.[8] Nevertheless, those printers who spoke up for art education were very influential. Potter was not alone in this. The Lancashire calico printer James Thomson sat on the council of the London School of Design when it was established in 1837, and the Manchester school was, to begin with, 'supported almost entirely by funds from local calico printers'.[9] What I am interested in is the role of the printers in that moment of early professionalisation in art education, and its counterpart, with its own 'calico connections', in the rise and institutionalisation of chemistry.

The first two volumes of the *Memoirs of the Literary and Philosophical Society of Manchester*, published in 1785 and containing papers read to the society over the previous four years, cover science, economics, manufacture and the arts. Here are some indicative titles: 'An essay on the ascent of vapour'; 'On crystallization'; 'Observations on blindness'; 'On the different quantities of rain which fall, at different heights, over the same spot of ground'; 'A description of a new instrument for measuring the specific gravity of bodies'; 'On economical registers'; 'A plan for the improvement and extension of liberal education in Manchester'; 'Observations on the use of acids in bleaching of linen'; 'Thoughts on the style and taste of gardening among the ancients'; 'On the influence of the imagination, and the passions, upon the understanding'; 'On the comparative merit of the ancients and moderns, with respect to the imitative arts'.[10] As several historians of intellectual life in Manchester have recorded, this late eighteenth-century culture of eclectic inquiry (in which, amongst other things, the same person might give lectures on more than one theme from science, manufacture, the arts and philosophy) did not survive long.[11] By the mid-nineteenth century, the papers delivered to the meetings of the 'Lit and Phil' were almost uniformly scientific. And by the end of the century, each field was highly professionalised and skills and knowledge narrowed (and deepened) in specific spheres, each defined and supported by institutional bodies – college, university, art school, art gallery, and so on. Robert Kargon points out that by 1846 the ratio of scientific to non-scientific papers in the Lit and Phil *Memoirs* was 95 per cent.[12] With the emergence of what he calls the 'devotee-scientist', especially in the 1840s and 1850s, 'the "gentlemanly" brand of amateur science ... was gradually giving way under an assortment of pressures'.[13] The style of presentation, too, changed: the 'literary flourishes' of earlier scientists were abandoned and, with them, the 'taint of amateurism'.[14] T.W. Heyck, citing Kargon's account, summarises this transformation in his overview of the development of literary and philosophical societies in the provinces:

> By the 1830s, the Manchester Literary and Philosophical Society was the most active and important. In the late-eighteenth century it had been a kind of club for the recreation of gentlemen – all amateurs in science. During the early-nineteenth century, the Society changed to reflect the commercial and industrial leadership of the city ... By the 1840s the city of Manchester had attracted a large number of men who sought to combine a devotion to science with industrial employment, and these 'devotees' assumed leadership of the Literary and Philosophical Society.[15]

For Heyck, this particular local story formed part of the great transformation of intellectual life in Victorian England, notably the emergence by the late nineteenth century of a distinct class of intellectuals. Central to this was the expansion and consolidation of professions, with their associated organi-sations, regulations and exclusionary practices.[16] Professionalisation in turn, together with the great expansion of scientific and technological knowledge in the following decades, provided the social and institutional (and perhaps ideological) conditions for the problem identified in the mid-twentieth century by C.P. Snow as the radical divide of the 'two cultures'.[17]

I want to focus, in this essay, on that key moment in the nineteenth century which was the turning point in the encouragement of arts and sciences in urban industrial society. The shift from eclecticism and amateurism to the initiation of professionalisation in both fields can be fairly precisely located in the period between the late 1830s and the early 1860s. Although the trend was, or would become, a national one, Manchester serves as an ideal case study, being in the forefront of economic and social changes in the period.[18] The transformation of the Lit and Phil is the clearest example of these developments, though as we will see, other cultural institutions also serve as registers of the broader changes. The case I want to make is for the central role of the calico printers – manufacturers and merchants – in instigating and facilitating the systematic development of the scientific and artistic fields in the first half of the nineteenth century. Research in dyeing and other chemical processes, as well as the rise of cultural institutions and art education, can be traced to the active and energetic involvement of these men. Although they retained their links with science and scientists as well as sustaining their involvement in and support for the arts, by then art school, college, university and research laboratory had asserted their autonomy from the interests of manufacturers and from the direct involvement of non-professionals. That autonomy, though, was founded in the activities of cotton producers only a few decades earlier.

That easy fluidity of movement between arts and sciences, which within decades came to be seen as mere amateurism, was evident across a range of institutions in early nineteenth-century Manchester. The University of Manchester Institute of Science and Technology had its origins in the Manchester Mechanics' Institution, founded in 1824.[19] Its purpose is made clear in the preamble to the rules:

> The Manchester Mechanics' Institution is formed for the purpose of enabling Mechanics and Artisans, of whatever trade they may be, to become acquainted with such branches of science as are of practical application in the exercise of that trade; that they may possess a more thorough knowledge of their business, acquire a greater degree of skill in the practice of it, and be qualified to make improvements and even new inventions in the Arts which they respectively profess.[20]

Its early years were precarious, despite strong support from a number of businessmen, engineers and bankers, and the solution appeared to lie in diversification. In 1831, the institution introduced classes in landscape, figure and ornamental drawing, and by 1840 'more than half of the lectures were on such subjects as poetry, travel, elocution, drama and history'.[21] As Mabel Tylecote records, most of the members wanted a general education, rather than a narrowly practical one; the library expanded its holdings in literature and history. Musical events, excursions and exhibitions were part of the institution's activities from the early 1830s.[22] Dances and dance classes proved popular too.[23] The transformation of this social-cultural-practical institution into a dedicated technical school occurred later in the century, the result of the expansion of state education in 1870, which negated some of its *raison d'être*, and of the appointment in 1879 of a new secretary, J.H. Reynolds, who re-defined the role of the Institution as a technical school closely related to local industries. By 1883, the original Mechanics' Institution had been transformed.[24]

The Royal Manchester Institution was founded in 1823 on the initiative of a group of artists, soon supported enthusiastically by local gentry and businessmen.[25] The objective was to encourage both exhibition and patronage for local artists. Fund-raising efforts were successful, royal patronage acquired in 1824, and, after a few years of operating in temporary premises, the RMI had its own building, designed by Charles Barry, from 1829. In 1882, when the building and its art collection were taken over by Manchester Corporation – it is now the City Art Gallery – the various activities of the RMI had been in decline, as lectures, art education and honorary professorships found their permanent homes in the dedicated institutions of Owens College and the School of Art. But it is worth noting, for example, the institution of those professorships at the RMI in 1843. Each professor was required to give four lectures each season, and science figured as prominently as the arts and literature.[26] The first two honorary professors, appointed in 1843, were Lyon Playfair in chemistry and Thomas Turner in physiology.[27] An analysis of the subjects of lecture courses given by visiting speakers at the institution from 1835–59 shows a preponderance of science themes – 24 in chemistry, 19 in physiology, 15 in natural history, 7 in geology and 6 in astronomy compared with 14 in music, 14 in art history, 7 in literature and 5 in history.[28] By the last quarter of the nineteenth century, in parallel with developments in science, professionalisation of knowledge had ensured a firm division of specialised function, and the new art gallery was to devote itself to the purchase and display of works of art, to be followed and joined by the Whitworth Art Gallery, founded in 1890.[29] Art education had followed a similar trajectory, from classes taught in a variety of institutions (including the Mechanics' Institution), through the emergence of a School of Design in the late 1830s and decades of debate about the pros and cons of practical design training versus fine art education, to the consolidation of independent art education in the re-named Manchester School of Art in the 1850s.[30]

The development and transformation of cultural and educational institutions in Manchester has by now been substantially recorded, and the story (local as well as national) of increasing specialisation and the rise of dedicated professional organisations has been fully rehearsed.[31] There is a different story, however, concerning the early intersections of art, science and manufacture that deserves to be told: one focusing on the central role of calico printers and other manufacturers in both science and art (or, more particularly, chemistry and the visual arts) in the first half of the nineteenth century. In the following sections of this essay I want to explore some of these connections, to suggest that we need to supplement both intellectual and institutional histories with a socio-economic account. This traces developments in art and science to the needs of the key manufacturing activities of the region, and particularly cotton manufacture and calico printing, and then engineering.[32] The push for both scientific knowledge (notably, but not only, chemical advancements in dyeing) and art education was very closely tied to manufacture, as the key involvement of merchants, calico printers and engineers in scientific and cultural institutions makes clear; the first epigraph to this essay illustrates this point of view. After a brief discussion of the early close connections between manufacture and chemistry, I will turn to the rather complex relationship between calico printers and cultural activities – part pragmatic, part disinterested – and then focus on the important case of the expansion of art education in Manchester. As historians of this field have shown, and as manifest in my second epigraph, art education in England had its origins in the needs of trade and manufacture, with the motivation to improve design in industry, in view particularly of competition with France. And as we would therefore expect, manufacturers and merchants took an active interest in this, always with an eye to the pay-off for industry in the training of artists. However, as I will explain towards the end of this essay, the utilitarian outlook was by no means philistine; nor was it absolute. Taking the calico printer Edmund Potter as a case study, we find him making the case for fine art training against those in favour of design and ornament – my third and final epigraph is an illustration of this.

Owens College was founded in Manchester in 1851, the precursor to the establishment of the Victoria University in 1880. From the mid-nineteenth century, scientific research was increasingly conducted in the academy.[33] Although the first four chairs were in classics, mathematics and natural philosophy, mental and moral philosophy, and English language and literature, a half-time chemistry chair was also established from the beginning, with funds to set up a chemistry laboratory. New science degrees were introduced in 1858, and

Henry Roscoe, appointed to the chemistry chair in 1857, worked to build a highly successful school, with strong links to local industry and the community.[34] Although the academic scientists were also likely to be members of the Literary and Philosophical Society, and sometimes presented papers at its meetings, this was a very different scenario from the earlier years, as Kargon points out:

> Unlike the great devotees such as Joule, Hodgkinson, Fairbairn, and Leigh, and those new professionals of the 1840s who remained in the city ... the academics eschewed what they saw as narrow parochialism and sought the larger stage. They published their important work exclusively in the journals which would capture international attention: while they did not ignore local duties, *Science* made upon them more compelling demands.[35]

At the same time as research in chemistry was being established in the academy, it was becoming detached in another way from the amateur and pragmatic practices of a civic mix of doctors, merchants, apothecaries and manufacturers, namely in the establishment of the chemical industry in Manchester, particularly in the field of dyeing. Independent, often immigrant, chemists set up important businesses in the region – Roberts, Dale & Co. in 1859, Levinstein & Co. in 1864, Clayton Aniline Co. in 1876 and several others.[36] Their work, as with Roscoe's research projects at the college, remained closely linked with the needs of local industry, particularly calico printing, and an active interchange between manufacturer, industrial chemist and academic scientist persisted through the nineteenth century.[37] But the emergence of the new professions, with the material and institutional consolidation of their identities, presented a radical contrast with the early decades of the nineteenth century.

The integral relationship between manufacture and chemistry is very evident in that earlier period, to which the origins of both industrial and academic science can be traced. At the turn of the nineteenth century, calico printers for the most part did their own bleaching, before bleaching became a commercial proposition and a distinct trade.[38] As Joseph H. Park and Esther Glouberman point out, the expansion of the textile industries from the late eighteenth century soon mandated innovations in chemistry to match the technological inventions in cotton manufacture:

> Just as hand looms became inadequate for the demand put upon them once the spinning-jenny had been invented, so, in a similar manner, bleaching, dyeing, and related chemical processes, but for improvements, must have been incapable of meeting the most urgent requirements as soon as textile inventions increased the output of woven goods ... In short, interdependence of mechanical and chemical developments led a mid-nineteenth-century writer justly to remark 'that almost every mechanical process requires the aid

of chemistry in its development while chemistry would be nothing without the aid of the machines, the furnaces, and the vessels which permit the processes to be carried on'.[39]

Thomas Barnes, Minister of the Cross Street Chapel, urged manufacturers, in a paper delivered to the Manchester Lit and Phil in 1782, to extend their knowledge of chemistry.[40] Thomas Henry, a year earlier, had spoken about the importance for merchants and manufacturers of developing their knowledge beyond trade, cultivating leisure and art pursuits, studying history and the classics, and, among other sciences, taking a special interest in chemistry – the 'corner stone' of the arts ('arts' here meaning the practical arts of manufacture):

> Bleaching is a chemical operation ... The same may be said of the arts of dying [sic] and printing, by which those beautiful colours are impressed on cloths, which have contributed so largely to the extension of the manufactures of this place. How few of the workmen, employed in them, possess the least knowledge of the science to which their profession owes its origin and support! The misfortune is, that few dyers are chemists, and few chemists dyers.[41]

The dependence of cotton manufacture and calico printing on the expertise of dyers meant that the north-west of England was, and long remained, the main area of concentration of the dye-making industry.[42] Indeed, many chemists, including from overseas (particularly Germany), came to the region because of the opportunities offered in relation to the textile industry.[43] Some chemists, who later went on to found their own companies or to work in the chemical industry, were brought to the region by calico printers themselves: an 1839 guide to Manchester noted that 'the arts of dyeing and calico printing have received great assistance from ... men of science ... and in most of the establishments in which these arts are wrought out, some one or more of the principals, are, practically, men of eminent scientific talent'.[44] Lyon Playfair, educated as a chemist in Scotland and Germany, was brought to Manchester by the calico printer James Thomson as manager of his dyeing works in Clitheroe.[45] (As we have seen, he become an Honorary Professor at the RMI in 1843, and he later went on to a distinguished career in London and Edinburgh, as a professor and a member of parliament, and eventually to a baronetcy.) Thomson himself had good scientific knowledge, as had John Mercer, another calico printer. Indeed, among the foremost chemists were some who had started out as calico printers, notably John Dale, Heinrich Caro and Henry Edward Schunck.[46] R. Brightman, in a paper read at the Manchester Section of the Society of Chemical Industry in 1956, makes a strong claim: 'The first modern chemical industry arose ... to meet the demands of the expanding textile industry for dyes, mordants and, above all, an efficient and rapid bleaching agent.[47] Roscoe's predecessor, the first professor of chemistry at Owens College, Edward Frankland, used his inaugural address in 1851 to stress that although the study of chemistry was essential in its own right ('for its own intrinsic excellence'), its great value for manufacture was clear: 'The advantages of chemistry to the chemical manufacturer, the dyer and the calico printer are almost too obvious to require comment.[48] But by that date, the actual segregation of science from manufacture was well under way.

In his 1957 essay on Manchester, published in *Encounter*, A.J.P. Taylor famously manages to damn the city he sets out to praise. Before commending the entrepreneurial brilliance of the 'merchant princes', and the independence of spirit of the people of Manchester and its region, he dismisses in a couple of sentences their taste in art and architecture. These new 'Renaissance' men, he claims, 'lack one Renaissance characteristic. Of all dominant classes, they were the least equipped with aesthetic taste.[49] Others have challenged his peculiar dismissal of Manchester's nineteenth-century architecture ('Manchester is irredeemably ugly', he says); its neo-Gothic town hall and its Italianate warehouses have long been admired by many.[50] More generally, it is not difficult to record the keen involvement in the arts by many of the bankers, merchants and manufacturers in the city throughout the nineteenth century, as well as their influential role in establishing each of Manchester's important cultural institutions. Their motives were a very productive mix of cultural taste with professional interests.

Studies of art patronage have established very clearly that manufacturers and other members of the middle class, in Manchester as elsewhere, were active as collectors and patrons from the early nineteenth century.[51] They also played an important role in the planning and execution of the great 1857 Art-Treasures Exhibition in Manchester, as lenders and organisers.[52] They were active in the Manchester Lit and Phil and in the RMI. Among the first 100 names on the membership list on the founding of the RMI were twelve owners of spinning mills and twelve dyers and calico printers; a tally of membership of the latter for the years 1825, 1845 and 1865 reveals numerous merchants, cotton spinners and manufacturers among the doctors, lawyers and bankers.[53] Throughout the century, too, manufacturers and engineers were great supporters of the musical life of the city. Hermann Leo, a Manchester calico printer, was instrumental in bringing Charles Hallé to Manchester from France in 1848; the conductor's permanent orchestra took shape ten years later, after performances at the 1857 exhibition. And the engineer Henry Simon was one of three businessmen who guaranteed the continuation of the Hallé Orchestra after the death of Charles Hallé in 1895.[54] Many other examples could be cited of the influential – and historically crucial – role of the new class in Manchester's cultural life. Here I want to turn to one specific area, and to return more particularly to calico printers and their connection with the development of art education in the city.

There were art classes in Manchester in the early years of the nineteenth century – at the Mechanics' Institution, as we have seen, and at the short-lived Manchester Academy for Drawing and Designing (1803–5).[55] But the initiative for a systematic art education was a national one, with the first School of Design opening in London in 1837. The Manchester School of Design, opened the following year, was the first provincial school in the system.[56] The original motivation for the schools was clear in the remit of the 1835–36 Select Committee, 'appointed to inquire into the best means of extending a knowledge of the arts and of the principles of design among the people (especially the manufacturing population) of the country'. The first paragraph of the committee's report, while noting the general lack of encouragement for the arts, stresses in particular the consequent problems for manufacture:

> The want of instruction in design among our industrious population, the absence of public and freely open galleries containing approved specimens of art, the fact that only recently a National Gallery has even been commenced among us, have all combined strongly to impress this conviction [that the arts receive little encouragement] on the minds of the Members of the Committee. In many despotic countries far more development has been given to genius, and greater encouragement to industry, by a more liberal diffusion of the enlightening influence of the Arts. Yet, to us, a peculiarly manufacturing nation, the connexion between art and manufactures is most important; – and for this merely economical reason (were there no higher motive), it equally imports us to encourage art in its loftier attributes.[57]

Indeed, despite a quarter century of debate about fine art versus practical training (with the former gradually winning out), a later Select Committee, convened in 1864–65 to review the Schools of Art, still refers to this crucial link with trade and manufacture:

> The period 1837 to 1852 may be regarded as a period of experiment, during which the Government endeavoured to supply a remedy for the alleged artistic inferiority of our manufactures to those of other countries, by the maintenance of a head school of Design in London, and of a limited number of provincial schools in the chief seats of manufacturing industry, with a view to the direct promotion of Ornamental Art.[58]

Quentin Bell and Stuart Macdonald have traced in detail the comings and goings of directors, inspectors and heads of school at the Normal School of Design in London, as well as the intervention from the very beginning of members of the Royal Academy (and notably the energetic promoter of art education, Benjamin Haydon) on the question of whether the schools should devote themselves to practical (ornamental) training or offer a broader fine arts education.[59] Another Select Committee on Schools of Design, in 1849, which took evidence from manufacturers amongst others, discussed the question and affirmed the need for industrial art education, noting that only a small proportion of designers working in industry had been educated at the schools.[60] One problem had been that those attending the schools, as Edmund Potter reported in his evidence to the 1865 Select Committee, tended not to be artisans, but 'families of people of the better class, residing in the neighbourhood'.[61] Although the debates continued, nationally and locally, by 1852 the Schools of Design had been re-designated Schools of Practical Art, in which the emphasis was on education in drawing, not design.[62]

The alignment of different interested groups on the issue makes fascinating reading. Cecil Stewart records a petition presented in 1850 by drawing masters and artists who had not found employment at the Manchester School of Design, arguing on the side of a narrower design training. Amongst other things, it notes:

> That the School was supposed to improve design for calico printing and that the government grant was given on this ground and this only.

> That the Manchester School of Design is a total failure and that the calico printers are dissatisfied with its results and that the masters themselves have publicly confessed its failure as an auxiliary to trade.

> That this lamentable result has been occasioned by the perversion of the School into an ordinary drawing academy.[63]

Even after the official change from Design School to Art School, objections appeared in the press. Stewart quotes Gabriel Tinto, who says: 'The moment the artisan student is taught to be an artist instead of a draughtsman, his mind becomes unsettled and aspirations arises in his bosom calculated to lead him out of the sure and solid path of commerce into the thorny and devious tract which leads to Fine Art.'[64] On the other hand, in 1845 students at the Normal School of Design in London submitted to the Board of Trade a challenge to the management of the school, among their grudges the objection that they were being guided into 'humbler occupations' – this despite the fact that on entering the school they had been obliged to accept that training was purely industrial, and to declare that they had no intention of becoming artists. Losing their case, they were again required to undertake 'to become designers for industry and nothing else'.[65] In all this, the calico printers were central, from the early debates about art education, through various committees, on the boards and councils of schools, and in the fraught issue of fine art/practical design. For the most part, they retained a dual commitment: to strong support for art education, with all its benefits for industry; and to the value of a fine arts training. The latter was notable in the context of their obvious investment in the supply of good designers.[66]

The 1835–36 Select Committee took evidence from merchants and manufacturers, including from the textile industries, in discussing the problem of the superiority of French design to British.[67] When the London School was established a year later, its council included the Manchester calico printer, James Thomson; later Thomson played a key role in the shift of emphasis from design to high art at the London School.[68] Thomson, together with Potter, was instrumental in setting up the Manchester School of Design (which had its own educational debates and wavering fortunes over its early decades, before its secure establishment by mid-century).[69] Both retained a national role in relation to art education, and though they were thus accredited because of their work – and needs – as calico printers, neither took the side of an industrial design education in either the national or the regional debate:

> Paradoxically, the manufacturers on the council of the Manchester School, especially the art-loving philanthropists Edmund Potter and James Thomson, were not in favour of a vocational school. They were proud of their art school … and thought that a fine art influence was what the artisans in calico printing needed.[70]

Potter, though we cannot assume he was typical of all Manchester calico printers, makes an illuminating case study of the particular links between manufacture and design in these decades. Records of his views provide an insight into a certain logic with regard to art education. Born in 1802, the son of a Manchester merchant, Potter established his printworks in 1825 at Dinting Vale, Glossop, in partnership with a cousin. The company's warehouse was in the centre of Manchester.[71] In his evidence to the 1864–65 Select Committee, he was able to claim that, having been engaged in calico printing for more than forty years, he was probably the largest producer in the world.[72] His successful career in the textile trade brought him various forms of recognition, including a medal of honour for his company at the 1855 Paris Exhibition, election as a Fellow of the Royal Society in 1856, and national recognition in various consultancy roles in relation to manufacture and design. At the Great Exhibition of 1851 in London, he was Reporter to the Jury for the Class on printed and dyed fabric.[73] In 1861 he was elected to parliament, representing Carlisle as a Liberal member. In Manchester, he was engaged in many cultural and institutional bodies: elected to the Lit and Phil in 1826, a member of the committee of the Athenaeum in 1835, a member of the first Grand Jury after the constitution of Manchester as a borough in 1838 (one of six calico printers), on the Executive Committee planning the Art-Treasures Exhibition of 1857 and President of the Chamber of Commerce in 1859.[74] He was also politically active in a number of campaigns, notably the repeal of the Corn Laws in the early 1840s.[75] Professionally, the work of his company was acknowledged by inclusion in the Great Exhibitions in 1851 in London, in Paris in 1855 and in Manchester in 1857.[76]

Potter's involvement in the question of art education dates at least from the early years of the schools of design.[77] He participated in the initial planning meeting for a Manchester School, in January 1838, and when the School opened in October that year he became a member of its Governing Council; in 1855 he took over as President of the school, by then known as the Manchester School of Art.[78] In his evidence to the 1864–65 Select Committee, he answers an opening question about the application of art to manufacture:

> I have watched it very closely for 40 years, partly from necessity, and partly from taste. I have done a good deal with the pencil myself in early life. I have watched the application of Art to the production of articles of manufacture for that entire period. I have taken a great interest naturally in all the Schools of Design, and, in fact, in everything relating to Trade Art and design, in my own and other manufactures, for the last 40 years.[79]

He went on to give detailed evidence about the origins of the school, its financial arrangements in terms of subscriptions, government aid, and student fees and payment to its masters, before turning back to the question of what was, or ought to be, taught in the school. His answer to a question about 'the general feeling of the manufacturers of Manchester with reference to the value of the school' is particularly interesting, recording his own change of mind, as a calico printer, about the question of technical training:

> It has been felt to be of very slight value. I will give the facts as briefly as I can: I have been connected, more or less, with the school from 1838 to 1861; perhaps for the last three or four years I have not paid the same close attention to it as formerly, but I have been aware of what has been going on. I admit that, as far as I was concerned, I advocated, first of all, technical teaching, and accordingly the object put forward in our first address was, the promotion of better designing; but my conclusion afterwards was, that technical teaching had a bad effect upon taste and art generally. I know nothing more distressing, or more annoying, or more degrading to an artist of any taste than to have to bring himself down to draw the sort of designs that the calico printers want to supply their demands.[80]

As he says in the answer quoted at the beginning of this essay, his view is that manufacture is likely to benefit more from a high art training.[81] As mentioned earlier too, he reports that the majority of students attending the Manchester School are in any case not destined to work in manufacturing:

> I do not deny that designers have gone into the school who have become figure drawers, and we have produced some artists of a high class, but not any great designers; we have produced artists, but not trade artists.[82]

He goes on to tell the committee that the only chance the school would have of local financial support would be as an art school, not a design school.[83] Arguing that government funds would be better spent supporting local technical schools, he suggests that Manchester would supply the necessary support for a school of high art. He holds his own in this exchange, in the face of a rather supercilious metropolitan prejudice:

> What do you mean when you speak of having a School of High Art at Manchester; do you mean one like the Royal Academy? – Yes, like the Royal Academy; I mean a school of pure Art …

> Do you think that Manchester would contribute the necessary funds for such a school? – If the connection with Kensington is thrown away, I think and I hope that the people of Manchester will do so.

> Do you think that the situation of Manchester is favourable for a school of high Art? – I think there is a great demand for modern Art in the district, and we have also sent out a great many first class artists from the School of Art in Manchester.

> Do you think that the sights and sounds in which people are surrounded in Manchester are favourable for the cultivation of taste and the perception of beauty? – Our school has succeeded very well in turning out artists of a high class.[84]

Potter's argument for a fine art school depends on a number of points: first, that the School of Design/School of Art in any case did not attract many artisans, who would be better placed to learn appropriate skills in a technical school; second, that there is a strong case for an art school, to educate taste and to train professional artists; and third, that the general elevation of taste which an art school (together with other local art institutions like an art gallery) would achieve should in any case benefit design indirectly. In a lecture he gave to the Society of Arts in 1852 he had made the case that the calico printer must not go beyond popular taste in designing the goods, giving examples of certain contemporary prints whose success was short-lived because they anticipated by too much the development of consumer taste.[85] Manufacturers, he suggests, must respect the preferences of 'the working and middle classes', who require 'quiet, modest, and useful' designs and 'cling to an inoffensive taste'.[86] But, he goes on, a more general art education will raise the standards of taste in the population and create a more adventurous demand for material goods.[87] Over the thirty years of his active involvement in questions of manufacture and art education one can see both the evolution and the consistency of his commitment, both to design improvements in calico printing and to the support of the arts and aesthetic ventures in Manchester. Although he is, of course, only one manufacturer among many, in him we can see in detail the changing role of the calico printer in the story of the professionalisation of art education: from active initiation, based on vested interest, to considered support for the emergence of this area of the aesthetic sphere, based on the civic engagement and refined taste of an enlightened member of the new middle class.[88]

During the nineteenth century the sciences and the arts developed their own professional and institutional characters, which materialised in college departments, dedicated branches of the chemical industry, art organisations, museums and art schools. In Manchester, by the end of the century, many of these retained their links with local manufacture in practice or in historical memory – even today the centrality of the textile industry is evident in the collections of the Whitworth Art Gallery and the Museum of Science and Industry, and the courses taught at the School of Art (now part of Manchester Metropolitan University). The case I have been making in this essay is that the well-known story of the professionalisation of intellectual life during this period should be supplemented by another social history: one that foregrounds the 'calico connections' that started the process in the early decades of the century and then continued to develop new relations with both chemistry and art education, adjusting along the way to the transformations they had helped to set in train.

Thanks, for advice, suggestions and comments, to Stella Butler, Laura Doan, Helen Rees Leahy, Jackie Stacey, Steve Milner, John Pickstone, Mike Savage, John Seed and an anonymous reviewer for the *Bulletin of the John Rylands University Library*. Thanks to my brother-in-law, David Kaiserman, for letting me raid his library of books about Manchester.

Notes

1 Thomas Henry, 'On the advantages of literature and philosophy in general, and especially on the consistency of literary and philosophical with commercial pursuits', p. 25.

2 Evidence to 1849 Parliamentary Select Committee on the School of Design,

quoted in Stuart Macdonald, *The History and Philosophy of Art Education*, p. 118.

3 Edmund Potter, Evidence to the Parliamentary Select Committee on Schools of Art, 1864–65, para. 2241, p. 126.

4 Geoffrey Turnbull, *A History of the Calico Printing Industry of Great Britain*, pp. 134–48.

5 *Ibid.*, pp. 148–9.

6 Anthony Howe, *The Cotton Masters 1830–1860*, p. 2. Howe's study of 351 textile masters, over the period 1830–60, includes 36 calico printers. See also Turnbull, *A History of the Calico Printing Industry*, Appendix Two, for a list of English calico printers in 1840, all of them in Manchester and the north-west (pp. 423–6). Turnbull also cites Edmund Baines's 1835 *History of the Cotton Manufacture in Great Britain* as estimating that calico printing represented 6.5 per cent of the total cotton trade (p. 82).

7 Howe, *The Cotton Masters*, p. 1.

8 *Ibid.*, pp. 4–5, 15.

9 *Ibid.*, pp. 289–90.

10 *Memoirs of the Manchester Literary and Philosophical Society*, Vols 1 and 2.

11 Thomas Barnes and Thomas Percival were particularly polymathic in this respect. See Richard Holmes, *The Age of Wonder: How the Romantic Generation Discovered the Beauty and Terror of Science* for a study of the intersections of science and the arts in the late eighteenth century.

12 Robert H. Kargon, *Science in Victorian Manchester: Enterprise and Expertise*, p. 45. C.P. Darcy makes the same point: 'In the early nineteenth century when the presence of Dalton dominated the meetings of the Manchester Literary and Philosophical Society, papers on science ousted all others': C.P. Darcy, *The Encouragement of the Fine Arts in Lancashire 1760–1860*, p. 98.

13 Kargon, *Science in Victorian Manchester*, p. 34

14 *Ibid.*, p. 78

15 T.W. Heyck, *The Transformation of Intellectual Life in Victorian England*, pp. 57–8.

16 *Ibid.*, pp. 21–2.

17 C.P. Snow, *The Two Cultures*.

18 Important earlier studies of social and cultural change in Manchester include A.J. Kidd and K. W. Roberts eds., *City, Class and Culture: Studies in Cultural Production and Social Policy in Victorian Manchester* and Simon Gunn, *The Public Culture of the Victorian Middle Class: Ritual and Authority in the English Industrial City, 1840–1914*.

19 In 2004 UMIST merged with the Victoria University of Manchester to form the University of Manchester.

20 Dame Mabel Tylecote, 'The Manchester Mechanics' Institution, 1824–50', p. 55.

21 Cecil Stewart, 'Art in adversity. A short history of the Regional College of Art, Manchester', p. 3; Kargon, *Science in Victorian Manchester*, p. 24.

22 Tylecote, 'The Manchester Mechanics' Institution', pp. 65, 72–3.

23 M.J. Cruickshank, 'From Mechanics' Institution to Technical School, 1850–92', p. 136.

24 *Ibid.*, pp. 142, 144, 146.

25 S.D. Cleveland, 'The Royal Manchester Institution: its history from its origin until 1882'; W.G. Sutherland, *The RMI: Its Origin Its Character and Its Aims*; R.F. Bud, 'The Royal Manchester Institution'; Stuart Macdonald, 'The Royal Manchester Institution'; Darcy, *The Encouragement of the Fine Arts in Lancashire*, especially Chapter IV which focuses on the RMI and is rather strangely titled 'Liverpool's Rival', pp. 63–79.

26 Cleveland, 'The Royal Manchester Institution', p. 15.

27 Kargon, *Science in Victorian Manchester*, p. 90

28 Bud, 'The Royal Manchester Institution', p. 125.

29 Francis W. Hawcroft, 'The Whitworth Art Gallery'.

30 Stewart, 'Art in adversity', p. 10; Quentin Bell, *The Schools of Design*, especially pp. 110–22; Macdonald, *The History and Philosophy of Art Education*, pp. 84–95 and Chapter 14, 'The swing to fine art', pp. 263–8.

31 Kidd and Roberts (eds), *City, Class and Culture*; Ann Brooks and Bryan Haworth, *Portico Library. A History*; John H.G. Archer (ed.), *Art and Architecture in Victorian Manchester*; D.S.L. Cardwell (ed.), *Artisan to Graduate: Essays to Commemorate the Foundation in 1824 of the Manchester Mechanics' Institution*; and other sources cited throughout this article.

32 Kargon notes that engineers increasingly figured in the Literary and Philosophical Society after 1840: *Science in Victorian Manchester*, p. 48.

33 *Ibid.*, Chapters 5 and 6: 'Academic science: Owens College born and reborn' and 'University science: Arthur Schuster and the organization of physics in Manchester'.

34 *Ibid.*, pp. 156–7, 169, 175–82.

35 *Ibid.*, p. 164.

36 L.F. Haber, *The Chemical Industry during the Nineteenth Century*, pp. 166–7. See also M.R. Fox, *Dye-makers of Great Britain 1856–1976: A History of Chemists, Companies, Products and Changes*, Chapter II: 'Ivan Levinstein (1845–1916): early years' and Chapter XIV: 'Lancashire's pioneers'.

37 For example, Ivan Levinstein was involved in Owens College and the Victoria University, as well as the Mechanics' Institute and the Technical School: Fox, *Dye-makers of Great Britain*, pp. 27ff; an early meeting of the committee to discuss the establishment of a college in Manchester included calico printers Richard Cobden, Edmund Potter and R.H. Greg as well as other manufacturers and merchants; and those involved in planning for an extension to Owens College in 1867 included businessmen and industrialists as well as scientists: Kargon, *Science in Victorian Manchester*, pp. 154, 191.

38 Joseph H. Park and Esther Glouberman, 'The importance of chemical developments in the textile industries during the Industrial Revolution', p. 1153.

39 *Ibid.*, pp. 1143–4.

40 Thomas Barnes, 'On the affinity subsisting between the arts'.

41 Henry, 'On the advantages of literature and philosophy', pp. 26–7.

42 Fox, *Dye-makers of Great Britain*, p. 125. As Kargon says, 'The cotton industry, the staple of Manchester, had long possessed a reputation for requiring chemists for its ancillary industries': *Science in Victorian Manchester*, p. 135.

43 Fox cites R. Brightman as believing that Levinstein 'was attracted to Blackley [in Manchester] because of its proximity to the textile dye-houses and printworks of Lancashire and the West Riding of Yorkshire. He would also know of the availability of the raw materials for dye-making in the Manchester area': Fox, *Dye-makers of Great Britain*, p. 2.

44 Kargon, citing Love and Barton's 1839 guide, *Manchester As It Is*: *Science in Victorian Manchester*, p. 135.

45 *Ibid.*, p. 88.

46 Fox, *Dye-makers of Great Britain*, pp. 97, 126; Kargon, *Science in Victorian Manchester*, pp. 95, 137.

47 R. Brightman, 'Manchester and the origin of the dyestuffs industry', p. 86.

48 Edward Frankland, 'On the educational and commercial utility of chemistry', quoted in Kargon, *Science in Victorian Manchester*, p. 159.

49 A.J.P. Taylor, 'Manchester', p. 309.

50 See John H.G. Archer, 'Introduction', in *Art and Architecture in Victorian Manchester*, p. 27.

51 Dianne Sachko Macleod, *Art and the Victorian Middle Class: Money and the Making of Cultural Identity*, especially pp. 88–110; Elizabeth Conran, 'Art collections', pp. 65–80; John Seed, '"Commerce and the liberal arts": the political economy of art in Manchester, 1775–1860', pp. 45–81; and the earlier publication, Darcy, *The Encouragement of the Fine Arts in Lancashire*, especially Chapter VII, 'Lancashire collections', pp. 122–55.

52 Tristram Hunt, 'Manufacturing consent: the 1857 Art Treasures Exhibition in historical context'; Ulrich Finke, 'The Art-Treasures Exhibition'.

53 Bud, 'The Royal Manchester Institution', pp. 121, 123.

54 Michael Kennedy, *The Hallé 1858–1983: A History of the Orchestra*, pp. 3, 7.

55 Stewart, 'Art in adversity', p. 3.

56 Bell, *The Schools of Design*, especially pp. 100–22; Macdonald, *The History and Philosophy of Art Education*, especially pp. 84–95.

57 *Report of Select Committee on Arts and Manufactures*, 1836.

58 *Report of Select Committee on Schools of Art*, 1864.

59 Bell, *The Schools of Design*; Macdonald, *The History and Philosophy of Art Education*.

60 Bell, *The Schools of Design*, chapter XII, pp. 224–39, especially p. 235.

61 Potter, Evidence to Select Committee, paras 2264, 2267.

62 Macdonald, *The History and Philosophy of Art Education*, Chapter 8, especially p. 176.

63 Stewart, 'Art in adversity', pp. 9–10.

64 Quoted in Stewart, 'Art in adversity', p. 10. Gabriel Tinto, an art critic for the *Manchester Guardian*, was a pseudonym for the landscape painter and art teacher, George Wilfred Anthon (1810–59).

65 Bell, *The Schools of Design*, pp. 163–5.

66 John Seed has recorded the employment of a number of artist-designers by the calico-printing industry in the period 1775–1860: Seed, '"Commerce and the liberal arts"', p. 61.

67 Macdonald, *The History and Philosophy of Art Education*, pp. 67–8.

68 Bell, *The Schools of Design*, pp. 66, 181.

69 The report of the 1849 Select Committee stated that Manchester had been 'the most signal failure while it ought to be the most important School we have'. Quoted in Bell, *The Schools of Design*, p. 235. See also *Ibid.*, pp. 111–12 for Potter's and Thomson's role in founding the Manchester School.

70 Macdonald, *The History and Philosophy of Art Education*, p. 86.

71 John G. Hurst, *Edmund Potter and Dinting Vale*, pp. 2, 4.

72 Potter, Evidence to Select Committee, para. 2207.

73 Hurst, *Edmund Potter*, pp. 27, 37, 21.

74 *Ibid.*, pp. 6, 13, 15–16, 39, 43.

75 *Ibid.*, pp. 18–19.

76 *Ibid.*, pp. 22, 27, 39.

77 Although his membership is not mentioned by Bell, Macdonald or Hurst, the report of the 1835–36 Select Committee on Arts and Manufactures, which first established art schools in Britain, includes a Mr Potter in its list of committee members; given the government's primary concern with design in industry (several textile and other merchants were called to give evidence), and Potter's already high profile and interest in the question, it is possible that it is him. *Report of Select Committee on Arts and Manufactures*; Macdonald, *The History and Philosophy of Art Education*, p. 67.

78 Bell, *The Schools of Design*, p. 111; Hurst, *Edmund Potter*, p. 32.

79 Potter, Evidence to Select Committee, para. 2209. Potter, by then an MP, was also a member of the committee, as well as a respondent.

80 Potter, Evidence to Select Committee, para. 2234. In answer to a later question, para. 2258, he refers again to his change of mind: 'I admit that at first I was an advocate for technical teaching; I very soon changed my opinion.'

81 See note 3.

82 Potter, Evidence to Select Committee, para. 2238.

83 *Ibid.*, paras 2246–50.

84 *Ibid.*, paras 2283–7.

85 Edmund Potter, 'Calico printing as an art manufacture', pp. 48–50.

86 *Ibid.*, p. 51.

87 *Ibid.*, pp. 58–60. As part of this general improvement, Potter cites illustrated periodicals like the *Illustrated London News*.

88 We know that Potter's friend and fellow calico printer, James Thomson, whom he mentions in his 1852 address as the foremost manufacturer in Lancashire

and who was equally active in the Manchester School of Design, shared his views in favour of a fine art education; Potter, 'Calico printing as an art manufacture', pp. 16–18; Bell, *The Schools of Design*, pp. 66, 115–17, 128–9.

Bibliography

Archer, John H.G. (ed.), *Art and Architecture in Victorian Manchester* (Manchester: Manchester University Press, 1985).

Baines, Edward, *History of the Cotton Manufacture in Great Britain* (London: R. Fisher and P. Jackson, 1835).

Barnes, Thomas, 'On the affinity subsisting between the arts', in *Memoirs of the Manchester Literary and Philosophical Society*.

Bell, Quentin, *The Schools of Design* (London: Routledge and Kegan Paul, 1963).

Brightman, R., 'Manchester and the origin of the dyestuffs industry', *Chemistry & Industry*, 4 (26 January 1957), pp. 86–91.

Brooks, Ann and Bryan Haworth, *Portico Library. A History* (Lancaster: Carnegie Publishing, 2000).

Bud, R.F., 'The Royal Manchester Institution', in Cardwell (ed.), *Artisan to Graduate*.

Cardwell, D.S.L. (ed.), *Artisan to Graduate: Essays to Commemorate the Foundation in 1824 of the Manchester Mechanics' Institution, Now in 1974 the University of Manchester Institute of Science and Technology* (Manchester: Manchester University Press, 1974).

Cleveland, S.D., 'The Royal Manchester Institution: its history from its origin until 1882, when the building and contents of the Institution were presented to the Manchester Corporation and became the City Art Gallery'. Printed by direction of the Council, and presented to the Governors at the Annual General Meeting, Monday 28 September 1931.

Conran, Elizabeth, 'Art collections', in Archer (ed.), *Art and Architecture in Victorian Manchester*.

Cruickshank, M.J., 'From Mechanics' Institution to Technical School, 1850–92', in Cardwell (ed.), *Artisan to Graduate*.

Darcy, C.P., *The Encouragement of the Fine Arts in Lancashire 1760–1860* (Manchester: The Chetham Society, 1976).

Finke, Ulrich, 'The Art-Treasures Exhibition', in Archer (ed.), *Art and Architecture in Victorian Manchester*.

Fox, M.R., *Dye-makers of Great Britain 1856–1976: A History of Chemists, Companies, Products and Changes* (Manchester: Imperial Chemical Industries PLC, 1987).

Gunn, Simon, *The Public Culture of the Victorian Middle Class: Ritual and Authority in the English Industrial City 1840–1914* (Manchester: Manchester University Press, 2000).

Haber, L.F., *The Chemical Industry during the Nineteenth Century* (Oxford: Clarendon Press, 1958).

Hawcroft, Francis W., 'The Whitworth Art Gallery', in Archer (ed.), *Art and Architecture in Victorian Manchester.*

Henry, Thomas, 'On the advantages of literature and philosophy in general, and especially on the consistency of literary and philosophical with commercial pursuits' (2 October 1781) in *Memoirs of the Manchester Literary and Philosophical Society.*

Heyck, T.W., *The Transformation of Intellectual Life in Victorian England* (London: Croom Helm, 1982).

Holmes, Richard, *The Age of Wonder: How the Romantic Generation Discovered the Beauty and Terror of Science* (London: Harper Press, 2008).

Howe, Anthony, *The Cotton Masters 1830–1860* (Oxford: Clarendon Press, 1984).

Hunt, Tristam, 'Manufacturing consent: the 1857 Art Treasures Exhibition in historical context', in Tristram Hunt and Victoria Whitfield, *Art Treasures in Manchester: 150 Years On* (Manchester: Manchester Art Gallery/Philip Wilson Publishers, 2007).

Hurst, John G., *Edmund Potter and Dinting Vale* (Manchester: Edmund Potter and Company Limited, 1948).

Kargon, Robert H., *Science in Victorian Manchester: Enterprise and Expertise* (Manchester: Manchester University Press, 1977).

Kennedy, Michael, *The Hallé 1858–1983: A History of the Orchestra* (Manchester: Manchester University Press, 1982).

Kidd, A.J. and K.W. Roberts (eds), *City, Class and Culture: Studies of Cultural Production and Social Policy in Victorian Manchester* (Manchester: Manchester University Press, 1985).

Macdonald, Stuart, *The History and Philosophy of Art Education* (London: University of London Press, 1970).

Macdonald, Stuart, 'The Royal Manchester Institution', in Archer (ed.), *Art and Architecture in Victorian Manchester.*

Macleod, Dianne Sachko, *Art and the Victorian Middle Class: Money and the Making of Cultural Identity* (Cambridge: Cambridge University Press, 1996).

Memoirs of the Manchester Literary and Philosophical Society, Vols 1 and 2 (Warrington: T. Cadel, 1785).

Park, Joseph H. and Esther Glouberman, 'The importance of chemical developments in the textile industries during the Industrial Revolution', *Journal of Chemical Education*, 9:7 (July 1932), pp. 1143–70.

Potter, Edmund, 'Calico printing as an art manufacture'. Lecture read before the Society of Arts, 22 April 1852 (Manchester: Johnson, Rawson, and Co., 1852).

Potter, Edmund, Evidence to the Parliamentary Select Committee on Schools of Art, 28 April 1864 (House of Commons Parliamentary Papers Online, 2005).

Report of Select Committee on Arts and Manufactures (1835–36), Parliamentary Papers, 1836.

Report of Select Committee on Schools of Art (1864–65), Parliamentary Papers, 1864.

Seed, John, '"Commerce and the liberal arts": the political economy of art in

Manchester, 1775–1860', in Janet Wolff and John Seed (eds), *The Culture of Capital: Art, Power and the Nineteenth-Century Middle Class* (Manchester: Manchester University Press, 1988).

Snow, C.P., *The Two Cultures* (Cambridge: Cambridge University Press, 1998 [1959]).

Stewart, Cecil, 'Art in adversity. A short history of the Regional College of Art, Manchester'. Address to the Royal Manchester Institution (Manchester: Council of the RMI, 1954).

Sutherland, W.G., *The RMI: Its Origin Its Character and Its Aims* (Manchester: RMI, 1945).

Taylor, A.J.P., 'Manchester', in *Essays in English History* (Harmondsworth: Penguin, 1976 [originally published in *Encounter*, 1957]).

Turnbull, Geoffrey, *A History of the Calico Printing Industry of Great Britain*, ed. John G. Turnbull (Altrincham: John Sherratt and Son, 1951).

Tylecote, Dame Mabel, 'The Manchester Mechanics' Institution, 1824–50', in Cardwell (ed.), *Artisan to Graduate*.

Counting the coppers: John Jennison and the Belle Vue Zoological Gardens

Michael Powell and Terry Wyke

In spite of the fact that it closed its gates to the public over a generation ago, Belle Vue remains one of Manchester's best-known popular attractions. Its memory has been kept green by a number of local historians in books and on websites and by sporadic campaigns in the local press for it to be brought back.[1] Nostalgic reminiscences of visiting Belle Vue – of the zoo, the shilling bobs and the rest – were a commonplace in the Manchester oral history projects begun in the 1970s[2] as well as in the columns devoted to local history in the *Manchester Evening News*.[3] It is thus surprising to note that Belle Vue has not attracted a major published academic study. Even the rise of the social history of leisure and leisure studies since the 1970s has not resulted in a substantial monograph.[4] There have been a small number of dissertations on aspects of the zoo's history but little else.[5] In the considerable research completed into leisure in the North West during and since the industrial revolution, Belle Vue, if mentioned at all, has been confined to a walk-on part, a place to illustrate an argument.[6]

Most nineteenth-century visitor attractions in Manchester have left little in the way of a documentary record. For Belle Vue however, we are fortunate to have a large business archive generated and maintained largely by successive members of the Jennison family who were responsible for creating and managing the zoological gardens. This includes financial records, day books, cash books, invoices and accounts and other business papers relating to the organisation and administration of the complex, as well as guides, photographs and other ephemera.[7] These papers were deposited in Chetham's Library, Manchester, between 1929 and 1939 by George Jennison, grandson of the founder, John Jennison, along with a narrative history of the zoo, 'A Century of Lancashire Open Air Amusements, 1825–1925', which, he claimed, was written from news items, private records and personal experience. To protect members of the family, this was not to be consulted until twenty-five years after his death. This short essay cannot cover all aspects of the history of Belle Vue, and certainly does not attempt to list or record all of the attractions of the site, but seeks to make the point that the archive allows Belle Vue to be studied in detail and in a depth that is open to few other nineteenth-century cultural institutions. It uses the archives to emphasise what was the fundamental feature of Belle Vue from its foundation by John Jennison in 1836 until the business was sold in 1925.

The keynote is money. Belle Vue was first and foremost a business, an entertainment business in a world of increasingly commercialised leisure. Profits were made out of providing entertainment for all classes who could afford the entrance fee. George Jennison recalled that 'the money counting was rather a boring business'.[8] Each Sunday the family would gather to count the week's takings. This became such a time-consuming task that a special sieve was made to separate the coppers from the silver. The coins were bagged, finding a ready market among local employers and shopkeepers who never questioned that there would be 200 sixpences in a Belle Vue five-pound packet. There was a neat symbolic circularity in the arrangement whereby the very money workers spent at Belle Vue in one week was paid out to them in wages in the following week. Manchester's mills spun cotton yarn; Belle Vue manufactured amusement.

Beginning in the eighteenth century one can trace in Manchester, as in other provincial towns, the opening of pleasure gardens. These gardens, as Peter Borsay has argued, followed the example of London where Ranleagh Gardens and, above all, Vauxhall Gardens, under the dynamic entrepreneurship of Jonathan Tyers, became the most successful and most influential.[9] In their design and in the amusements provided they followed London, their development based in part on first-hand experience of the London gardens as well as reading the metropolitan news that featured so prominently in the rising provincial press. Norwich had four pleasure gardens by the 1760s.[10] The parvenu northern towns followed. Both Liverpool and Newcastle-upon-Tyne had their Ranleagh Gardens by the 1760s whilst Birmingham took the alternative nominal route by opening its Vauxhall Gardens.

Manchester's best-known pleasure garden was opened by Robert Tinker in about 1795. Located in the suburb of Collyhurst close to the river Irk, its origins were similar to many others in that it began as a small garden attached to a public house. Tinker increased its attractions, re-naming it Vauxhall Gardens after the end of the Napoleonic wars. Tinker provided the conventional entertainments interspersed with more spectacular ones: firework displays and balloon ascents.[11] In spite of high admission charges, the gardens appear to have

Figure 1: John Jennison (1793–1869), founder of Belle Vue. Small photographic print c.1860.

become popular among a working class with disposable income and a desire for spectacle and novelty. Efforts were made to maintain its appeal to the more genteel visitor but as its popularity increased Tinker struggled to maintain the social tone. As in other industrialising towns there was to be a long struggle to control the excesses of plebeian leisure:[12] in the early nineteenth century Whitsun, the first major holiday of the year in Manchester, was described as a time when 'pleasure reigns with almost Parisian despotism'.[13] Tinker's Gardens, as it was popularly called, also faced competition from other pleasure gardens. These recreational spaces were an important part of an expanding urban leisure economy though they have tended to be overlooked both in contemporary accounts and by historians. Publicans with contiguous land invested in popular amusements, including sporting attractions. The White House, New Stretford Road in Hulme attracted customers with cricket and wrestling matches.[14] An admission charge was usual though as at the Victoria Gardens in Tanner's Lane in Seedley it was returned in refreshments.[15] Gardens in rising suburban districts could cause friction, as was the case with the Grove Inn Gardens when complaints were made about drunken visitors disturbing residents on a Sunday.[16] John Jennison entered the world of commercialised leisure by developing a pleasure garden on land next to his house in Adswood, between Stockport and Cheadle. Birds were displayed in the garden and these proved to be sufficient an attraction that the family house was converted into a pub. The location was also important – it was rural but within easy walking distance for Stopfordians looking to escape the town.

John Jennison's experience at Adswood appears to have inspired him to establish a more ambitious leisure business. In 1835 he took the opportunity to lease and develop the land on which the Belle Vue Tea Gardens stood. The location was decisive. The thirty-five acre site was on the boundary of Ardwick and Kirkmanshulme, some two miles from the centre of Manchester. Jennison was naturally cautious and Belle Vue was initially taken on for a six-month trial. Fortunately for him, the trial period proved successful and the following December he took a ninety-nine-year lease on the property at an annual rent of £135. A year later he sold his property and gardens at Adswood, committing himself fully to his new venture.

Some twenty acres of the site at Belle Vue had been used for rabbit coursing and these were considered by Jennison to be the most valuable part of the business. But Jennison's aim from the first was to establish a zoo and a botanical garden in addition to the racing and shooting ground. In doing this Jennison was aware that Manchester lacked such an attraction, an omission that was pointed up by the commercial zoo established in Liverpool by Thomas Atkins in 1833 as well as proposals to establish zoological gardens in Leeds. Jennison, an imitator rather than innovator, was probably more influenced by Liverpool than the metropolis, though he would have been aware of the success of the Surrey Zoological Gardens which blended the conventional entertainments of the pleasure garden and a zoo.[17] His menagerie at Adswood was modest and his financial situation did not allow him to add significantly to it. Thus when the new zoo opened in May 1837, the paying customer was invited to inspect a variety of plumage birds and small common mammals.[18] The zoo and gardens were seen as attracting a different audience from those who attended the race grounds and the attraction was set up as separate and distinct from the sporting grounds. Jennison regarded the sporting grounds, where the events were to include athletic races and pigeon shooting matches, as attracting a different class of visitor from those who would visit the gardens. The latter included the more genteel middle classes and the 'steadier, more serious section of the working class' who would pay the 3d admission.[19] At first the gardens and zoo offered only non-alcoholic refreshments[20] but Jennison soon relented. Drunkenness was incompatible with his idea of the gardens and zoo but it was an important source of revenue in any commercial pleasure gardens.

Jennison's venture was an enormous risk. He had no business partners and had taken out a substantial mortgage of £3,000 on the Belle Vue site, on top of the mortgage on his Stockport property. Moreover, within months of opening Belle Vue he was faced with a new competitor, the Manchester Zoological Gardens, situated in the fashionable suburb of Higher Broughton, which offered the public a far larger and more sophisticated attraction. In comparison to Jennison's motley assembly of birds and mammals, Broughton boasted among other things a lion house, a bear pit and an elephant house. Fortunately for Jennison, what might have been a major competitor was to fail. The Manchester Zoological, Botanical and Public Gardens Company set out to develop a zoo on land leased from Reverend John Clowes. Opened in May 1838, it enjoyed an initial period of success but it soon became evident that it had underestimated the costs of establishing and operating a zoo. In spite of public pronouncements that it would provide a much-needed improving recreation for the working classes, its principal audience were the polite middle classes. But the latter did not turn up in sufficient numbers to fund the zoo. Sunday opening would have helped, but Clowes had forbidden this when selling the land. The idea of establishing a botanical garden also alienated potential supporters, putting Broughton in competition with the Manchester Botanic Gardens in Old Trafford which had the patronage of some of the most powerful local individuals.[21] The zoo's finances deteriorated, resulting in the company becoming one of the more publicised local bankruptcies in the maelstrom of 1842. Unfortunately for Jennison, his own financial problems meant that he was unable to take advantage of the bargain prices at the auction of the animals and fittings in November 1842.[22]

The opening of the Manchester Zoological Gardens had threatened Belle Vue's very survival and within a few months Jennison had been forced to default on the payments of his leases. After his initial trial success, Jennison had chosen to expand his land by taking out additional leases on adjacent lands, but payment on these could not be serviced. Broughton had made a profit of over £2,000 in its first six months of operations and had attracted over 42,000 visitors,[23] many of whom were the sort of patron that Jennison wished to attract. Jennison struggled on but made little money and even the rabbit coursing events failed. All this was occurring as Manchester experienced one of the severest economic depressions of the century and by 1842 the cotton towns were convulsed by protests and riots that resulted in a crackdown on the gathering of large crowds.[24] In December of that year matters were brought to a head when bankruptcy proceedings were brought against him. His debts were estimated at £1,340 and his total assets at £652 plus the value of the gardens themselves.[25] Two attempts were made to sell the gardens early the following year but no sale took place. Some of the creditors seem to have decided that their best chance of recovering the money was to wait for it to be earned by Jennison.[26] The land on which the zoo was situated was attractive but disposing of animals, birds, cages, and twelve tons of hay was more problematic. Jennison obtained a loan to pay off his creditors, and one creditor allegedly accepted his dues in beer brewed by Jennison. Jennison was forced to cut back and to give up the additional land that he had leased.

Jennison learned the lessons of his lucky escape from bankruptcy and above all, the need to avoid expanding too quickly. Competitors had to be taken seriously and their success and failure analysed. Good ideas introduced elsewhere would be introduced into Belle Vue. Jennison brought out an advertisement for the Zoological Gardens at Belle Vue, thanking the public for their liberal support, and detailing additional attractions. Notably, a quadrille band, conducted by the Cambrian family, which had proved very successful at Higher Broughton, was available every day during Whitsun week.[27] More significantly Jennison laid emphasis on the importance of transport to the zoo: excursions were laid on for large parties by railway for 3d. The Longsight railway station, which had initially disappointed Jennison by being located too far from the entrance, was now merely 300 yards from the grounds, thanks to a new entrance which he opened. A regular omnibus service from Manchester and back was organised on race days.

In addition to the quadrille band, Jennison also seemed to have picked up other ideas from the bankrupted Manchester Zoological Gardens: the need for more exotic animals, the value of a large water feature, and the importance of opening on a Sunday. Jennison brought out the first guide in 1847 – a four-penny guide printed by George Bradshaw of Manchester. The guide confirmed the central role of the zoo: from then on Jennison's venture would be known as Belle Vue Zoological Gardens. Jennison expanded the collection of animals with the introduction of dingos, raccoons, monkeys, wildcats and armadillos which were displayed in a series of cages and paddocks instead of being grouped together in a large shed. Geese and swans were present on the lake, as at Higher Broughton, and aviaries were situated at various points throughout the garden. The zoo proved to be a star attraction and helped to set the social tone of the gardens.[28] A visit, for example by Sunday Schools, could be defended on the grounds that it combined 'instructive recreation' with entertainment. Moreover these educational visits by schools, mechanics' institutes and societies helped create an image of Belle Vue as a safe place, one posing no threat to the authorities in the uneasy post-Chartist period. Yet there were limits, and in the Belle Vue guide of 1847 Jennison made it clear

Figure 2: Group of children, keeper and orang-utan outside the monkey terrace in the early 1900s, an illustration of the way in which animals were not simply left to be observed in cages but were brought out to be handled by the public.

that whilst the plant and animal specimens had Latin names, they were not listed. More exotic and dangerous animals were purchased and through adept publicity some of these became local celebrities.[29] New arrivals were seen as crowd-pullers. An orang-utan, for example, was said to have more than paid its way (it had cost £150) during the six weeks that it lived in the zoo.[30] Moreover the zoo provided the public with an opportunity to interact with the animals. Animals were brought out of cages to be petted or ridden and some large animals featured in large firework displays or pyrodramas. Setting a zoo in the middle of a garden, alongside other entertainments and amusements, not least sporting events and the evening firework displays, made the zoo completely different from other leisure attractions.

Jennison continued to provide sport.[31] Part of his unused land was converted into tracks for horse racing and athletics and Belle Vue quickly became one of a number of sporting venues in the town. Betting was profitable, and the family received commission of 6d in the pound, but racing also caused Belle Vue problems of policing, with sporting events attracting a less respectable clientele. The size of the gardens, however, lent themselves to spatial or temporal zoning, allowing the rough and the respectable to be kept apart, and those who entered the races had a separate entrance from those entering the gardens. Admission charges for the races were also increased, presumably to deter the more undesirable elements. This recognition of separate consumers of leisure was one of the pillars of Belle Vue's success. In fact Jennison had already begun to identify specific groups of pleasure-seekers, having in his very first season provided a field and a band free of charge to local Sunday Schools who chose to bring their children there in the all-important Whitsun holidays.

Investment also went into other attractions, many of which had their roots in the previous century. Once again, Jennison was willing to follow the examples set by other gardens, and ballooning continued to provide a spectacle, drawing the crowds even after a fatal accident in 1852. In 1851 Jennison began to employ George Danson, one of the country's leading scenery painters, who had worked on the firework displays at Surrey Gardens and London Colosseum, to design a series of huge tableaux, covering 30,000 square feet, depicting military episodes and historical events. Danson and his sons began with 'The Bombardment of Algiers', a suitably patriotic military battle of 1816, and the panoramas became another star feature of the gardens. Re-enactments were accompanied by ever more brilliant firework displays, and employed large casts of extras. The historical tableaux were changed each year, providing the spectacle and novelty the public demanded.[32] By staging these shows as the last attraction of the day, Jennison ensured that the people coming into the zoo and gardens would stay as long as possible, and would spend more on refreshments and other paid attractions. Firework displays lasting twenty minutes were shown at peak times, and ran from Whit Monday until 5 November, a total of eighty shows a season. Those who wished to get the best views were required to pay extra for a seat in the covered grandstand and a penny guide which explained the event taking place before them.

Jennison also recognised the importance of investing in the garden, and land which he had been forced to give up in the early 1840s was bought back and the gardens enlarged. Re-invested profits drove the business. New features such as a maze (claimed to be modelled on that of Hampton Court) were built, whilst the size of the grounds allowed the creation of new walks. A viewing tower built in 1882, if not quite the equivalent of the seaside pier, did provide a vantage point to survey the surrounding countryside. A trip on the boating lake may not have been as exciting as a boat trip around a seaside bay but in the winter the lake provided a skating rink. Like the maze and the museum of curiosities, the boat ride also had the advantage of incurring an extra charge to customers. Money was also spent on renovating existing buildings. Each year parts of the gardens that had not brought in sufficient return or parts that were simply in the way were removed to make space for new attractions or a better through-flow of visitors. This policy of continuous improvement

Figure 3: Postcard, probably from the 1920s, of the wooden outdoor dancing platform located in front of the lake and firework island. The picture shows men dancing together, the subject of frequent complaints about dancing at Belle Vue.

usually took place in the winter months, and was based on an awareness of the importance that visitors placed on the general appearance of the grounds and the buildings and that improving the layout of the gardens helped ensure that people would return.

Establishing a series of regular events was seen as one way to attract the public year after year. Annual flower shows began to be organised in the 1840s, but it was to be the brass band contests, the first of which was in 1853, that proved especially popular. The Belle Vue contests became a key event in the banding calendar, helping to strengthen Lancashire and Yorkshire's predominance nationally.[33] But as the regular advertisements in the press for contests for handbell ringers, dog shows, bird shows, horticultural shows and small sporting matches indicate, there were many other events by which Belle Vue could increase attendances. By the 1870s political demonstrations and trades union gatherings had become part of Belle Vue's programme of events.

Of all the attractions that Jennison introduced after the zoo, perhaps the most important was the dancing pavilion. Belle Vue provided dancing out of doors and inside the pavilion. The hiring of a superior band was no less important. Dancing took place throughout the day but was especially popular in the evening, and the dancing platform was located next to the lake, opposite the island on which the pyrodramas were staged. The two biggest evening attractions were thus placed next to one another. The dancing platform, however, was one part of the gardens where there was the opportunity for social mixing, and as early as 1848 there were complaints in the Manchester press that coarsely dressed 'roughs' were attempting to dance with middle-class ladies.[34] Postcards issued by the Jennisons depict well-groomed middle-class couples attired in evening dress, gliding around spacious dance floors, but the reality was somewhat different. There were repeated complaints throughout the nineteenth century that working-class men were dancing together.[35] The creation of the grandstand, entry to which was a penny, may have been an attempt by the Jennisons to separate the classes in the dancing arenas, but the evidence suggests that the meeting of the classes on the dance floors was not a serious problem. The Jennisons operated a dress code and a day trip to Belle Vue saw workers in their Sunday best.[36] Rather the problem was that groups of working men, often worse for wear from drink, would take over the dance floor.

Central to the success of Belle Vue was its geographical location. In the 1830s it was on the frontier of the built-up town, and within walking distance for the majority of the population. As the city spread outwards it could no longer be considered in the country, but it remained highly accessible. It developed excellent transport links. At first there was no direct railway link but there was an omnibus service. Details were included in the Belle Vue guides of the locations of cabstands and the prices to and from the gardens. To protect the gardens from ever-growing encroachment the Jennisons continued to acquire land on which they built houses and commercial properties. By 1905 the Belle Vue estate consisted of 68 acres within the walls with a further 42 freehold acres and 58 leasehold acres acquired outside the walls. By investing in land the Jennisons protected Belle Vue from growing assimilation into Manchester and the rural character of the site survived at least into the early twentieth century.

It was to be the railway that most obviously transformed Jennison's business. As the railway network developed across the north of England Jennison was one of the first leisure entrepreneurs to negotiate the running of cheap excursion trains. These negotiations became crucial to the business as, importantly, they involved including admission to the gardens in the price of the excursion ticket. These arrangements reflected Jennison's understanding of the importance of the 'wakes' calendar which meant that different towns took their holidays in different weeks over the summer.[37] In 1854 Jennison received payments totaling £709 from the railway companies. By 1876 this had increased to almost £5,000. Admission money was of course only part of the benefit of the excursions. Once inside the excursionists had to pay extra for admission to the various attractions as well as for refreshments. In 1837 the closest station to Belle Vue was London Road, a couple of miles from the gardens; by the 1880s there were four stations close to the gardens, the first having opened in June 1840.[38] Belle Vue Station was built specifically to serve the gardens and opened in 1876. Locals might still choose to walk to Belle Vue but they did so in the knowledge that one could now reach it by train from the centre of Manchester in two minutes.

The railway extended the catchment area that Belle Vue served, making the gardens less dependent on the pleasure-seekers of Manchester and the immediate towns. We can track in the local press across the north of England and the Midlands references to visits to Belle Vue, especially at Whitsun. By the 1870s, as competition from the seaside for the all-important day-trippers continued to increase, the Jennisons were making more effort to attract new customers, and they had some success in establishing Belle Vue as a tourist destination among the Welsh. Excursion trains ran from as far as Neath and Milford Haven in South Wales to Belle Vue, a twelve- or fourteen-hour trip each way, and it was a Welshman who was reputed to have replied to the question 'Where is Manchester?', that it was a place near Belle Vue. By the 1850s excursionists had become and were to remain a key part of the visiting public: according to George Jennison, in one year alone over 325,000 people came on excursions to Belle Vue.[39]

The railway, of course, was also a threat to the gardens, providing as it did the opportunity for potential visitors to travel to other parts of the country. The extraordinary rise of the Lancashire seaside resorts in the Victorian period was facilitated by the railways, with the annual seaside trip depending on a railway network and companies willing to operate excursion trains. This took some business away from Belle Vue, though it is important to recall that large as the numbers carried by the railway companies to the coast became, even by the beginning of the twentieth century not all of the working classes could afford even a day trip to the seaside. For many people a trip to Belle Vue was their holiday. It should also be recognised that those who visited the seaside as day-trippers or visitors may also have had sufficient funds to treat themselves and their families to a day out at Belle Vue.

Competition was also found closer to home. One threat came from other gardens, including those smaller pub gardens in which sports and gambling continued, of which the Copenhagen Grounds in Newton Heath was one of the best known in the mid-century years.[40] Collyhurst's Tinker's Gardens continued to operate until at least the early 1850s, but Belle Vue's main Victorian competitor was Pomona Gardens in Stretford. What had begun life as another pub garden within easy walking distance of Manchester was taken over and transformed by the Beardsley family in the 1840s and 1850s. They made good use of its riverside location by helping to organise the annual Manchester and Salford Regatta. By the 1860s Pomona was offering a diet of entertainment similar to Belle Vue though its lower admission charges suggested that the Beardsleys were more concerned to attract the masses rather than the classes. Its newspaper adverts ran next to those for Belle Vue and the Jennisons noted those days when a special attraction at Pomona reduced their takings (Blondin, the tightrope walker who had become a household name following his crossing of Niagara, appeared there in 1861). Pomona did not have a zoo but it boasted extensive walks and above all music and dancing. It had a more racy reputation which was seen in the knowing looks given to hasty weddings involving 'Pomona brides'.

In 1868 James Reilly, a chair manufacturer, purchased the gardens, investing heavily in new buildings, including the Pomona Palace and the Agricultural Hall.[41] The dancing platforms were extended – the Leviathan Platform was nearly 1.5 acres in area – and Reilly took care to provide good bands at what was now the Royal Pomona Palace and Gardens. Reilly was an astute businessman and he took every opportunity to organise events that would attract visitors.[42] Political demonstrations drew large numbers – Disraeli attracted over 25,000 people in 1872. An even larger number gathered to support the Manchester Ship Canal scheme in 1884; in fact attendance was so numerous that meetings were held simultaneously in the two main halls.[43] Horse shows, dog shows and industrial exhibitions were used to draw the crowds that kept the refreshment bars busy. That Pomona took business away from Belle Vue is not in doubt, and helps to explain the investment in even larger dancing pavilions and superior bands at Belle Vue. Fortunately for the Jennisons this heavyweight battle of leisure entrepreneurs ended when it was announced that Pomona was on the line of the proposed Ship Canal.[44] Its closure in 1888 resulted in almost a doubling of Belle Vue's profits. The Jennisons were also fortunate in that other potential local competitors – the Aquarium and Manley Park – did not survive long.

But there was always competition. The new municipal parks were heavily promoted, especially at holiday times, as recreational spaces, whilst for some the wakes provided the opportunity to enjoy more socially exclusive outdoor attractions such as the Botanical Gardens in Stretford. Outside the city there were commercialised leisure attractions other than the seaside. Hollingworth Lake – the 'Weighvers Seaport' – was popular, offering a range of entertainments, many of its day-trippers arriving on scheduled as well as excursion services run by the Lancashire and Yorkshire Railway Company.[45]

Belle Vue watched its competitors closely. Establishing a new pleasure park similar to Belle Vue might have appeared a sound investment but as those Manchester businesses that sank money into the Clough Hall Pleasure Gardens, Kidsgrove in the 1890s found, developing a money-making 'Paradise in the Potteries' required more than capital and good transport.[46] Location could be as important as the attractions, a factor that helps explain why Raikes Pleasure Gardens in Blackpool, which had been modelled in part on Belle Vue, eventually gave up its struggle to attract visitors. In Edwardian Manchester a new local competitor was White City, which was said to attract a higher class of visitor than those going to Belle Vue. But the White City management made the mistake of charging couples for dancing, and the place immediately suffered in comparison. As more people had more disposable income to spend on leisure and recreation in the second half of the nineteenth century there was more competition for that money and leisure entrepreneurs needed to be aware of new crazes, of new competitors.[47] In a business where novelty was important, it was easy to become out of date and to see profits disappear. New entertainments, however, needed to be assessed. The Jennisons appear to have been slow in introducing amusement rides such as the switchback railway which was to be found at Crystal Palace and Alexandra Palace in the 1880s. An aquarium could also have been added to the garden's attractions, particularly after the closure of the Manchester Aquarium in 1877.

Another important reason for the success of the gardens was that Jennison controlled his costs. As already noted, he was willing to invest heavily in improving the gardens but he adopted a business model in which as few as possible of the services necessary to the gardens were contracted outside. This was most obvious in catering, with the establishment of a bakery and brewery in the grounds. So strong was the demand for beer that a new brewery was opened in 1872. A smithy was in operation from the 1840s and the gardens had their own gas and electricity supply. Catering profits were to become, in George Jennison's words, 'the sheet anchor' of the business. Importantly, a catering service was also provided for events outside Belle Vue, and Jennison provided the catering for many public events in and around Manchester as well as in other parts of the country, for many years catering for the shooting trials at Wimbledon.

Belle Vue was intended to provide a source of income for all of John Jennison's children: seven sons and two daughters. All were expected to work. George was in charge of the Hyde Road entrance, followed by his brother James who managed this for over twenty years. The tea room was overseen by wives and daughters. Following an argument with the contractor of the fireworks factory in 1862 Jennison installed his youngest son, James, a man with no training or technical knowledge, as a manufacturer of fireworks, John Jennison the younger carried out bricklaying and George worked as a slater and builder. Most building work was carried out in-house. Bricks for building were baked on the site from clay dug out from the site of the lake. Third generation Jennisons, James, Charles, William and George, were all employed to take gate money.

A printing works, dating from the 1850s, produced the ubiquitous penny guidebooks, ephemeral handbills and the posters which were displayed across the north of England. Posters were printed on a distinctive arsenical green paper, also made in-house, the colour becoming so well known that it was named Belle Vue green. Money spent on advertising was regarded as an essential part of the business. Jennison employed his own bill stickers in a world where the sheer volume of posters was making bill posting a more competitive and organised business. Newspaper advertising was also important and there must have been long-term contracts with the local press, an arrangement that was reciprocated by favourable reviews of the garden's attractions at the beginning of each season.

Another of Jennison's strengths as a leisure entrepreneur was that he grasped the importance of attracting different classes of visitor to the gardens. As John Walton has argued in explaining the rise of the seaside, it was not possible for resorts 'to grow on the grand scale by concentrating on one visiting public to the exclusion of all others'.[48] Belle Vue was never socially exclusive. Jennison recognised that it was possible, given the size of the gardens and with careful management, to offer entertainments that would be attractive to different social groups. Above all, he recognised the rising demand for entertainment among the urban working class, not least those young working boys and girls who had coppers to spend. At Belle Vue the money from admissions was for a number of years paid back in refreshments. Jennison understood his market by allowing visitors to bring their own food, a practice that caused restaurateurs and publicans in seaside towns to grumble. Not all did so, preferring to eat the good value food available in Belle Vue.

The Jennisons could not only feed and water thousands on a busy day, they also kept a quiet order and respectability. Belle Vue was not generally a place associated with the kind of coarse working-class behaviour that disturbed sections of the middle classes. It is noteworthy that Belle Vue featured in the Manchester guidebooks as a suitable place for strangers to visit. More will be discovered about the social and demographic characteristics of the pleasure-seeking crowds that filled the gardens but from George Jennison's account they appear to have been generally well behaved, in part due to monitoring admission as well as behaviour in the gardens. There was some drunkenness and pick-pocketing but if we can rely on the court cases reported in the local press,[49] anti-social behaviour does not seem to have been a significant problem. In any case, as John Jennison knew, rough hands did not always mean rough manners. 'We saw many family parties,' wrote one visitor on a busy Monday in August, 'and all seemed to be enjoying themselves, without any of that coarse or indecorous conduct, which we are too apt to imagine inseparable from such assemblages.'[50] All this contributed to a good day out. Visitors left

Belle Vue with a sense of having enjoyed themselves and having had value for their money. Jennison understood that a satisfied customer was more likely to return.

John Jennison died in 1869 after a battle with cancer. He settled control of the zoo on his sons, and on his eldest daughter Ann. They were to hold the proceeds of the business in trust for themselves and for one of his grandsons. The eldest son, John, was paid an equal share but was bought out after his wife upset her father-in-law with a comment about his appearance. George Jennison had been his father's right-hand man and he continued to manage the business on the same principles as his father, adopting the motto, 'if there were no money, no-one could have it'.[51] George built a new wall around the entire site, ending once and for all the problem of non-paying customers. His premature death at the age of 46 in 1878 ushered in a series of problems. James Jennison took over, a man who was more timid than cautious, and one who introduced fewer changes, failing to adapt the zoo and to invest in new attractions at a time when the amusement park was changing rapidly. Nonetheless the period from George's death until the end of the century was among the most profitable period in Belle Vue's history, with the best years in 1891, 1899 and 1900.

Belle Vue as a business

What then of the archive? According to George Jennison, John Jennison and his sons did not produce proper accounts of the zoological gardens. This, however, is simply not true and owes more to George Jennison's attempts to persuade other family members to make Belle Vue into a limited company. The reality is that the Jennisons produced a remarkable business archive, full of detail; indeed Belle Vue's success, one might argue, is because of the way that the family audited all aspects of the garden's finances. At a stroke they could compare day-on-day takings and could see which parts of the zoo were profitable and which were a drain on investment.

The accounts begin with a cash book from 1844–50 which includes details of admission prices, firework costs and lists of printed guides and programmes. There are eleven files of receipts from the 1850s until 1925 which contain receipts for all aspects of the zoo, including payments for animals, animal feeds, foodstuffs, carriage, dinners and refreshments, posters and stationery, fireworks, band fees, policing, indeed for all aspects of expenditure. These cover the smallest, most incidental of purchases – two Indian rubber balls (6 September 1869), nutmegs and mace (22 July 1859), umbrellas, bicycles, prizes for shows and bands and payments to one of the Jennison wives for washing shirts. The receipts often provide additional information that serves to explain good or bad days. These may be reports on poor weather: 'Mizzly morning.

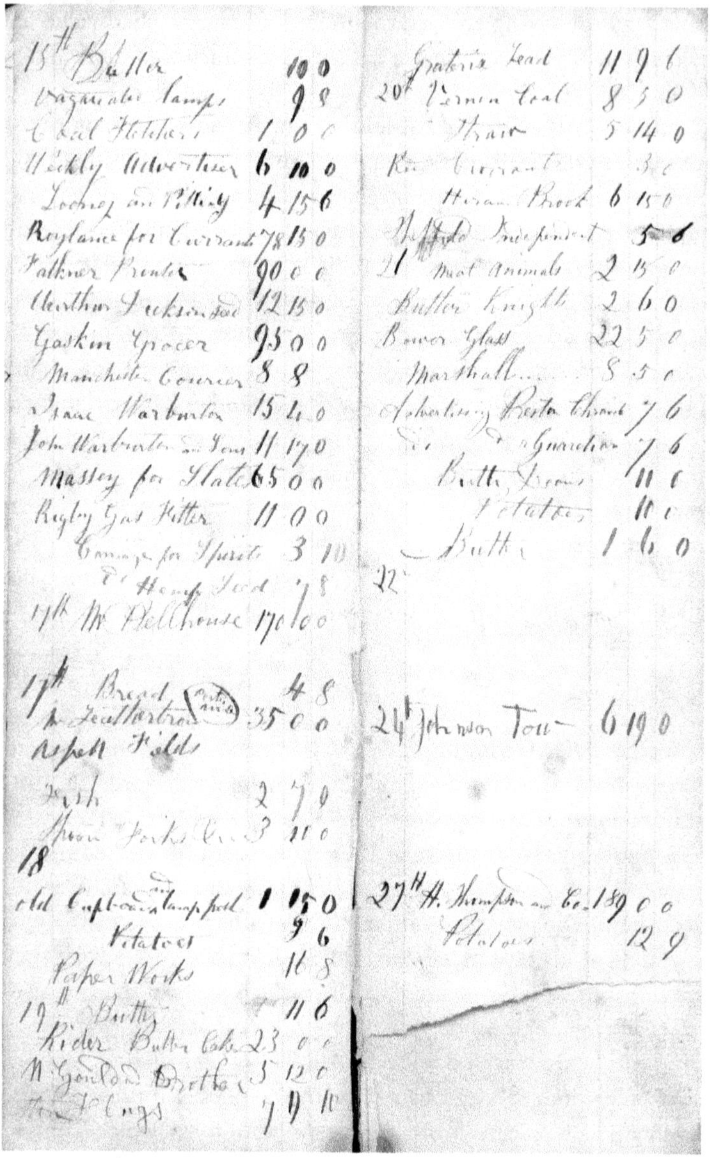

Figure 4: Summary of expenditure in the hand of John Jennison, 15–27 July 1854. A figure of £78-15s-0d for currants illustrates the huge amounts of foodstuffs needed to feed Belle Vue's visitors.

Very wet and windy all afternoon from one o'clock, impossible to imagine much worse, dry boats could not be got round new lake for the wind' (2 June 1860); they may also take note of rival attractions – a special event taking place at Pomona (first Saturday of tramcars, 8 May 1880) or the football match between Manchester City and Newcastle United at Ardwick (26 December 1905).

The daily receipts list payments as well as income, essential to a business that was built on coppers rather than on sovereigns. These receipts enabled the Jennisons to keep a control over cash flow. The receipts are supplemented by a series of large ledgers in which the Jennisons record daily, weekly and monthly income and expenditure for the years 1869–94 and 1906–15: these were written in code. All of the receipts and all of the accounts at Belle Vue were compiled by members of the family. Every single item of expenditure, no matter how small, was signed off by a Jennison and, as we have noted, each Sunday there was the family ritual of counting the takings. Clerks were not employed and cryptic letters were used in the ledgers to keep the workforce ignorant of the firm's business. The codes are not hard to crack: A stands for the main Hyde Road entrance and B for Longsight; M – the museum; S – the stand for fireworks; B – boats on the fireworks lake; I – ice, 1T – 1 shilling teas and 2T – 2d tea room (2d was the charge for hot water). But the sheer weight of detail enabled the family to track money on a day-to-day basis much in the same way as the large supermarkets today can determine expenditure and income by the hour. Moreover, by adding reports to the accounts of weather, excursions and attractions, both in the zoo and at other rival parks and sporting arenas, the Jennisons could explain, for example, why a particular afternoon had seen poor attendance or why an evening had been a great success. The entry for 6 June 1880 is typical: 'Fine morning to 3 heavy cloud 3.40 showery /fine/ fireworks at 9.30'.

From a survey of the ledgers, it is clear that entrance fees accounted for approximately a quarter of the total income. Over half of Belle Vue's income came from catering, with the single biggest income stream coming from the bars. The 1861 receipts, for example, show that more than £7,604 came in from bar takings. The Jennison family were often quick to quash the complaint that Belle Vue was a gigantic public house, George Jennison pointing out, for example, that its drink licence probably covered a larger area than anywhere in Great Britain, but that this did not mean that Belle Vue saw too much drinking. Whilst drunkenness was frowned upon, the Jennisons were still happy to make significant profit from the sale of drink. Indeed catering as a whole was always a big money-spinner, simply because of vast quantities of goods sold. On Whit Sunday 1859 Belle Vue got through 17,000 biscuits, 19,000 two-penny cakes, 10,000 one-penny cakes, 15,000 bottles of ginger beer, 11,000 of cider, 2,000 of lemonade and 500 of soda water. George Jennison estimated that the sale of Belle Vue's celebrated veal pies brought in a profit of over two thousand pounds a year.

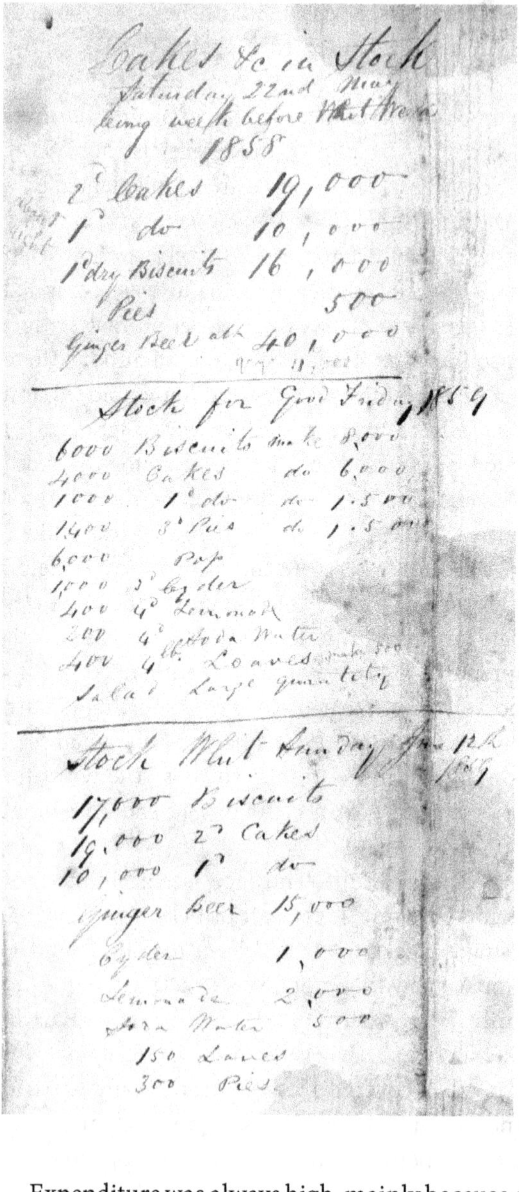
Cakes &c in Stock
Saturday 22nd May
being week before Whit Week
1858
2d Cakes 19,000
1d do 10,000
1d dry Biscuits 16,000
Pies 500
Ginger Beer &c 40,000

Stock for Good Friday 1859
6000 Biscuits make 8,000
4000 Cakes do 6,000
1000 1d do do 1.500
1,400 3d Pies do 1.500
6,000 Pop
1,000 3d Cyder
400 4d Lemonade
200 4d Soda Water
400 4lb Loaves make 500
Salad Large quantity

Stock Whit Sunday June 12th 1859
17,000 Biscuits
19,000 2d Cakes
10,000 1d do
Ginger beer 15,000
Cyder 1,000
Lemonade 2,000
Soda Water 500
150 Loaves
300 Pies

Figure 5: Extract from summary of catering stocks for 1858–60, showing the enormous quantites of cakes, biscuits and ginger beer in store for special holidays.

Expenditure was always high, mainly because of the difficulty in maintaining an increasingly complex business enterprise that was open all year. In the quieter winter months expenditure invariably exceeded income. In 1875, for example, out of a total income of £88,645, over 60 per cent (£54,693) came from the four months May, July, August and September. The firework displays could extend the season into the winter but Belle Vue was essentially an open-air attraction, and winters were the time for carrying out maintenance and upgrades. Catering accounted for most costs, although it also brought in the highest returns. Wages accounted for less than 20 per cent of all costs. Belle Vue certainly needed a large workforce. In 1876, for example, 196 staff were recorded at an average weekly wage of one pound.[52] Many casual staff were also taken on in the summer months, mainly to work in the refreshment rooms and in the historical re-enactments. Many staff stayed on the payroll for decades; the Jennisons were seen as good employers and cultivated a loyal workforce. The animals and the zoo, one of the main attractions, accounted for only about 5 per cent of the costs. New animals were regularly acquired but expenditure on feeding and maintaining the livestock was relatively low. This is surely a mark of the family's business acumen: their ability to run attractions at very little cost which would draw in large numbers of paying customers.

How much money was made by the Jennisons cannot be assessed in this brief paper although the financial records are available to enable us to determine the profitability of the zoo. Just before John Jennison's death in 1869 the sum of £80,000 was divided between his children, a huge return on his initial mortgages of 1836. In relation to other industries the returns were enormous. Taking three years' accounts at random we find that in 1880 Belle Vue made an operating profit of £13,231 out of a turnover of £77,793. This amounted to a 17 per cent profit, enabling six family members to take dividends of £12,447 on top of their salaries. In 1889 Belle Vue had expenditure of £57,283 and receipts of £86,241, an astonishing profit of almost £30,000, and a margin of 34 per cent. This was an exceptional year in which profits almost doubled because of the closure of their main competitor, Pomona Gardens. By 1909 profits had returned to a more modest but still remarkable 16 per cent, with a profit of £12,346 out of a turnover of £76,131. This level of profit and return on investments would have been the envy of any engineering or cotton enterprise in Textile Lancashire.

The accounts are more than institutional records and detail family expenditure – family trips and holidays, clothing bills, such as John Jennison's shoe repairs, magazine subscriptions (*All the Year Round* and others were bought on 5 November 1870) and George Jennison's personal accounts for wine and champagne. More importantly they show how more and more family members came to be dependent on the zoo: John Jennison's children, their wives and husbands, and then their sons and daughters, all came to rely on Belle Vue profits. One failing of the period 1878–1925, identified by George Jennison, was that the family failed to reinvest sufficiently in the zoo but were content to take bigger and bigger dividends and profits. His point that increasing amounts were taken out is supported by the accounts: in 1886, for example, four members of the family took out salaries of £200 each on top of dividend payments of £3,500 each.

Figure 6: Richard Jennison, son of the founder, in his customary garb of frock coat and top hat, mingling with customers, 1899.

To some extent Belle Vue followed an almost classic model where if not the second then the third generation family members failed to heed the lessons and failed to follow the pattern set by the first. Richard Jennison left an estate worth £225,000, whilst James left almost as much in cash, plus a large country house. For John Jennison's sons, Belle Vue had become a cash cow. There was no longer any question of working for nothing as in the days of the founder. Now most of the family did virtually nothing for large sums of money. Even so, James Jennison created large reserves for the time that the ninety-nine-year lease would have to be renegotiated. This was negotiated early and the freehold was purchased in 1915 for the bargain sum of £35,000. With this out of the way there was no reason why Belle Vue could not have continued indefinitely under Jennison control.

It is important to note that Belle Vue was not sold by the family in 1925 because it had in any sense failed. Profits *were* falling, and there was no doubt that the First World War had had a major impact: in the early 1920s the excursion trade was declining and the numbers coming into the zoo fell sharply. For the second- and third-generation Jennisons, however, Belle Vue had served its purpose and had provided them with material rewards and with a sharp rise in social status.[53] The zoological gardens was a high-maintenance enterprise that required considerable managerial input, and a

Figure 7: George Jennison (1872–1938), grandson of the founder, the last Jennison to manage the zoo, and author of the unpublished history of the zoological gardens.

commitment of investment and of labour that the younger Jennisons were simply reluctant to make.

In assessing John Jennison's business skills and also the skills of the Jennison family, it is important to set the success of Belle Vue in context and acknowledge that it took place at a time when there was an increasing demand for leisure and more people had money they were willing to spend on traditional and new forms of leisure.[54] Paralleling what Trollope recognised as the emergence of 'the largest and wealthiest leisure class that any country, ancient or modern, boasted'[55] was the rise of a working class with an appetite for more leisure and the means to realise it. John Walton's research into the Lancashire seaside has established one of the most visible features of this leisure revolution among the working classes, especially among those northern textile families with more than one wage earner.[56] But whilst acknowledging these changes we should recognise that they did not reach right down into the working classes, and even in the Edwardian period not all sections of the working class could afford a day trip, let alone an annual stay at the seaside. Holidays for some workers still meant seeking entertainment closer to home. Workers were also benefiting from a reduction in working hours, notably the creation of the Saturday half day. This came much sooner in Manchester than in many other towns thanks to the campaign for early closing: the fact that admissions peaked at Belle Vue on Saturdays was due in part to this. The same was true of other changes in the holiday calendar. The rapid adoption of the August bank holiday following the Bank Holiday Act of 1871 was also reflected in the Belle Vue ledgers.

After a nervous start Belle Vue thrived as a business concern, principally due to the acute but careful management of John Jennison and his sons. By controlling costs, expanding only as resources permitted, investing in advertising, cultivating customers from far and near, and diversifying Belle Vue from a zoo and garden into a broader entertainment complex, the Jennisons were able to withstand rising competition and establish Belle Vue as one of Manchester's or, more accurately, one of the North West's most popular destinations; a place described in a newspaper of the 1860s as one of the most remarkable institutions of which Manchester, or indeed any other city or town in the kingdom could boast.

John Jennison also deserves recognition as one of the important Manchester businessmen of the nineteenth century. He was more enterprising than strictly entrepreneurial but given his contribution to the leisure economy of one of the country's leading cities and industrial regions, his omission from the histories of Manchester, as well as the current *Oxford Dictionary of National Biography* and the earlier *Dictionary of Business Biography* is puzzling. Jennison had clear and bold ideas about the rapidly changing and increasingly competitive world of commercialised leisure but demonstrated a flexibility to alter them when necessary. The origins of the business in the small pub garden made him aware of the importance of investing in attractions to bring in the public and the importance of providing his visitors with an experience that would make them his most effective advertisers. Jennison also had a clear understanding of which parts of the business generated the profits and he was quick to appreciate the advantages that the railways offered for his business. There were setbacks but he also had the good fortune to have access to capital at critical points and to see two of his major competitors go out of business.

The disappearance of the Pomona Gardens was to be especially important for the family business. In less than thirty years Jennison built up a leisure business that can be considered to be one of the earliest people's playgrounds. Belle Vue's direct influence on other leisure businesses deserves closer consideration, although even from this preliminary analysis it appears that it needs to be more closely integrated into discussions of the rise of the modern amusement park.[57] A closer examination of the business accounts and family papers will be needed to clarify Jennison's role but from this initial survey of the Belle Vue Zoological Gardens there seems to be a strong case for placing him alongside Jonathan Tyers, George Carstensen, Fred Thompson and William George Bean in the pantheon of leisure entrepreneurs.

Notes

1 Robert Nicholls, *The Belle Vue Story; Looking Back at Belle Vue Manchester*; Jill Cronin and Frank Rhodes, *Belle Vue*; Heather Stackhouse, *Belle Vue: Manchester's Playground*; C.H. Keeling, *Belle Vue Bygones: A Farewell to the Manchester Zoological Gardens*; *The Life and Death of Belle Vue* and *The Fragments that Remain*; Chris Osuh 'Bring back Belle Vue'. The best website is the remarkable 'Belle Vue Revisited' set up by David Boardman: http://manchesterhistory.net/bellevue/menu.html (accessed 26 January 2012).

2 Manchester Studies oral history tapes (Tameside Local Studies Library).

3 One of the latest campaigns is The Belle Vue 2020 Vision, drawn up by campaign group Communities 4 Stability (C4S). See Deborah Linton, 'Bring back Belle Vue magic'.

4 Peter Bailey, 'Leisure, culture and the historian: reviewing the first generation of leisure historiography in Britain'; Eileen Kennedy and Helen Pussard (eds), *Defining the Field: 30 Years of the Leisure Studies Association*.

5 Donald Roach, 'John Jennison – a study in Manchester entrepreneurship', remains by far the best study, and this essay draws on Roach's research. Others include Helen Pussard, 'A mini Blackpool: Belle Vue and the cultural politics of pleasure and leisure in interwar Manchester'; Gemma Lawrence, 'Re-thinking "rational recreation": a study of Victorian attitudes to leisure at Manchester's Belle Vue Zoological Gardens from 1850–1900'; and Nichola Mundy, 'The Belle Vue revolution: a case study of the evolution of an entrepreneurial mass leisure facility'.

6 An exception should be made for some interesting work carried out by Helen Pussard on Belle Vue in the inter-war period. See 'The blackshirts at Belle Vue: fascist theatre at a north-west pleasure ground' and '"50 places rolled into 1": the development of domestic tourism in inter-war England'.

7 The Jennison archive is part of Chetham's Library Belle Vue archive, which comprises thirty-six archival boxes and several dozen volumes of ledgers and scrapbooks Mun. F.4.1–F.6.10. In addition to the Jennison collection, there are substantial collections of papers on the post-Jennison era. The collection can be searched at the A2A Access to Archives database at the National Archives: www.nationalarchives.gov.uk/a2a.

8 George Jennison, 'A century of Lancashire open air amusements, 1825–1925'. Zoe Willock has produced an illustrated ebook of Jennison's history that is available at Chetham's Library website: www.chethams.org.uk.

9 Peter Borsay, *The English Urban Renaissance: Culture and Society in the Provincial Town 1660–1770*, Chapter 6; David Coke and Alan Borg, *Vauxhall Gardens: A History*.

10 Sarah Jane Downing, *The English Pleasure Garden 1660–1869*, pp. 39–42.

11 There is no modern account of the history of these gardens; see T. Swindells, *Manchester Streets and Manchester Men*, pp. 149–53.

12 Robert W. Malcolmson, *Popular Recreations in English Society 1700–1850*,

Chapter 7; J.M. Golby and A.W. Purdue, *The Civilisation of the Crowd: Popular Culture in England 1750–1900*.

13 Joseph Aston, *A Picture of Manchester*, p. 190.

14 Advertisements in *Manchester Courier*, 29 June 1844; 5 April 1845; 20 October 1847.

15 Advertisement in *Manchester Guardian*, 3 June 1843.

16 Editorial Notice in *Manchester Times and Gazette*, 12 August 1843 condemning the gardens as a 'great public nuisance'.

17 Richard D. Altick, *The Shows of London*, pp. 323–31.

18 Advertisement in *Manchester Guardian*, 10 May 1837.

19 Jennison, 'Amusements', p. 17.

20 Nicholls, *Belle Vue Story*, p. 5.

21 Ann Brooks, *'A Veritable Eden': The Manchester Botanic Garden: A History*, pp. 27–34.

22 *Manchester Guardian*, 19 November 1842; *Manchester Times*, 26 November 1842.

23 Nicholls, *Belle Vue Story*, p. 6.

24 Mick Jenkins, *The General Strike of 1842*; Arthur G. Rose, 'The Plug Riots of 1842 in Lancashire and Cheshire'.

25 Details of the case including Jennison's creditors and also his assets are given in Jennison, 'Amusements', pp. 22–7.

26 Nicholls, *Belle Vue Story*, p. 7.

27 Advertisement in *Manchester Guardian*, 20 May 1843, p. 1.

28 For the zoo, see a number of studies for the Bartlett Society by David Barnaby and his book, *The Elephant who Walked to Manchester*.

29 The star attraction was Consul, a chimpanzee, bought from a sale of one of the Wombwell's travelling menageries in the 1890s. Dressed in a smoking jacket and cap, Consul smoked a cob pipe and drank a glass of beer. So popular was he with visitors that on his death in 1894 a successor, Consul II, was obtained. Consul's death was given an obituary in verse by the dialect poet Ben Brierley. Harriet Ritvo, *The Animal Estate: The English and Other Creatures in the Victorian Age*, pp. 228–9.

30 At one point, the Jennisons had to employ six policemen to control the crowds coming to see the animal. Nicholls, *Looking Back at Belle Vue*, p. 22.

31 Jennison opened an archery ground in 1856.

32 David Mayer, 'The world on fire … pyrodramas at Belle Vue, Manchester, c.1850–1950'.

33 Dave Russell, *Popular Music in England 1840–1914: A Social History*, pp. 164–6.

34 *Manchester Guardian*, April and June 1848, cited in Mayer, 'The world on fire', p. 181.

35 See *The Critic*, 15 June 1872, cited in Mayer, 'The world on fire', p. 181.

36 In the 1890s ladies in the ballroom were presented with a 'Dance appointment

card', attached to which was a small present, by which men formally requested an appointment to dance. Nicholls, *Looking Back at Belle Vue*, p. 23.

37 One of the earliest (and cardinal) documents in the archive is a list of the wakes holidays in different Lancashire and Yorkshire towns. 'Admissions from April 1851', Chetham's Library Belle Vue Archive, F.4.2 (3). For the wakes, see Robert Poole, 'Oldham Wakes'.

38 The railway stations serving Belle Vue were Longsight (1840), Gorton (1841), Ashburys (1846) and Belle Vue (1875).

39 The actual year is not given but appears to be 1919. Jennison, 'Amusements', p. 97.

40 Another venue in which sport and gambling co-existed in mid-Victorian Manchester was the City Grounds, Ashton Road.

41 Article in *Manchester Times*, 30 May 1868.

42 See Gregory Anderson and Barbara Ferguson, 'James Reilly: an artisan manufacturer in Victorian England', pp. 93–6.

43 *Manchester Guardian*, 23 June 1884.

44 Bosdin Thomas Leech, *History of Manchester Ship Canal: From its Inception to its Completion, with Personal Reminiscences, Volume 1*, p. 209.

45 A.W. Colligan and George Kelsall, *The Weighvers Seaport*; and *Davenport's Illustrated Guide to Hollingworth Lake* (1861–1875).

46 The rise and crash of Clough Hall Park and Gardens Company was widely covered in the Manchester press because of the involvement of Stephen Chesters Thompson and Chesters Brewery; see, for example, *Manchester Guardian*, 14 February 1894; 3 May 1894.

47 Jennison, 'Amusements', pp. 150–2. They appeared to be slow in introducing amusement rides such as the switchback railway and toboggan slide which were to be found at Crystal Palace and Alexandra Palace in the 1880s. They were also a crowd pleaser at the Manchester Jubilee Exhibition in 1887. We do not know from the Jennison papers whether these and other potential attractions such as an aquarium – the Manchester Aquarium had closed in 1877 – were discussed.

48 John K. Walton, *Riding on Rainbows: Blackpool Pleasure Beach and its Place in British Popular Culture*, p. 3.

49 At least the issues of those titles that are currently searchable online.

50 *Manchester Guardian*, 8 August 1849.

51 Jennison, 'Amusements', p. 136.

52 In the 1871 census George Jennison states that he employed 153 men and 24 boys.

53 George Jennison, grandson of poor, barely literate John, was educated at the King's School, Pontefract, read law at Balliol College, Oxford, and became a Fellow of the Zoological Society.

54 W. Hamish Fraser, *The Coming of the Mass Market 1850–1914*; John Benson, *The Rise of Consumer Society in Britain 1880–1980*.

55 Anthony Trollope, *British Sports and Pastimes*, p. 18.

56 The starting point in an extensive literature is John K. Walton, 'The demand for working-class seaside holidays in Victorian England'.
57 Walton, *Riding on Rainbows*, p. 146; Gary S. Cross and John K. Walton, *The Playful Crowd: Pleasure Places in the Twentieth Century*; Scott A. Lukas, *Theme Park*.

Bibliography

Altick, Richard D., *The Shows of London* (New Haven: Harvard University Press, 1978).

Anderson, Gregory and Barbara Ferguson, 'James Reilly: an artisan manufacturer in Victorian England', *Manchester Region History Review*, 8 (1996), pp. 93–6.

Aston, Joseph, *A Picture of Manchester* (Manchester: Self-published, 1816).

Bailey, Peter, 'Leisure, culture and the historian: reviewing the first generation of leisure historiography in Britain', *Leisure Studies*, 8:2 (1989), pp. 107–27.

Barnaby, David, *The Elephant who Walked to Manchester* (Plymouth: Basset Publications, 1988).

Benson, John, *The Rise of Consumer Society in Britain 1880–1980* (London: Longman, 1994).

Borsay, Peter, *The English Urban Renaissance: Culture and Society in the Provincial Town 1660–1770* (Oxford: Oxford University Press, 1989).

Brooks, Ann, 'A Veritable Eden': The Manchester Botanic Garden: A History* (Oxford: Windgather Press, 2010).

Coke, David and Alan Borg, *Vauxhall Gardens: A History* (New Haven: Yale University Press, 2011).

Colligan, A. W. and George Kelsall, *The Weighvers Seaport* (Littleborough: G. Kelsall, 1977).

Cronin, Jill and Frank Rhodes, *Belle Vue* (Stroud: The History Press Ltd., 1999).

Cross, Gary S. and Walton, John K., *The Playful Crowd: Pleasure Places in the Twentieth Century* (New York: Columbia University Press, 2005).

Downing, Sarah Jane, *The English Pleasure Garden 1660–1869* (Oxford: Osprey Publishing Ltd., 2009).

Fraser, W. Hamish, *The Coming of the Mass Market 1850–1914* (London: Archon Books, 1981).

Golby, J.M., and A.W. Purdue, *The Civilisation of the Crowd: Popular Culture in England 1750–1900* (London: Sutton, 1984).

Jenkins, Mick, *The General Strike of 1842* (London: Lawrence and Wishart, 1980).

Jennison, George, 'A century of Lancashire open air amusements, 1825–1929', Chetham's Library Belle Vue archive F.4.11.

Keeling, C.H., *The Life and Death of Belle Vue* (Shalford: Clam Publications, 1983).

Keeling, C.H., *Belle Vue Bygones: A Farewell to the Manchester Zoological Gardens* (Shalford: Clam Publications, 1990).

Keeling, C.H., *The Fragments that Remain* (Shalford: Clam Publications, 1992).

Kennedy, Eileen and Helen Pussard (eds), *Defining the Field: 30 years of the Leisure Studies Association* (Eastbourne: Leisure Studies Assocation, 2006).

Lawrence, Gemma, 'Re-thinking "rational recreation": a study of Victorian attitudes to leisure at Manchester's Belle Vue Zoological Gardens from 1850–1900', MA History thesis, University of Manchester, 2007.

Leech, Bosdin Thomas, *History of Manchester Ship Canal: From its Inception to its Completion, with Personal Reminiscences, Volume 1* (Manchester: Sherratt and Hughes, 1907).

Linton, Deborah, 'Bring back Belle Vue magic', *Manchester Evening News*, 12 October 2008.

Lukas, Scott A., *Theme Park* (London: Reaktion Books, 2008).

Malcolmson, Robert W., *Popular Recreations in English Society 1700–1850* (Cambridge: Cambridge University Press, 1973).

Mayer, David, 'The world on fire … pyrodramas at Belle Vue, Manchester, c.1850–1950', in John M. MacKenzie (ed.), *Popular Imperialism and the Military: 1850–1950* (Manchester: Manchester University Press, 1992).

Mundy, Nichola, 'The Belle Vue revolution: a case study of the evolution of an entrepreneurial mass leisure facility', MA History thesis, Manchester Metropolitan University, 2011.

Nicholls, Robert, *Looking Back at Belle Vue Manchester* (Timperley: Willow Publishing, 1989).

Nicholls, Robert, *The Belle Vue Story* (Radcliffe: Neil Richardson, 1992).

Osuh, Chris, 'Bring back Belle Vue', *Manchester Evening News*, 7 April 2008.

Poole, Robert, 'Oldham Wakes', in John Walton and James Walvin (eds), *Leisure in Britain 1780–1939* (Manchester: Manchester University Press, 1983).

Pussard, Helen, 'A mini Blackpool: Belle Vue and the cultural politics of pleasure and leisure in interwar Manchester', MA Cultural History thesis, University of Manchester, 1997.

Pussard, Helen, 'The blackshirts at Belle Vue: fascist theatre at a north-west pleasure ground', in Julie V. Gottlieb and Thomas P. Linehan (eds), *Cultural Expressions of the Far Right in 20th Century Britain* (London: I.B. Tauris, 2003).

Pussard, Helen, '"50 places rolled into 1": the development of domestic tourism in inter-war England', in John K. Walton (ed.), *Histories of Tourism: Representation, Identity, and Conflict* (Clevedon: Channel View Publications, 2005).

Ritvo, Harriet, *The Animal Estate: The English and Other Creatures in the Victorian Age* (Cambridge, Mass.: Harvard University Press, 1987).

Roach, Donald, 'John Jennison – a study in Manchester entrepreneurship', MA History of the Manchester Region thesis, Manchester Metropolitan University, 2005.

Rose, Arthur G., 'The Plug Riots of 1842 in Lancashire and Cheshire', *Transactions of the Lancashire and Cheshire Antiquarian Society*, 67 (1951), pp. 75–112.

Russell, Dave, *Popular Music in England 1840–1914: A Social History* (Manchester: Manchester University Press, 1987).

Stackhouse, Heather, *Belle Vue: Manchester's Playground* (Altrincham: First Edition Ltd., 2005).

Swindells, T., *Manchester Streets and Manchester Men* (Manchester, 1908).

Trollope, Anthony, *British Sports and Pastimes* (London: Virtue and Company, 1868).

Walton, John K., 'The demand for working-class seaside holidays in Victorian England', *Economic History Review*, 34:2 (1981), pp. 249–65.

Walton, John K., *Riding on Rainbows: Blackpool Pleasure Beach and its Place in British Popular Culture* (St Albans: Skelter Publishing, 2007).

Manufacturing the Renaissance: modern merchant princes and the origins of the Manchester Dante Society

Stephen J. Milner

A few months after arriving in Manchester as Serena Professor of Italian in August 2006 I came across two boxes in the west-wing corridor of the Samuel Alexander Building where my office is located, both of which had been put out for the cleaners by an incoming academic member of staff who was clearing out material left by the previous incumbent. Curious as to the contents of these old boxes, I examined them and discovered they contained the minute books, membership lists, correspondence, press cuttings, off-prints, and annual programme cards of the Manchester Dante Society which was founded in 1906 and continued its programme of activities until its merger with the Manchester branch of the *Società Dante Alighieri* in the early 1990s. Thence began the process of listing and enlisting, of inventory and invention as I began to reconstruct the particular social and cultural milieu that drew Dante to the manufacturing centre that was nineteenth- and early twentieth-century Manchester.

By way of guide, and acting as Virgil to my Dante, was a chapter written by David Wallace in his volume *Premodern Places: Calais to Surinam, Chaucer to Aphra Behn*. Entitled 'Dante in Somerset', the study sought to recreate the cultural milieu of medieval Somerset which hosted the phenomenon 'so furious and all-enveloping' as Dante.[1] In the chapter Wallace addresses the seeming disjuncture between contemporary Somerset imagined as a sleepy, deeply rural 'place', and its status in the Middle Ages as an international cultural centre and intellectual melting pot linked with cities such as Constance and Urbino. Assuming a method somewhat akin to that of W.G. Sebald (himself a sometime academic in the School of Languages at the University of Manchester who was famed for taking tickets and photographs as points of departure for his own stories and novelistic journeys), Wallace takes as his point of departure a Dante manuscript known to have been at Wells Library but now lost: a Latin translation of the *Commedia* discovered there in the 1530s. Seeking to reconstruct the story of how it got there, not as a philological exercise in textual emendation but rather as part of a process of re-membering (in the literal sense of reconstituting), Wallace aims to reconstruct the nexus of social, political and religious relations which brought Dante to Somerset in the first place and then domesticated him in the library for over one hundred years until the dispersal and disruption of those relationships during the Reformation.

For Wallace this disjuncture serves as an instance of the sort of temporal discontinuities and ruptures which he charts through a host of locations to illustrate his wider thesis concerning the recovery of voices and milieu lost in the developmental historicist narratives of nation and national cultures and literatures. In the place of such teleological accounts, he seeks to weave alternative paths through history, re-membering a precolonial and premodern, rather than modern and postcolonial, narrative frame. The Dante manuscript, therefore, serves as an instance of what Barthes terms the *punctum*, 'a sign or detail in a visual field provoking some deep – yet highly subjective – sense of connectedness with people in the past'.[2] This 'moment', this coming together as self-consciously willed subject positioning, forms what Benjamin refers to as a 'constellation', understood as a sort of astral star burst or flash of lightning in which associations, insights and realisations combine past and present in the generation of meaning.[3] Such heightened emotion and cognitive activity is a consequence of actually being in a place, being stimulated by what human geographers refer to as the haptic of happening.

It is this experience of being in a place, of possible encounter (of memory and archive) that I want to examine, translating Wallace's paradigm to nineteenth- and early twentieth-century Manchester and replacing the Cathedral Library at Wells with the John Rylands Library in Spinningfields in the centre of Manchester. Discovering the boxes that contained the archive of the Manchester Dante Society served as my own *punctum* or moment of heightened emotion and subjective encounter that initiated the process of re-collecting scattered fragments and references in order to tell another Dante story. In what follows, therefore, the aim is to reconstruct the cultural milieu which conjured forth the ghost of Dante in nineteenth- and early twentieth-century Manchester and begin the process of understanding how the proponents and critics of the new political economy drew variously on the poet's prophetic vision in engaging with industrialisation, cultural patronage, and the social inequality of the shock city of modernity. At the centre of the narrative stand the library itself, the persons of John and Enriqueta Rylands, and Dante, who still looks down on the visitors and readers from the stained-glass south window in the Historic Reading Room.

Figure 8: C.E. Kempe, stained-glass portrait of Dante
(c.1897–99). South window, John Rylands Library,
Manchester.

Industrial Florence

To imagine Dante, the medieval Florentine poet, in Manchester, the shock
city of modernity, may initially seem as incongruous as setting him down in
contemporary Somerset. Yet on many levels the city furnished an accommo-
dating reception context. Capital of capital, home of free market economics
and nursery of the new political economy, Manchester in the 1800s was
often characterised as a modern metropolis shorn of cultural and aesthetic
sensibilities. Yet the analogy between medieval and Renaissance Florence and
nineteenth-century Manchester was regularly made. It was to Italy and to
Florence, as the cloth, wool processing and financial capital of late medieval

and Renaissance Italy, that the industrialist entrepreneurs turned when seeking a cultural paradigm that fused capital accumulation with cultural production in a civic context. Gradually the new moneyed entrepreneurial elite began to follow in the footsteps of the aristocracy for whom the Grand Tour had always been a rite of passage, a necessary step in the education of an English gentleman. In the words of another son of Manchester, A.J.P. Taylor, writing in the 1950s, it was in Manchester that 'the ghosts of merchant princes walk in the twilight' as 'these were the men who gave Manchester its historical character'.[4] In the figures of the Medici and Strozzi, this new industrial class saw fellow merchants who demonstrated a high level of cultural discernment and civic pride in their roles as patrons of the arts. Such a trajectory was earlier embodied in the career of Liverpudlian lawyer and banker William Roscoe (1753–1831) who formed an outstanding collection of Italian medieval and Renaissance paintings, manuscripts and early printed books, published lives of both Lorenzo de' Medici and Pope Leo X and spent his latter years at Holkham Hall, the ancestral seat of his friend Thomas Coke, 1st Earl of Leicester (1754–1842), cataloguing the library which had been collected by successive generations of the family on their Grand Tours. Whilst distinctions were drawn between the model patrician Liverpudlian Gentleman whose riches derived from seaborne commerce and the industrial self-made Manchester Man whose riches derived from manufacture, both looked to Italy in seeking to rebut the charges of cultural philistinism.[5]

Many subsequent Mancunian industrial patrons like Richard Cobden (1804–65) and Thomas Fairbairn (1823–91) spent time in Italy, as did many of the architects responsible for the city's burgeoning architectural development. Sir Charles Barry (1795–1860) undertook a three-year Grand Tour between 1817 and 1820 and consciously drew on Raphael's Palazzo Pandolfini in Florence in designing the Manchester Athenaeum in 1837–39 (to house the Manchester Athenaeum for the Advancement and Diffusion of Knowledge – one of many societies formed for social settlement and reform, and further evidence of the voluntarism and co-operative mentality of the time), initiating a Renaissance revival architecture that became known as the 'Palazzo-style'. This style was subsequently adapted and deployed by the likes of Edward Walters and J.E. Gregan in their work on the city's trading architecture, from its banks to its copious warehouses.[6] When the Corn Laws were repealed in 1846, the city commissioned Walters to build its most ideological building, The Free Trade Hall, as a monument to the proposition that underpinned the city's economic ethos. According to one historian of the city's Italian diaspora community, it was modelled in a 'stile pretamente Lombardo', a decidedly north-Italian style.[7] Similarly Salford-born Thomas Worthington (1826–1909) undertook a grand architectural tour to Italy in 1848, and in

1876 described Manchester as 'the Florence of the nineteenth century' in his presidential address to the Manchester Society of Architects. His many public commissions for the city, from baths to hospitals, bear ample witness to his Italian expeditions.[8]

This association of Manchester with the Italian palace style was most clearly stated when the House of Commons debated the designs for the new Foreign Office in July 1861. In discussing the relative merits of Renaissance and Gothic styles, the Puginite Lord John Manners read an extract from a newspaper article to the House that cited Manchester as 'the city *par excellence* of Italian Renaissance'.[9] Significantly, the later vogue for High Victorian Gothic found ample expression in Manchester and also drew on Italian sources for inspiration, albeit the more Venetian and medieval forms popularised by John Ruskin. Alfred Waterhouse (1830–1905) was responsible for the Assize Courts (1858–59), the Town Hall (1867–77) and the Victoria University (1878) whilst Basil Champney (1842–1935) oversaw the design and construction of the John Rylands Library, which was completed in 1899.[10] The architectural debt to Italy and its impact on the city's built environment testified to Manchester's wealth and its sense of historical genealogy. It also showcased the city as an enlightened architectural patron, willing to back young architects who were setting the stylistic pace and who subsequently went on to design iconic buildings further afield. In the words of a more recent historian, 'In this sense the foolish-sounding allusions that liken Manchester to the cities of the Italian Renaissance are justified.'[11]

Manchester as underworld

Whilst Dante predated the original construction of such built forms, the analogy of Manchester with late medieval and Renaissance Florence extended beyond the aesthetic of its palace façades to encompass the city's mercantile activities, its public preaching and its social inequalities. For late medieval and Renaissance Florence also had its underclass. Just as every mill-owner and merchant employed a mass of workers, so every Florentine mercantile dynasty employed numerous lesser guildsmen and wool-carders. The uprising and seizure of power by the so-called *Ciompi* wool workers against their patrician overlords in 1378 is often given pride of place in western histories of social insurrection and industrial dispute, as the so-called *popolo minuto* and minor guilds sought wider political participation within the governance of the city's affairs.[12] Parallels with the Chartists abound. Behind the great palaces of both cities, the living and working conditions of the labouring poor were abject. Life expectancy for the urban poor in Manchester was just twenty-six and a half years by the mid-nineteenth century, the lowest level since the Black Death as chronicled by Boccaccio in the opening of his *Decameron*. The Poor Law Commissioners in 1842 reported that 57 per cent of those born to the working classes in Manchester died before reaching five years of age.[13]

For both cities there were two faces to the social consequences of urban expansion. Manchester, taken as a conglomeration of all the surrounding industrial centres such as Bolton and Oldham, was an international tourist attraction that drew travellers and commentators to voyeuristically examine its sprawling Gothic horror.[14] As tourist spectacle it was the aesthetic antithesis to Florence as described by William Hazlitt in 1825: 'a city planted in a garden'.[15] In 1835 the aesthetic analogy was applied in reverse by Alexis de Tocqueville who described Manchester as 'a medieval town with the marvels of the nineteenth century in the middle of it'. Such was the novelty of this new urban industrial world that finding an appropriate narrative register was seen as a challenge. As de Tocqueville asked 'who could describe the interiors of these quarters set apart, home of vice and poverty, which surround the huge palaces of industry and clasp them in their hideous folds?'[16] Sir Charles James Napier, writing in 1839, tried in the following terms: 'Manchester is the chimney of the world. Rich rascals, poor rogues, drunken ragamuffins and prostitutes form the moral; soot made into paste by rain the physique, and the only view is a long chimney: what a place! The entrance to hell realized.'[17]

Similar descriptions are found in the Victorian novels that took the form of social and cultural commentary. Benjamin Disraeli used Manchester as the setting for *Coningsby* (1844), describing how the protagonist travels to Manchester passing over 'the plains where iron and coal supersede turf and corn, dingy as the entrance to Hades, and flaming with furnaces' to arrive in the streets of the city 'among illuminated factories, with more windows than Italian palaces'.[18] The following year in *Sybil or the Two Nations* Disraeli has the Chartist leader Walter Gerard contemplate how there could co-exist in one place 'Two nations; between whom there is no intercourse and no sympathy; who are as ignorant of each other's habits, thoughts, and feelings, as if they were dwellers in different zones, or inhabitants of different planets; who are formed by a different breeding, are fed by a different food, are ordered by different manners, and are not governed by the same laws ... the Rich and the Poor.'[19] The inhabitants of Mowbray, Disraeli's Manchester, dwelled in 'the subterranean nation of the cellars' but passed down streets along which 'rose huge warehouses, not as beautiful as the palaces of Venice, but in their way not less remarkable'.[20] In 1854 Charles Dickens also used Manchester and nearby Preston as the mise-en-scène for *Hard Times*, initiating a phenomenon that became known locally as 'the Coketown slur'. Dickens's description of the alienating routinisation of modernity figured the cities' inhabitants as caught within the same eternal cycle of damnation as Dante's sinners:

Inhabited by people equally like one another, who all went in and out at the same hours, with the same sound upon the same pavements, to do the same work, and to whom every day was the same as yesterday and to-morrow, and every year the counterpart of the last and the next.[21]

The most famous chronicler of life amongst the city's poor, however, was Friedrich Engels (1820–95) whose polemical *The Conditions of the Working Class in England* drew on his experiences working at a branch of his father's cotton mills in Manchester between 1842 and 1844, and charted the fortunes of those deemed surplus to requirements once deemed incapable of generating surplus-value. Their literal and metaphorical 'abasement', to use his own term, is the focus of his study. According to a report of the Manchester Statistical Society in 1835, 3,500 cellar dwellings housed 15,000 people equating to 12 per cent of the labouring population of Manchester. Engels's partner, the working-class Irish radical Mary Burns, acted as both Virgil and Beatrice in leading him through the slums of Cottonopolis and its 'subterranean dens' and 'smokiest holes'.[22]

In this context it should perhaps come as no surprise that Dante should haunt this architectural and social landscape, lurking behind William Blake's 'dark satanic mills'.[23] For viewed from this perspective, Dante's *Inferno* furnished a literary trope for the evocation of the Gothic horror of industrial Manchester that challenged the sensibilities of the outsider who came to town. In Engels's description, it is as if Dante's fictional landscape has been translated into literal fact. The settlements which surround the darkest core of the city's centre are described as 'a girdle' evoking the circles of Hell, Stalybridge is shown perched on a crooked ravine, the chimneys of Stockport 'belching forth black smoke', the river Irk 'a narrow, coal-black, foul-smelling stream'. The 'swarm' of inhabitants embody depravity in their abjection, giving themselves up to alcohol, licentiousness, fraud, and violence: 'only a physically degenerate race, robbed of all humanity, degraded, reduced morally and physically to bestiality, could feel comfortable and at home'. Many in their desperation, he notes in a manner redolent of Dante's seventh circle, commit suicide in the face of 'the frightful condition of this Hell on Earth'.[24]

The parallel was not lost on George Jacob Holyoake, one of the early pioneers of the co-operative movement, who wrote in his working-class journal *The Reasoner* in the mid-1840s: 'As you enter Manchester from Rusholme, the town at the lower end of Oxford-road has the appearance of one dense volume of smoke, more forbidding than the entrance to Dante's *Inferno* … It struck me that were it not for previous knowledge, no man would have the courage to enter it.'[25] It is precisely this sense of looming threat that haunts William Wyld's painting *Manchester from the Cliff, Higher Broughton, Salford (1830)*,

Figure 9: William Wyld, *Manchester from the Cliff, Higher Broughton, Salford* (1835).

the dark clouds of industrial smoke and towering chimneys disrupting the pastoral idyll.

Significantly Marx also had recourse to Dante as he too stood at a more symbolic threshold, that of seeking to overturn the established political and economic order which he held responsible for sustaining such inequality. In the introduction to his *A Contribution to the Critique of Political Economy* written in 1857, he invoked Canto III of the *Inferno* in his call to arms:

> This account of the course of my studies in political economy is simply to prove that my views, whatever one may think of them, and no matter how little they agree with the interested prejudices of the ruling classes, are the result of many years of conscientious research. At the entrance to science, however, the same requirement must be put as at the entrance to hell:
> 'Qui si convien lasciare ogni sospetto
> Ogni viltà convien che qui sia morta.'
> ['You needs must here surrender all your doubts.
> All taint of cowardice must here be dead.']²⁶

The words are those of Virgil to Dante as they stood at the entrance to Hell and contemplated the journey before them. No doubt they would have served George Jacob Holyoake just as well as he stood in Rusholme figured as gateway to Manchester.

Both Dante's epic poem and Marx's epic critique can be read as prophetic texts, albeit offering very different roads to deliverance. Indeed, the parallels between these two temporally distinct salvific narratives are telling, as both offered paths through the moral economies of their respective cities. Yet whilst Marx sought a revolutionary uprising to seize the means of production and establish an earthly paradise in the industrial heartlands, Dante damned his own city as embodiment of sin and vice. For as has been argued by many critics, Dante's *Inferno* and his description of the city of Dis can be read as a portrait of Florence; Dante's revenge against the birth city that exiled him being to represent it as a hell-hole to be passed through along the road to salvation and, ultimately, citizenship in the city of God figured as the new Jerusalem.[27]

Cultural redemption: a Mancunian Renaissance?

Opinions differed concerning the responsibilities of the new class of mercantile entrepreneurs to the burgeoning underclass of the urban poor. Whilst laissez-faire Utilitarianism held that slums, pollution, poverty and disease were simply the opportunity cost of surplus labour, many in Victorian Britain were clearly exercised by the moral cost of capital accumulation in terms of its impact on social and cultural capital. An increasing engagement in politics by a broadening social constituency, combined with an emergent class-consciousness, led to an increased discussion of the role of culture as social mediator and the respective politics and economics of cultural production.[28] Once again it was to Italian history that contemporary observers turned when seeking exemplary cases that demonstrated the happy union of industry, labour and art to rebut the charges of cultural philistinism levelled against the great industrial centres. Disraeli, speaking at the Manchester Athenaeum in 1843 in a paper entitled 'The liberalizing tendencies of commerce and manufacturers', attacked the defamatory conjunction of mercantilism with philistinism. He declared, 'the pages of history have shown that literature and the fine arts have ever discovered that their most munificent patrons are to be sought in the busy hum of industry'.[29] He eulogised the merchants of Venice who had nurtured the works of Titian and Tintoretto. In his view, the act of commerce and the art of manufacture sympathise with the inventiveness and skill needed in artistic creativity. In conclusion, he announced that he was certain that a future as great as the Florentine past was destined for the great cities of Lancashire. Many contemporaries were well aware of the apparent paradox that it was major trading centres that often produced great culture. In 1847, Archibald Alison, the Chair of the Athenaeum, declared at the Annual General Meeting 'that it was in the manufacturing city of Florence that a rival was found in Dante to the genius of ancient poetry; in the merchant city of Venice that painting rose to its highest lustre on the canvas of Titian'.[30]

Ten years later Manchester staged the first fine-art blockbuster exhibition, the magnificent Art-Treasures Exhibition of 1857 at Old Trafford. Organised by an executive committee of the city's mercantile and political leaders, and underwritten by ninety-two citizens who raised £74,000 by subscription, it constituted one of the key moments in challenging the 'Coketown slur'. It drew together works of art from private collections across the United Kingdom and was seen by over 1.3 million visitors who perused the 16,000 exhibits over five months.[31] The Ancient Masters held pride of place, including thirty-three exhibits attributed to Raphael and thirty to Titian. Whilst Manchester may well have been the capital of laissez-faire economic practice, the organisers of the Art-Treasures Exhibition were keen to emphasise the civilising force of culture and its agency as a catalyst for aesthetic and mechanical invention in addition to its role as a means of moral re-creation. In a revocation of the ethos of civic pride which animated both the city-states of medieval and Renaissance Italy and those of the industrial north of England, the official magazine of the event, *The Art-Treasures Examiner*, opened its weekly coverage of the exhibition claiming that Manchester now 'steps forward in her aggregate character to emulate the glorious example of Florence of old, under her Prince-merchants the de' Medici, to display to the world the richest collection of fine arts the resources of the country allow'.[32] The great figures of the past are embraced by the city as 'our manufacturers woo our artists to their looms'. Whilst the city's cotton-lords cry 'Thrice welcome saintly Raphael!', *The Art-Treasures Examiner* asks 'How proud should we be to grasp old Michael Angelo, if he could step upon the scene once more and, turning past yonder Raphael tapestry, stand before us!'.[33] The Renaissance master's link with the city is still maintained as a result of the sensation caused by the display at the Art-Treasures Exhibition of a painting which had only been recently attributed to him, the *Madonna and Child with St. John and Angels*. Such was the stir created that it is still known as the 'Manchester Madonna', and was brought for the nation and now resides in the National Gallery, London.

This complex juxtaposition of art, culture, social reform and the fashion for all things Italian is best summed up in the remarks of one contemporary observer of the exhibition who remarked: 'Everyone up here is an art lover just now and the talk is all of pictures at the exhibition ... Amongst the finest is a magnificent portrait of Ariosto by Titian ... you and your wife ought to come up this summer and see the thing.'[34] The commentator was none other than Engels himself, urging his correspondent, one Karl Marx, to visit the show. Whilst Engels may have decried the social injustices of everyday life, he was a fervent consumer of culture and liked nothing better than attending one of the many events organised by his fellow German émigré Charles Hallé, whose orchestra was originally founded to provide the musical entertainment at the

Art-Treasures Exhibition. Engels was also a member of the Athenaeum, the Albert Club, the Manchester Foreign Library and the Royal Exchange amongst other associations and clubs.[35] Whether he attended Hallé's 1891 staging of Bazzini's symphony *Francesca da Rimini*, based on the famous episode in Canto V of Dante's *Inferno*, is unknown. Yet while Engels may have decried the 'cloak of charity' with which the Mancunian industrial bourgeoisie shielded itself from the reality of the working poor, he frequented and participated in the activities of institutions established by that self-same social constituency. If he had attended two lectures purposely programmed to coincide with the Art-Treasures Exhibition and held at the Athenaeum in July 1857, he would have heard another critical voice use Dante to remind his audience of the difference between exchange value and cultural value.

The invited speaker was John Ruskin, and his lectures were subsequently published under the title *The Political Economy of Art*.[36] What he had to say may well have affronted his hosts, for rather than talk about the art objects then on display he lectured them on the relation of aesthetic to exchange value within a moral economy of the arts. At the outset of the first lecture Ruskin cites Dante as furnishing a medieval instance of the condemnation of the pursuit of wealth for its own sake, 'the purse round the neck is, then, one of the principal signs of condemnation in the pictured *Inferno*'.[37] As his lecture built, Italy and the works of Renaissance master craftsmen such as Ambrogio Lorenzetti, Ghiberti, Leonardo da Vinci, Michelangelo, and Veronese figure as exemplary instances of the primacy of cultural worth over exchange value in the battle between monetary and cultural capital. Significantly, Ruskin chooses Dante and Homer as the authors made available to the poor man as a result of the invention of mechanised printing and moveable type. He also placed the opening words of Dante's *Divine Comedy* above the entrances to the continent's great galleries as testament to their neglect of Europe's cultural patrimony: 'They are the places of execution of pictures: over their doors you only want the Dantesque inscription, "Lasciate ogni speranza, voi che entrate"' ('Abandon all hope, ye who enter here').[38] The hope was that Manchester would be a more careful and discerning custodian of the nation's art treasures during their sojourn in the city, and that its cotton magnates would prove more discerning investors in cultural capital in their guise as enlightened patrons in the image and likeness of Lorenzo de' Medici.

Living in Manchester, therefore, involved engaging with a moral universe that obviated the distinctions between wealth and poverty, charity and exploitation, faith and secularism, indulgence and abstinence. Hellish in many ways, it struggled for redemption through reform, through education, through religion and through political action. In the poetry of Dante as citizen, prophet and pilgrim, the Victorians found a spirit guide who engaged with human vices and human worth, the civic and the transcendent.[39] It was this Dante that Manchester welcomed and to whom it offered a home amongst friends.

Dante wholesale

And so to John Rylands (1801–88) and his third wife Enriqueta Rylands (1843–1908) and their philanthropy, charitable works and faith. For central to the accession of Dante to Manchester was their interest in things Italian, their religious fervour as Congregationalists and their understanding of the interrelation between trade, education and religion. Nowhere is this better encapsulated than in the fine sculptural relief commissioned and overseen by Enriqueta herself, and mounted on the wall facing the John Rylands Library's original main entrance. Executed by John Cassidy, it represents Theology directing the labours of Science and Art.[40] It was this nexus which was responsible for the passage of Dante's body of works, his textual corpus, to the North West as the great Christian, albeit Catholic, poet.

The story of the Rylandses as Italophiles has yet to be written, but clearly they were, undertaking their own Grand Tours which combined business and pleasure. The two life-size statues of John and Enriqueta which stand at either end of the Historic Reading Room were commissioned by Enriqueta and executed by Cassidy in marble imported specially from the Carrara region. Not only did the Rylands's business have offices in Genoa, Alessandria and La Spezia, but the couple also made a number of trips to Italy, including to Florence in 1874.[41] John's interest seemed to have originated back in 1866 with the establishment of a Baptist mission in La Spezia under the guidance of James Wall, a Baptist missionary who persuaded Rylands to supply him with 10,000 copies of the New Testament in Italian. Ever one to deal wholesale, he supplied 20,000 and then financed the publication and import into Italy of 50,000 copies of Giovanni Diodati's 1603 Italian translation of the bible from Hebrew and Greek: Diodati being an Italian Protestant theologian from Geneva whose family were originally from Lucca. At the relatively late age of 70 years old, John Rylands took an increasingly personal interest in the evangelisation of Italy in the aftermath of the 1870 entry of Italian troops into the capital of the Papal monarchy.[42] In addition, he established an orphanage in Trastevere in Rome for which he was awarded a knighthood of the Order of the Crown of Italy in 1880, the charter still hanging on the library's walls. It was in Rome that he and Enriqueta adopted an Italian girl named Maria Castiglioni, who came and resided with them at their residence at Longford Hall, Stretford.[43] They both learnt Italian, and the purchase of over 730 volumes of Italian dictionaries, grammars and texts in various dialects in 1906 suggests that Enriqueta had more than a passing interest in Italian language and linguistics.[44]

Figure 10: John Cassidy, *Theology directing the labours of Science and Art* (1898).

On the death of John Rylands in 1888, Enriqueta decided to use her inheritance to build a major ecumenical theological library to commemorate her husband and to house their collection of bibles, religious texts and hymnals held in the large library at Longford Hall. There is no mention of any Dante texts in the 1881 catalogue of Longford Hall, but with the wholesale purchase of the Spencer collection by Enriqueta for £210,000 in 1892, now equivalent to over £150 million given the price inflation in rare books and manuscripts, the most significant Grand Tour private collection of early printed books in the world migrated from the Spencers' ancestral seat in Althorp to Stretford, just yards from the original site of the dismembered 1857 Art-Treasures pavilion.[45] In excess of 41,000 volumes were combined with the 10–15,000 books purchased since the death of her husband, causing huge storage problems. The most valuable items were stored warehouse-style in a strong room in the cellar of Longford Hall, including a vast number of Italian texts and one of the largest and most complete sets of Aldines, books printed by the Venetian printing house established by Aldus Manutius in the late fifteenth century. As the collection grew, so did the ambition of the library project, outstripping the original scope of a purely religious collection. Enriqueta commissioned agents across the UK to purchase volumes and collections, establishing in the process a library holding which still rivals the great industrial philanthropic libraries of the USA: the Pierpont Morgan, the Newberry and Huntington Libraries. It is difficult in the absence of Enriqueta's correspondence, which she ordered burnt on her death, to gauge when exactly her interest in Dante flourished and whether the impressive volumes which arrived with the Spencer collection, combined with the visits to Florence, acted as a catalyst to her collecting. That Dante figured as one of Enriqueta's *uomini illustri*, however, is apparent from his subsequent inclusion in the library's stained-glass window together with Raphael and Michelangelo.

The richness of the Spencer collection in terms of early printed editions of the *Divine Comedy* is witnessed by that fact it contained at least eleven of the fifteen incunable editions of the text (printed before 1500) as well as the 1502 Aldine 'vulgate' printed on vellum.[46] Overall the John Rylands Library holds fourteen of the fifteen incunable editions; only the exceptionally rare Naples edition of 1474, known in just three extant copies, is missing.[47] The acquisition of the manuscript portion of the Bibliotheca Lindesiana, the library of the Earls of Crawford and Balcarres, for £155,000 in 1901 allowed Enriqueta to add two Dante manuscripts to the collection, an exquisite Trecento Strozzi manuscript of Petrarch and Dante's *canzoni*, which was consulted by the famous German *dantista* Karl Witte, and a copy of the *Divine Comedy* previously owned by Seymour Kirkup, who famously discovered Giotto's portrait of Dante in 1840.[48] The genesis of the Crawford collection also bore testimony to the nexus of relations between the Grand Tour, mercantile capital and enlightened patronage as manifest in the Art-Treasures Exhibition. In 1865, Lord Lindsay, an ardent Florentinist like Roscoe, wrote a report on his library in the form of a long letter to his son composed at his villa near San Domenico on the road from Florence to Fiesole. In it he remarked:

> I little thought in my boyhood when Cosimo and Lorenzo were the object of my worship at Eton, that I should one day dwell beside their favourite San Domenico, look up at their villa and point to my son a parallel and a moral from their history. The parallel is this: – What commerce did, directly, for the Medici in the fifteenth century, commerce has done indirectly for our own family in the nineteenth.[49]

The wealth generated by the Lindsays' coalfields in Wigan permitted them to build up 'our old Library after the example of the Medici, and in the mode they would themselves have acted upon had they been now living'. Lindsay's particular interest in early Renaissance art and his love of Florence combined in his desire to emulate the library-building activities of Cosimo and Lorenzo. It was fitting that two late medieval and early Renaissance texts of Dante should migrate from the family's seat at Haigh Hall to the more modest seat of a like-minded philanthropist and library builder at Longford Hall, just twenty-two miles away and all within the county of Lancashire.

In 1905 the link between Dante, Florence, the Medici library and Manchester became even more tangible as Mrs Rylands purchased a *Biblioteca dantesca* wholesale from a Florentine book merchant, in all likelihood the famous publishing and auction house of Leo S. Olschki. The purchase is recorded in the sixth annual report of the library which notes that 'the most considerable gift, as usual, is due to the unflagging interest and continued generosity of Mrs Rylands' and runs to 'about 5,000 volumes'. The report continues:

> The collection was formed by Count Passerini, the eminent Dante scholar during a period covering twenty-five years. It is rich in early editions of the original text, and together with the remarkable copies of the earliest printed editions which were formerly the property of Lord Spencer, gives to the Library the distinction of possessing a collection of the *Divina Commedia* which is almost unrivalled.[50]

Indeed, in terms of depth and scale, the Manchester Dante collection was second only to that presented by the librarian and bibliophile Willard Fiske to Cornell University between 1893 and 1896.[51] The intention was to produce and publish a catalogue 'which will enable the Dante scholar, both at home and abroad, to appreciate the value and importance of this gift' and also mount an exhibition for public consumption.[52]

Count Giuseppe Landi Passerini is a fascinating character who deserves a study in his own right. A life-long librarian and *dantista*, he began his career as a junior librarian at the Biblioteca Nazionale in Florence before rising to end his career as Head Librarian of the Biblioteca Laurenziana in Florence, the library established by none other than the Medici family and designed by Michelangelo (the wheel comes full circle). He was a member of the Accademia della Crusca, founder and editor of the *Giornale Dantesco*, first Secretary of the *Società dantesca italiana*, close personal friend of Olschki the book merchant, correspondent of Pascoli, Carducci and Papini and close associate of D'Annunzio – who incidentally came to Manchester as a guest of Lord Newton at Lyme Hall in 1914 to buy greyhounds – and author and editor of numerous volumes on, and by, Dante.[53] Significantly, given the direction the cult of Dante took in the early fascist period, he partook in the March on Rome, was secretary of the *fascio* in Trento and then administrative secretary of the *Federazione fiorentina*. In 1915, ten years after auctioning off part of his

Dante collection, he gave the remaining part, which was of similar size, to the Accademia Petrarca in Arezzo together with his personal correspondence of over 8,000 letters dating back to 1881. The *Biblioteca dantesca* 'Giulio Luigi Passerini' was inaugurated there in October 1927 where it is still housed.[54] Significantly, no mention is made of the earlier sale of his Dante collection to Manchester in 1905. Given the scale of the collection and its complementing of the Spencer holdings, Dante was eventually granted lodgings in a room of his own within the library, the so-called Dante Room which stands alongside the Spencer and Crawford rooms. However, the catalogue promised by Guppy in 1906 never materialised and the task of identifying and reconstituting the collection is still a work in progress, the library's accession registers showing that the Dante collection was still being entered in the mid-1920s. An exhibition was held in 1909 for which a summary catalogue was produced.[55]

Enriqueta's agents clearly established direct contact with Passerini concerning the potential purchase of a precious fifteenth-century manuscript copy of the *Divine Comedy* in 1905. At this stage it appears he was unaware that his collection had been purchased by the Mancunian industrial heiress and benefactor. In a letter dated 1 February 1906 that accompanied the codex on its transfer to Manchester, Passerini wrote:

> Gentlemen,
> In compliance with your request I beg to declare once more that the ancient MS. of the 'Divine Comedy' by Landi purchased by your esteemed firm is absolutely unique and extremely interesting. It was exported from Italy with all the legal formality and attention and everything is in perfect order. The number of the ancient MS. of the 'Div. Comedy' is very small and the collector that owns one of them will greatly enhance the value of his collection.
> The codex secured by you, Gentlemen, has never been studied by scholars and being unknown to them would serve as a basis for new studies on the Divine poem.
> I am faithfully yours,
> Count G.L. Passerini.[56]

The significance of this purchase becomes clear on reading the minuted account of a gathering on 13 September 1906 at the Grosvenor Hotel on Deansgate. For it was there that a 'Meeting of Gentlemen interested in Dante Studies' was convened 'for the purpose of discussing the formation, here in Manchester, of a Dante Society'.[57] The meeting was chaired by the Right Reverend Dr Louis Charles Casartelli, Roman Catholic Bishop of Salford, who was born in the multi-ethnic and textile processing area of Cheetham Hill, north Manchester. He was the son of Italian immigrants from Como who settled in the city in the mid-nineteenth century and his father was a precision instrument maker

Figure 11: Giovanni Alberti, Dante bust (1906).

and optician. A prodigious scholar theologian, he secured a doctorate in Oriental Studies from the University of Louvain, lectured in Iranian at the University of Manchester and was Rector of St Bede's College, alma mater of another more recent Mancunian *dantista*, Zygmunt Baranski.[58] The meeting was attended by a broad cross-section of interested parties, amongst others: Major John Sington, the Italian consul; Mr Carl Collmann, the German consul; Mr Godbert from industry and commerce; Mr Guppy, Librarian of the John Rylands Library; Signor Valgimigli from the university; Mr Hughes, a bookseller; the Rev. Cossio from St Bede's College; Signor Alberti, a sculptor; Mr Lodge, a schoolmaster; Mr Sutton, the city's Librarian; Professor Herford of the English department, in whose memory the Herford Memorial Lecture in Italian Studies was established in 1932; and Mr George Milner, President of the Manchester Literary Club and expert on Lancastrian dialect poetry who co-authored studies with Elizabeth Gaskell. Signor Alberti presented the meeting with 'a beautiful bust of Dante with pedestal' that is still held by the Department of Italian Studies at the University.

In his introductory address to the meeting, Bishop Casartelli noted that

Manchester was an appropriate place for a Dante Society as 'the city is the seat of a great University', adding 'In every University in which the Humanities were well represented the study of the great Italian poet should find a place'. He also noted that the Rylands Library possessed a fine collection of Italian literature, before mentioning the prospect of an important addition: 'There was the prospect that the Manchester University would shortly acquire a valuable Dante Codex which would, he hoped, be known in time as the "Codex Mancuniensis".'[59] When the provisional committee met again on 19 September Casartelli was duly elected President of the Society and Mrs Rylands, together with Vice-Chancellor Sir Alfred Hopkinson of the University, were nominated Vice-Presidents. The inaugural meeting of the Manchester Dante Society was finally held in the university's Whitworth Hall on 24 October 1906 and an audience of over 400 listened to the Honorable William Warren Vernon deliver a lecture entitled 'The contrasts in the *Divina Commedia*'.[60] Afterwards letters wishing the society success were read out together with 'a communication from Count Passerini in which he announced a handsome gift of books to the Library of the Society'.[61] Through the agency of Passerini and the *Giornale Dantesco*, the event and establishment of the society gathered international news coverage and the Count was nominated an Honorary Member of the Society.[62] From this rousing beginning the Manchester Dante Society organised a full annual programme of events and lectures well into the 1990s, hosting leading international figures from the world of Dante studies.

The Manchester Dante Society was not the first to be established outside Italy but was certainly one of the most enduring and ambitious in its enterprises. In 1865 Karl Witte established the *Deutsche Dantegesellschaft*, while in 1876 Edward Moore established the Oxford Dante Society, and a London Dante Society was formally constituted in 1898. In America, Dante societies were established in 1881 at Harvard University, by Henry Wadsworth Longfellow and Charles Eliot Norton, and in Philadelphia. The respective fortunes of these groups varied considerably. The German society had ceased to meet by 1885, the Philadelphia society within two years of foundation, and the London society died out in about 1910. The Oxford Dante Society continued to meet into the 1980s, its long-time president Cecil Grayson editing a centenary volume of essays in 1980, whilst the Harvard society became the Dante Society of America which still meets and publishes the annual journal *Dante Studies*.[63]

Importing Dante: Florence to Manchester

The particularity of the Manchester Dante Society, however, lay in its foundational link with Florence, with Passerini, and, by association, with the activities of the *Società dantesca italiana* which was established in Florence in

1888 as a scholarly association committed to the study, research and editing of Dante's works. Unlike the nationalistic *Società Dante Alighieri*, founded by Giosuè Carducci in 1889 as an international organisation for the promotion of Italian culture overseas, the Florence-based *Società dantesca italiana* organised conferences, lectures, readings and excursions, establishing a branch network across Italy.[64] Passerini's connection with Manchester did not simply end with the purchase of his library and launch of the Manchester Dante Society. On 6 November 1906 he wrote to the Head Librarian, Henry Guppy, in Manchester, noting how he had recently read an account of the foundation of the John Rylands Library whilst in the Reading Room of the Biblioteca Laurenziana in Florence and asked for a copy to be sent to him. He also expressed his satisfaction that his personal collection had been purchased by the library and kept intact, offering a further 1,000 Dante volumes to the library, 'alcune delle quali di molta rarità' (some of which are extremely rare), and most importantly 'a prezzi assai convenienti' (at manageable prices).[65] Such an arrangement had the added benefit of dispensing with the services of an intermediary or book agent. Guppy obviously sent his brief history of the library to Passerini, who in a further letter of 26 November 1906 replied, thanking Guppy for his history but withdrawing the offer of his 1,000 volumes about which Guppy may well have been less than enthusiastic.[66]

Enriqueta's purchase of the so-called 'Codex Mancuniensis' brought a text of major significance to Manchester on which the rest of the collection hinged. On the flyleaf of the manuscript is written 'codice dantesco del sec. XV finora ignoto alla bibliografia G.L. Passerini'. An extraordinary manuscript containing a full version of the *Divine Comedy* together with a number of other works in Latin and the vernacular, it is a sophisticated early Quattrocento *zibaldone*, a compendium of texts for private use and consumption. The text is characterised by extensive marginal glossing by the copyist, in both Latin and the vernacular, measures 212 × 219mm and is in its original binding of wooden boards and stamped brown leather, with five metal studs on the front board and remnants of two clasps on the fore-edge.

The text is centred in a single column with double vertical boundaries ruled with a hard point, leaving plenty of scope for glossing and paratextual data. The main text is in a fairly neat *mercantesca* hand with the marginal notes in a more cursive style. Dated 1416, the text is autographed: 'Scripta fuit per me Bartolomeo Landi de Landis de Prato notarium. Et conplecta fuit die XXVIIII Junii Anno MCCCCXVI'.[67] In a review of the Rylands Dante Collection written in 1961 by Kathleen Speight, an indefatigable champion of Italian Studies at Manchester and long-time Secretary of the Manchester Dante Society until her retirement in 1970, it is noted how earlier plans to edit and bring this remarkable text to the attention of Dante studies had not borne fruit:

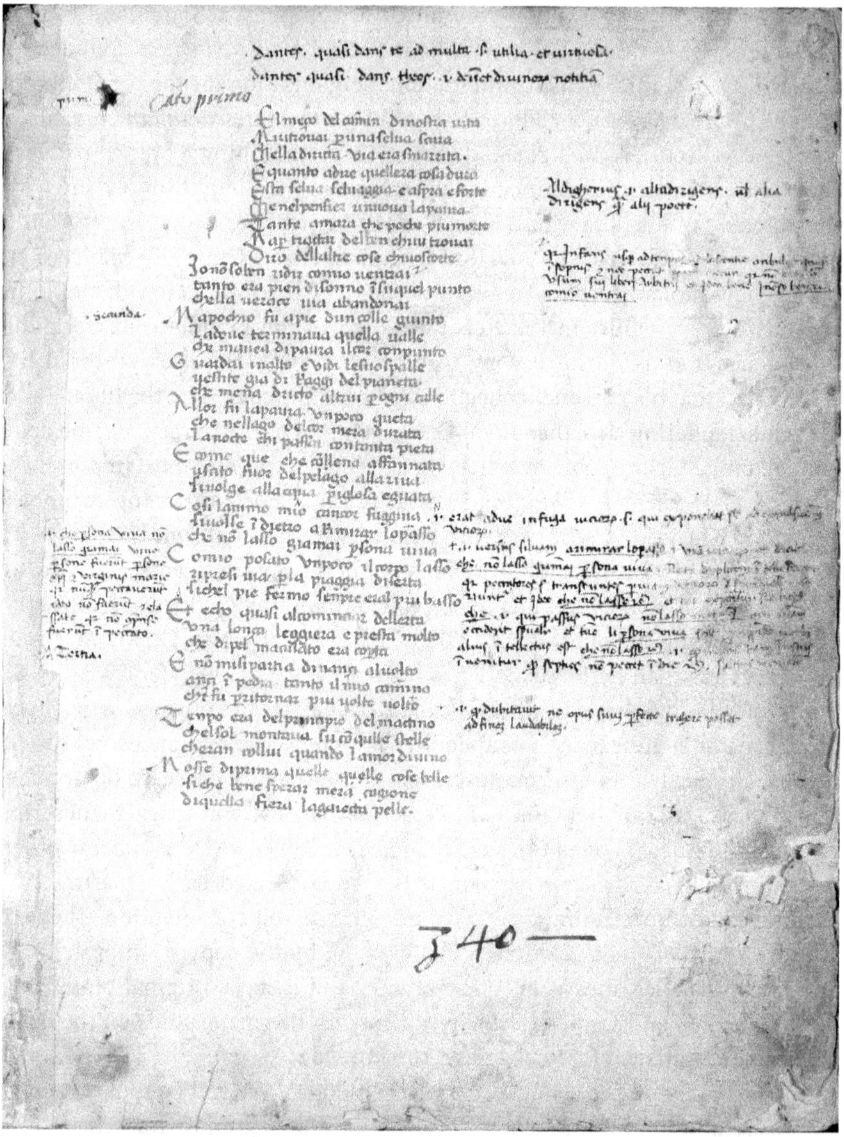

Figure 12: Italian MS 49, fol. 1r. Bartolomeo Landi de Landis da Prato 1416–26 (the so-called 'Codex Mancuniensis').

It is very much hoped that before 1965 Bartolomeo Landi may have found his editor, so that the omission of 1865 (the year of the great Dante Exhibition) may be made good and he may emerge from his undeserved obscurity to become part of the septem-centenary celebrations, thus bringing further honour to the Library where he is so carefully preserved.[68]

Figure 13: Italian MS 50, fol. 1r. Attilio Razzolini, *La Divina Commedia* (1902).

Although the manuscript was overlooked in a number of recent catalogues of fifteenth-century manuscripts of the *Divine Comedy*, it is now fully listed in the recently published *Censimento dei commenti danteschi: I commenti di tradizione manoscritta (fino a 1480).*[69]

A further unique modern Dante manuscript was also acquired by Mrs Rylands, again through the agency of Passerini. A sumptuous and vast modern manuscript copy on vellum, it consists of 104 folios measuring 595 × 470mm and fully illustrated with one canto to each page.[70] The border decoration and illuminated capitals are by Attilio Razzolini of Florence, who subsequently illustrated in 1906 an edition of the *Vita Nuova* as edited in 1897 by Passerini.[71] The individual paintings are by a number of other artists – A. Alessandrini, S. Bicchi, I. Olivotto, G. Tetti and V. Pochini – and the text in the Italian *textualis libraria* style presented in four columns using the Petrocchi edition of the poem 'secondo l'antica vulgata'. A postcard edition of the work based on chromolithographs of the original manuscript was published in 1903 and a facsimile of the Manchester manuscript in 2008.[72]

These two manuscripts were the most notable items in Enriqueta's last gift of books to the library from Longford Hall prior to her death in 1908. In listing that year's accessions, the Librarian noted:

Again, it is necessary to report that the most important gift of the year is due to the continued generosity of the founder. It consists of two manuscripts of Dante's *Divina Commedia*; the first written by Bartolomes Landi de Landis, a learned notary of Prato, and completed in the year 1416. Nothing is known of the transcriber save what is revealed in the manuscript itself. Having transcribed the poem, he seems to have delighted himself in translating Cicero, and in copying other classics. The manuscript is of very considerable importance to Dante scholars, since it is one of the very few dated manuscripts of the poet, and apparently has never been studied by the modern editors. The second is a modern illuminated copy of the poem produced by Signor Razzolini of Florence, assisted by other artists, and completed in 1902. It is a fine volume containing upwards of two hundred illuminations, illustrating passages from the various cantos of the poem.[73]

Produced nearly five hundred years apart, they act as bookends to the present study and collapse time in their simultaneous translation from Florence to Manchester. The transfer of these prestige items from Longford Hall in Stretford to the John Rylands Library in 1908 was subsequently followed by the accession of the rest of the Dante Collection as part of Enriqueta's bequest.

Space militates against a rehearsal of the numerous activities undertaken by the Manchester Dante Society from its foundation in 1906 to its amalgamation in the 1990s with the Manchester branch of the *Società Dante Alighieri* of which Professor Gwynfor Griffiths, former Serena Professor of Italian and the last President of the Manchester Dante Society, is still Honorary President. Reading through their papers I am struck by the extent to which their activities permeated all aspects of social life in Manchester and the North, from the talks given to such institutions as the Workers College in Chorley, and the Colonia Universitaria di Ancoats, to the tutorial classes in Salford, the lectures to branches of the Workers' Educational Association, and their participation with the Ateneo di Leeds in the University Extension Lecture programme and tutorial classes which toured Wakefield, Brighouse, Castleford and even Hebden Bridge in 1912. In April 1913 they even organised an outing to see the screening of Bertolini, Padovan and Liguoro's feature-length *Dante's Inferno* during its sell-out two-week run at the Manchester Free Trade Hall. After the war they continued to sponsor Anglo-Italian relations, organising evenings of song to entertain the Italian workers who came to work on the rail network in the 1950s and even a Manchester 'Italy' day in the 1960s which involved a cortège of over 200 Vespas driving through the city centre.[74]

One of the continuing legacies of the Manchester Dante Society, however, is the foundation of an endowed Chair in Italian Studies at the University of Manchester. For it was they who, in conjunction with the members of the Manchester branch of the British-Italian League, had already raised £3,000

Reserved Seats, 2s. & 1s.

BOOK IN ADVANCE.

Box Office Telephone 6465 Central.

DANTE'S "INFERNO"

A treasure, for six hundred years known to but a few scholars, now placed in unsurpassable beauty before all mankind. Presented by the film maker just as conceived by the immortal poet. Occupying more than two hours, telling in most artistic and realistic manner the great story of Dante, like animated paintings of living statuary.

The pictures give you in a few hours all the pleasure and knowledge it takes months to acquire through books.

WILL BE PRESENTED AT THE LARGE

FREE TRADE HALL,

MANCHESTER,

Commencing Monday, April 28th,

Three Performances Daily,
at 3, 7, and 9.

Figure 14: 1913 poster advertising *Dante's Inferno* (1911) directed by Francesco Bertolini, Adolfo Padovano and Giuseppe de Liguoro.

in 1918 through donations and pledges. On being informed that the shipping magnate Arturo Serena was intent upon establishing endowed chairs in Italian at Oxford, Cambridge and Birmingham, they determined to add his patronage to their endeavour. Through the agency of the London branch of the British-Italian League and the intervention with Serena of Edward Hutton, editor of the *British-Italian Review* and co-founder of the British Institute in Florence, Serena agreed to a gift of £5,000 on condition that the Manchester chair committee raised the same amount. This they duly did and the university agreed to the establishment of a Serena Chair in 1919, appointing Dr Edmund Garratt Gardner, Reader in Italian at University College London, to the first Manchester Chair. As noted in the *Manchester Guardian* in August 1919, 'Dr Gardner is well known in this country and ranks with veteran scholars Dr Arnold Toynbee and Dr Philip Wicksteed as one of the most distinguished students of Italian literature in Europe.'[75] Fittingly, Gardner was a noted Dante scholar and Florentinist who had previously addressed the Manchester Dante Society. His standing was confirmed when he was awarded the Serena Medal in 1922, made a Fellow of the British Academy and invited to give the British Academy Genius lecture on Dante in 1927.[76] Subsequent Serena professors, from Mario Praz, Pietro Rebora and Walter Bullock – who gave his own valuable collection of early Italian printed books to the John Rylands Library – to Giovanni Aquilecchia and Gwynfor Griffiths have maintained a Mancunian tradition in bibliography, history of the language, and comparative literature and translation which still endures.[77]

Dante's ghost, cultural rebirth, and the spinning of yarns

Fittingly, there is no conclusion to the present study, no casting off. Instead there are further threads to be picked up as the ongoing weaving of narrative continues to produce a larger textual fabric. The story taken up in this study has sought to collapse the seeming difference between text and place in the same manner as commentators in the Middle Ages. For they understood reading as a process whereby the reader inhabits the world of the page, proceeding from word to word as the storyteller proceeds from topic to topic, or the traveller from place to place. In the words of Tim Ingold:

> to tell a story, then, is to *relate*, in narrative, the occurrences of the past, retracing a path through the world that others, recursively picking up the threads of past lives, can follow in the process of spinning out their own. But rather as in looping or knitting, the thread being spun now and the thread picked up from the past are both of the same yarn. There is no point at which the story ends and life begins.[78]

Texts and textiles, spinning yarn and spinning yarns in Spinningfields is, as purveyors of the word, the business of historians of Manchester. From the chance encounter with dusty boxes destined for the bin to commencing the reconstruction and reanimation of a tradition and a history that tells a story about Manchester's past, its possible futures, and the place of Italian culture in its self-imagination, there is still work to be done. Inventories need drawing up, new texts need adding, and collections built upon as living entities. Dante's translation to Manchester is a story whose places of invention are topical, trope based, and as discursive as they are locational. For invention has the dual sense of imagination and re-collection as in the word 'inventory', the listing and ordering of materials, their enlisting. And cities and libraries, as we have seen, are nothing if not places of inventories and invention.

In a final piece of spinning I want to trace one particular thread I discovered during my researches which binds my own past and present. For this piece is a meditation on Manchester based on my own encounter with the city and its cultural heritage, and is conditioned by my own literary and historical interests and my simply being there. My attempts to read it are largely a result of a sensitivity derived from spending time with Michael Baxandall, my teacher and mentor whilst at the Warburg Institute as a postgraduate student in the late 1980s. As a supervisor he encouraged me to read Engels, as well as Gramsci, and awoke in me a curiosity about the complex interrelation of artisanal practice, social experience, and language. Significantly, Michael grew up in Manchester before going to Cambridge to study with F.R. Leavis. Whilst working on the current study I discovered the following entry in the minute book of the Manchester Dante Society from 1947:

> Wed, Dec. 3rd (1947): Mr. D. R. Baxandall (Curator of the City Art Gallery) gave a lecture on *Italian Painting of the Early Renaissance* which was illustrated by lantern slides. A record number of people present, 42, heard a most instructive and stimulating lecture which traced the history of Italian painting from the 13th to the end of the 15th centuries. A wealth of slides was shown, including works of Cimabue, Giotto, Fra Angelico, Duccio, Simone Martini, Paolo Uccello, Piero della Francesca, Sassetta, Baldovinetti, Luca Signorelli, Ghirlandaio, and Botticelli; and with Mr. Baxandall's expert guidance and able interpretation we discussed beauties not seen before in pictures already familiar, and we were able to understand and appreciate others seen for the first time. Entertaining anecdotes of the artists quoted from Vasari added to the pleasure given by a lecture which, as Professor Atkinson said in his vote of thanks, seemed to come to an end all too soon.[79]

The interest of Baxandall's father in Renaissance masters and word and image, combined with the experience of growing up in a city of industry, labour and art, clearly impacted on his own thinking. That he subsequently reflected on the Manchester years as a Renaissance scholar is apparent in his posthumously published memoirs: 'When, years later, I read Leon Battista Alberti's great treatise *On Architecture* I realised that one way of understanding Manchester is to adapt his fifteenth-century sense of buildings as many-dimensioned moral behaviour within a class-coded public/private functional system, but I did not know Alberti then.'[80] It was in seeking to make sense of these same streets, buildings and basements that the ghost of Dante was variously conjured by Mancunian merchant princes, the critics of the new political economy and Nonconformists in a transposition of the Roman rhetorical topos *mortuos excitare* to the industrial landscape of the metropolis of labour. Given that the voicing of ghostly figures is the master trope of the Renaissance, what they effectively produced was a Renaissance 'Made in Manchester'.

Notes

1 David Wallace, *Premodern Places: Calais to Surinam, Chaucer to Aphra Behn*, pp. 139–80.
2 *Ibid.*, p. 2.
3 See the comments of Janet Wolff, 'Memories and micrologies: Walter Benjamin's artwork essay reconsidered'.
4 A.J.P. Taylor, 'Manchester', p. 309.
5 Arline Wilson, *William Roscoe: Commerce and Culture* and '"The Florence of the North"? The civic culture of Liverpool'. Roscoe's catalogue of the collection still constitutes the main finding list as kept at Holkham Hall.
6 Marcus Whiffen, 'The architecture of Sir Charles Barry in Manchester and neighbourhood' and Stuart Macdonald, 'The Royal Manchester Institution'.
7 Azeglio Valgimigli, *La colonia italiana di Manchester (1794–1932)*, p. 12.
8 Anthony J. Pass, 'Thomas Worthington', p. 81.
9 'New Foreign Office', Vol. 164, c. 531, 8 July 1861, *Hansard's Parliamentary Debates* (online): http://hansard.millbanksystems.com/commons/1861/jul/08/resolution (accessed 10 September 2012).
10 John J. Parkinson-Bailey, *Manchester: An Architectural History*, especially '1840–1860. The architecture of commerce', pp. 56–95; in the footsteps of Ruskin see also Cecil Stewart, *The Stones of Manchester*.
11 John H.G. Archer, 'Introduction', in *Art and Architecture in Victorian Manchester*, p. 24.
12 Patrick Lantschner, 'The Ciompi Revolution constructed: modern historians and the nineteenth-century paradigm of revolution'.
13 See Gary S. Messinger, *Manchester in the Victorian Age: The Half-Known City*, pp. 33–64.
14 See the excellent survey of descriptions of Victorian Manchester in Steven Marcus, *Engels, Manchester, and the Working Class*, pp. 28–66.
15 Cited in Cecilia Powell, *Turner in the South: Rome, Naples, Florence*, p. 92.
16 Cited by Marcus, *Engels*, pp. 60–6.
17 *Ibid.*, p. 46.
18 Benjamin Disraeli, *Coningsby or The New Generation*, p. 135.
19 Benjamin Disraeli, *Sybil or The Two Nations*, pp. 65–6.
20 *Ibid.*, pp. 85–6.
21 Charles Dickens, *Hard Times*, p. 26.
22 Friedrich Engels, *The Condition of the Working Class in England*, p. 55. Engels repeatedly cites statistics drawn from various reports he accessed as part of his research.
23 The phrase was first used by William Blake in the preface to his epic 'Milton: a poem', pp. 110–12. Both Blake and John Milton drew extensively on Dante's own epic poem in their work. See the exhibition catalogue *Dante Rediscovered: From Blake to Rodin*, edited by David Bindman, Stephen Hebron and Michael O' Neil.

24 For the description of Manchester and its surroundings, see Engels, *The Condition of the Working Class*, pp. 53–86.

25 Cited in Tristam Hunt, *The Frock-Coated Communist: The Life and Times of the Original Champagne Socialist*, p. 81.

26 See Lewis S. Feuer (ed.), *Marx and Engels: Basic Writings on Politics and Philosophy*, p. 87. The translation of lines 14–15 of Canto III of the Inferno are taken from Dante Alighieri, *Inferno*, p. 21.

27 See Catherine Keen, *Dante and the City* and Claire Honess, *From Florence to the Heavenly City: The Poetry of Citizenship in Dante*. For the translation of this paradigm to Victorian Britain see Tristram Hunt, *Building Jerusalem: The Rise and Fall of the Victorian City*.

28 See the essays collected in Alan J. Kidd and K.W. Roberts (eds), *City, Class and Culture: Studies of Social Policy and Cultural Production in Victorian Manchester*.

29 Cited in Tristram Hunt and Victoria Whitfield (eds), *Art Treasures in Manchester: 150 Years On*, p. 54.

30 'Address of Archibald. November 18th, 1847', *Manchester Athenaeum Addresses 1835–1885*, p. 73.

31 See Elizabeth A. Pergam, *The Manchester Art Treasures Exhibition of 1857: Entrepreneurs, Connoisseurs and the Public*; Ulrich Finke, 'The Art-Treasures Exhibition'; and the essays in Helen Rees Leahy (ed.), *Art, city, spectacle: the 1857 Manchester Art-Treasures Exhibition revisited*.

32 *The Art-Treasures Examiner*, p. i.

33 *Ibid.*, pp. 2, 23.

34 Finke, 'The Art-Treasures Exhibition', p. 102 and Hunt, *The Frock-Coated Communist*, p. 210.

35 Roy Whitfield, *Frederich Engels in Manchester: The Search for a Shadow*, pp. 210–12.

36 John Ruskin, *The Political Economy of Art: Being the Substance (with Additions) of Two Lectures Delivered at Manchester, July 10th and 13th, 1857*.

37 *Ibid.*, p. 4.

38 *Ibid.*, pp. 91, 131. On the reception of Ruskin's thesis see David Throsby, 'The political economy of art: Ruskin and contemporary cultural economics'.

39 On the cult of Dante see the seminal study by Alison Milbank, *Dante and the Victorians*, and the essays collected in Nick Havely (ed.), *Dante in the Nineteenth Century: Reception, Canonicity, Popularization*. On Dante's moral universe see Patrick Boyde, *Human Vices and Human Worth in Dante's 'Comedy'*.

40 See John Maddison, 'Basil Champneys and the John Rylands Library'.

41 D.A. Farnie, *John Rylands of Manchester*, pp. 53–4, 91.

42 The Rylands's interest in Italy and travel is apparent from the volumes and guidebooks to Italy held in their library at Longford Hall. See *Catalogue of the Library of John Rylands at Longford Hall*. See, for example, *Italy Revisited* by A. Gallenga, Vol. 1, No. 946–7; *Something of Italy* by W. Chambers, No. 1216;

Italy, Sketches and Stories of Life in Italy, No. 471; *Travels through Italy* by John Northall, No. 769.

43 Farnie, *John Rylands*, p. 37.

44 *Governor's Minute Book*, I (1899–1910), p. 210.

45 Farnie notes that only five out of the nineteen bookcases were listed in the 1881 catalogue: Farnie, *John Rylands*, p. 22. On the creation of the John Rylands Library by Enriqueta see *ibid*., pp. 56–64, and Henry Guppy, *The John Rylands Library: 1899–1935. A Brief Record of its History*.

46 The reason I say 'at least' is that although eleven are listed in the first printed John Rylands Library catalogue of 1899, Mrs Rylands retained books for her own library at Longford Hall, many of which she then gifted prior to her death in 1908. There is, to my knowledge, no known catalogue of her retained personal library. See *Catalogue of the Printed Books and Manuscripts in the John Rylands Library Manchester*, I, p. 509. On the Spencer collection, see Anthony Lister, 'The Althorp Library of Second Earl Spencer'. The Spencer 1502 Aldine vellum vulgate *Divina commedia*, one of only six in the world, was sold in the 1988 Rylands auction. See *Books from the John Rylands University Library of Manchester, London Thursday 14th April 1988*, pp. 58–9.

47 For a summary description and assessment of the Dante holdings see Kathleen Speight, 'The John Rylands Library Dante Collection'.

48 Italian MS 1 and Italian MS 2, John Rylands Library, Manchester. See Moses Tyson, 'Hand-list of the collections of French and Italian manuscripts in the John Rylands Library', pp. 6–7, 37–8.

49 I would like to thank my colleague, John Hodgson, Collections and Research Support Manager (Manuscripts and Archives) at the John Rylands Library, for bringing this quotation to my attention. See Nicolas Barker, *Bibliotheca Lindesiana: The Lives and Collections of Alexander William, 25th Earl of Crawford and 8th Earl of Balcarres, and James Ludovic, 26th Earl of Crawford and 9th Earl of Balcarres* pp. 195–6.

50 'Gifts to the Library' (1906), p. 182.

51 *Catalogue of the Dante Collection presented by Willard Fiske*, compiled by Theodor Wesley Koch, and M. Fowler, *Catalogue of the Dante Collection Presented by William Fiske: Additions 1898–1920*.

52 'Gifts to the Library' (1906), p. 182.

53 See Ettore Bonora (ed.), *Dizionario della letteratura italiana: gli autori, i movimenti, le opere*, II 448, pp. 96–105; Alberto Petrucciani, 'Storie di ordinaria dittatura: I bibliotecari italiani e il fascismo', pp. 417–40; and Valgimigli, *La colonia italiana*, p. 75.

54 'Giuseppe Lando Passerini e l'Accademia Petrarca. L'archivio e la biblioteca di un "aretino" ritrovato. Atti della Giornata di Studio, Arezzo, Casa del Petrarca, 5 giugno 2007'.

55 *Catalogue of an Exhibition of the Works of Dante Alighieri March to October, MCMIX*.

56 I would like to thank Anne Young, former curator of the John Rylands Library archive, for bringing this letter to my attention.

57 *Minute Books of the Manchester Dante Society*, Vol. 1, 1.

58 See Martin John Broadley, *Louis Charles Casartelli: A Bishop in Peace and War*.

59 *Minute Books*, 1, 13 September 1906, p. 4.

60 William Warren Vernon, *The Contrasts in Dante. A Lecture Delivered at the University on 24th October 1906*.

61 *Minute Books*, 1, 24 October 1906, p. 10.

62 *Minute Books*, 1, 7 November 1906, p. 16; 11 April 1907, p. 36.

63 See Cecil Grayson (ed.), *The World of Dante. Essays on Dante and His Time* and George H. Gifford, 'A history of the Dante Society'.

64 See Patrizia Salvetti, *Immagine nazionale ed emigrazione nella Società Dante Alighieri*. For the *Società dantesca italiana*, see www.dantesca.it/eng (accessed 10 September 2012).

65 Two letters of Passerini to Guppy concerning Dante books, 6 November 1906, 4/1/4/4/, John Rylands University Library Archive, Manchester. Handwritten: 'Ho ammirato, nella Biblioteca Laurenziana di Firenze, un esemplare della Storia della J. Rylands Library dalla S. V. illma. Compilata, e mi permetto di pregarla, se ciò è possibile, di volermene inviare in dono un esemplare, che mi sarebbe gratissimo'.

66 'About my books on Dante, I do not care to sale them for the present: so, when You will be disposed to make some addition to the Dante section, I will be glad if You will remember of them', *ibid.*, 29 November 1906.

67 See Italian MS 49, John Rylands Library, Manchester, and A. Cossio, 'The Landi Dante Codex at Manchester'. Cossio's description of the manuscript draws heavily on the description sent to Manchester by Passerini together with the manuscript itself.

68 Speight, 'John Rylands Library Dante Collection', p. 179.

69 See, for example, the manuscript's omission from Sandro Bertelli, *La Commedia all'antica* although there is a discussion of Rylands Italian MS 48 (Veneto, sec. XV–XVI), p. 170. For the most recent description see Enrico Malato and Andrea Mazzucchi (eds), *Censimento dei commenti danteschi: I commenti di tradizione manoscritta (fino a 1480)*, II, pp. 852–3. The aim is to add the 'Codex Mancuniensis' to the early printed editions of Dante's epic poem which have been digitised as part of the 'Manchester Digital Dante' project led by Dr Guyda Armstrong, which seeks to make Manchester's Dante holdings more accessible. See http://manchesterdante.wordpress.com/ (accessed 10 September 2012).

70 Dante Alighieri, *La Divina Commedia, illustrata dall'ingegnere Attilio Razzolini di Firenze. A.D. 1902*. A brief description is in Tyson, 'Hand-list of the collections of French and Italian manuscripts in the John Rylands Library', p. 56.

71 Dante Alighieri, *La Vita Nuova (The New Life) secondo la lezione del Cod. Strozziano VI, 143 trascritta e illustrata da A. Razzolini*.

72 Dante Alighieri, *La Divina Commedia: illustrata da Attilio Razzolini*. For the recent facsimile edition see, *La Divina Commedia: illustrata da Attilio Razzolini con la trascrizione del poema 'secondo l'antica vulgata' a cura di Giorgio Petrocchi*.

73 'Gifts to the Library', (1908), pp. 360–1.

74 Kathleen Speight, *Manchester Dante Society: Founded 1906. A Short Account of the First Fifty Years*. Details of the Manchester Dante Society's activities are contained in the series of Minute Books and scrapbooks of press clippings held by the Department of Italian Studies, University of Manchester.

75 *Manchester Guardian*, 23 August 1919. See *Minute Books*, 2, p. 14.

76 See, amongst his works, Edmund D. Gardner, *Dante; The Story of Florence*; and *Italy: A Companion to Italian Studies*.

77 See Walter L. Bullock, 'A collection of cinquecento books'.

78 Tim Ingold, *Lines: A Brief History*, p. 90 (italics in original), and Suzanne Reynolds, *Medieval Reading: Grammar, Rhetoric and the Classical Text*.

79 *Minute Books*, 3, 3 December 1947, p. 34.

80 See Michael Baxandall, *Episodes: A Memory Book*, pp. 45–62, 61.

Bibliography

Alighieri, Dante, *La Divina Commedia, illustrata dall'ingegnere Attilio Razzolini di Firenze. A.D. 1902*, Italian MS 50, John Rylands Library, Manchester.

Alighieri, Dante, *La Divina Commedia: illustrata da Attilio Razzolini* (Milan: Alfieri e Lacroix, 1902–03).

Alighieri, Dante, *La Vita Nuova (The New Life) secondo la lezione del Cod. Strozziano VI, 143 trascritta e illustrata da A. Razzolini* (Florence: Tipografia Domenicana, 1906).

Alighieri, Dante, *Inferno*, trans. Robin Kirkpatrick (London: Penguin, 2006).

Alighieri, Dante, *La Divina Commedia: illustrata da Attilio Razzolini con la trascrizione del poema 'secondo l'antica vulgata' a cura di Giorgio Petrocchi* (Florence: Il Polistampa, 2008).

Archer, John H.G. (ed.), *Art and Architecture in Victorian Manchester* (Manchester: Manchester University Press, 1985).

The Art-Treasures Examiner: A Pictorial, Critical, and Historical Record of the Art-Treasures Exhibition at Manchester in 1857 (Manchester: Alexander Ireland and Co., 1857).

Barker, Nicolas, *Bibliotheca Lindesiana: The Lives and Collections of Alexander William, 25th Earl of Crawford and 8th Earl of Balcarres, and James Ludovic, 26th Earl of Crawford and 9th Earl of Balcarres* (London: Bernard Quaritch, 1978).

Baxandall, Michael, *Episodes: A Memory Book* (London: Frances Lincoln, 2010).

Bertelli, Sandro, *La Commedia all'antica* (Florence: Mandragora, 2007).

Bindman, David, Stephen Hebron and Michael O'Neil (eds), *Dante Rediscovered: From Blake to Rodin* (Grasmere: Wordsworth Trust, 2007).

Blake, William, 'Milton: a poem', in Robert N. Essick and Joseph Viscomi (eds), *The Illuminated Books of William Blake*, Vol. 5 (Princeton NJ: Princeton University Press, 1998).

Bonora, Ettore (ed.), *Dizionario della letteratura italiana: gli autori, i movimenti, le opere*, 2 vols. (Milan: Rizzoli, 1977).

Books from the John Rylands University Library of Manchester, London Thursday 14th April 1988 (London: Sotheby's, 1988).

Boyde, Patrick, *Human Vices and Human Worth in Dante's 'Comedy'* (Cambridge: Cambridge University Press, 2000).

Broadley, Martin John, *Louis Charles Casartelli: A Bishop in Peace and War* (Manchester: Koinonia, 2006).

Bullock, Walter L., 'A collection of cinquecento books', *Italica*, 8:4 (1931), pp. 1–6.

Catalogue of the Dante Collection presented by Willard Fiske, compiled by Theodore Wesley Koch (Ithaca, NY: The Library, 1898–1900).

Catalogue of an Exhibition of the Works of Dante Alighieri March to October, MCMIX (Manchester and London: Sherratt and Hughes, 1909).

Catalogue of the Library of John Rylands at Longford Hall, 1881, 2 vols, English MS 1140, John Rylands Library, Manchester.

Catalogue of the Printed Books and Manuscripts in the John Rylands Library Manchester, 3 vols (Manchester: J.E. Cornish, 1899).

Cossio, A., 'The Landi Dante Codex at Manchester', *The Antiquary* 6 (1910), pp. 209–13.

Dickens, Charles, *Hard Times* (Oxford: Oxford University Press, 2008 [1854]).

Disraeli, Benjamin, *Sybil or The Two Nations* (Oxford: Oxford University Press, 1981 [1845]).

Disraeli, Benjamin, *Coningsby or The New Generation* (Oxford: Oxford University Press, 1982 [1844]).

Engels, Friedrich, *The Condition of the Working Class in England* (Oxford: Oxford University Press, 1993 [1845]).

Farnie, D.A., *John Rylands of Manchester* (Manchester: John Rylands Library, 1993).

Feuer, Lewis S. (ed.), *Marx and Engels: Basic Writings on Politics and Philosophy* (Glasgow: Collins, 1969).

Finke, Ulrich, 'The Art-Treasures Exhibition', in Archer (ed.), *Art and Architecture in Victorian Manchester*.

Fowler, M., *Catalogue of the Dante Collection Presented by William Fiske: Additions 1898–1920* (Ithaca, NY: The Library, 1921).

Gardner, Edmund D., *Dante* (London: J.M. Dent, 1900).

Gardner, Edmund D., *The Story of Florence* (London: J.M. Dent, 1901).

Gardner, Edmund D., *Italy: A Companion to Italian Studies* (London: Methuen, 1934).

Gifford, George H., 'A history of the Dante Society', *Annual Reports of the Dante Society*, 74 (1956), pp. 3–27.

'Gifts to the Library', *Bulletin of the John Rylands Library*, 1:4 (1906), pp. 182–3.

'Gifts to the Library', *Bulletin of the John Rylands Library*, 1:6 (1908), pp. 360–1.

'Giuseppe Lando Passerini e l'Accademia Petrarca. L'archivio e la biblioteca di un "aretino" ritrovato. Atti della Giornata di Studio, Arezzo, Casa del Petrarca, 5 giugno 2007', *Atti e memorie dell'Accademia Petrarca di lettere, arti e scienza di Arezzo*, 69 (2007), pp. 335–471.

Governor's Minute Book, I (1899–1910), John Rylands University Library, Manchester.

Grayson, Cecil (ed.), *The World of Dante. Essays on Dante and His Time* (Oxford: Clarendon Press, 1980).

Guppy, Henry, *The John Rylands Library: 1899–1935. A Brief Record of its History with Descriptions of the Building and its Contents* (Manchester: Manchester University Press, 1935).

Havely, Nick (ed.), *Dante in the Nineteenth Century: Reception, Canonicity, Popularization* (Oxford: Peter Lang, 2011).

Honess, Claire, *From Florence to the Heavenly City: The Poetry of Citizenship in Dante* (Oxford: Leggenda, 2006).

Hunt, Tristram, *Building Jerusalem: The Rise and Fall of the Victorian City* (London: Weidenfeld and Nicolson, 2004).

Hunt, Tristram, *The Frock-Coated Communist: The Life and Times of the Original Champagne Socialist* (London: Penguin, 2009).

Hunt, Tristram and Victoria Whitfield (eds), *Art Treasures in Manchester: 150 Years On* (Manchester: Manchester Art Gallery, 2007).

Ingold, Tim, *Lines: A Brief History* (London: Routledge, 2007).

Keen, Catherine, *Dante and the City* (Stroud: Tempus, 2003).

Kidd, Alan J. and K.W. Roberts (eds), *City, Class and Culture: Studies of Social Policy and Cultural Production in Victorian Manchester* (Manchester: Manchester University Press, 1985).

Lantschner, Patrick, 'The Ciompi Revolution constructed: modern historians and the nineteenth-century paradigm of revolution', *Annali di storia di Firenze*, 4 (2009), pp. 277–97.

Leahy, Helen Rees (ed.), *Art, city, spectacle: the 1857 Manchester Art-Treasures Exhibition revisited*, themed issue of the *Bulletin of the John Rylands Library of Manchester*, 87:2 (2005).

Lister, Anthony, 'The Althorp Library of Second Earl Spencer', *Bulletin of the John Rylands Library*, 71:2 (1989), pp. 64–86.

Macdonald, Stuart, 'The Royal Manchester Institution', in Archer (ed.), *Art and Architecture in Victorian Manchester*.

Maddison, John, 'Basil Champneys and the John Rylands Library', in Archer (ed.), *Art and Architecture in Victorian Manchester*.

Malato, Enrico and Andrea Mazzucchi (eds), *Censimento dei commenti danteschi: I commenti di tradizione manoscritta (fino a 1480)*, 2 vols, with the collaboration of Massimiliano Corrado (Rome: Salerno, 2011).

Manchester Athenaeum Addresses 1835–1885, also Report of Proceedings of the Meeting of the Members in Celebration of the 50th Anniversary of the Institution, October 28th, 1885 (Manchester: Printed for the Directors, 1888).

Marcus, Steven, *Engels, Manchester, and the Working Class* (London: Weidenfeld and Nicolson, 1974).

Messinger, Gary S., *Manchester in the Victorian Age: The Half-Known City* (Manchester: Manchester University Press, 1985).

Milbank, Alison, *Dante and the Victorians* (Manchester: Manchester University Press, 1998).

Minute Books of the Manchester Dante Society, Department of Italian Studies, University of Manchester.

Parkinson-Bailey, John J., *Manchester: An Architectural History* (Manchester: Manchester University Press, 2000).

Pass, Anthony J., 'Thomas Worthington', in Archer (ed.), *Art and Architecture in Victorian Manchester*.

Pergam, Elizabeth A., *The Manchester Art Treasures Exhibition of 1857: Entrepreneurs, Connoisseurs and the Public* (Basingstoke: Ashgate, 2011).

Petrucciani, Alberto, 'Storie di ordinaria dittatura: I bibliotecari italiani e il fascismo, 1922–1942', *Bollettino della Associazione italiana biblioteche*, 4 (2004), pp. 417–40.

Powell, Cecilia, *Turner in the South: Rome, Naples, Florence* (New Haven and London: Yale University Press, 1987).

Reynolds, Suzanne, *Medieval Reading: Grammar, Rhetoric and the Classical Text* (Cambridge: Cambridge University Press, 1996).

Ruskin, John, *The Political Economy of Art: Being the Substance (with Additions) of Two Lectures Delivered at Manchester, July 10th and 13th, 1857* (London: Smith, Elder and Co., 1857).

Salvetti, Patrizia, *Immagine nazionale ed emigrazione nella Società Dante Alighieri* (Rome: Bonacci, 1995).

Speight, Kathleen, *Manchester Dante Society: Founded 1906. A Short Account of the First Fifty Years* (Manchester: Morris and Yeaman, 1957).

Speight, Kathleen, 'The John Rylands Library Dante Collection', *Bulletin of the John Rylands Library*, 44:1 (1961), pp. 175–212.

Stewart, Cecil, *The Stones of Manchester* (London: Arnold, 1956).

Taylor, A.J.P., 'Manchester', in *Essays in English History* (Harmondsworth: Penguin, 1976).

Throsby, David, 'The political economy of art: Ruskin and contemporary cultural economics', *History of Political Economy*, 43 (2011), pp. 275–94.

Tyson, Moses, 'Hand-list of the collections of French and Italian manuscripts in the John Rylands Library', *Bulletin of the John Rylands Library*, 14:2 (1930), pp. 3–68.

Valgimigli, Azeglio, *La colonia italiana di Manchester (1794–1932)* (Florence: Enrico Ariani, 1932).

Vernon, William Warren, *The Contrasts in Dante. A Lecture Delivered at the University on 24th October 1906* (Manchester: Manchester University Press, 1906).

Wallace, David, *Premodern Places: Calais to Surinam, Chaucer to Aphra Behn* (Oxford: Blackwell, 2004).

Whiffen, Marcus, 'The architecture of Sir Charles Barry in Manchester and neighbourhood', in Archer (ed.), *Art and Architecture in Victorian Manchester.*

Whitfield, Roy, *Frederich Engels in Manchester: The Search for a Shadow* (Salford: Working Class Movement Library, 1988).

Wilson, Arline, '"The Florence of the North"? The civic culture of Liverpool in the early nineteenth century', in Kidd and Nicholls (eds), *City, Class and Culture.*

Wilson, Arline, *William Roscoe: Commerce and Culture* (Liverpool: Liverpool University Press, 2008).

Wolff, Janet, 'Memories and Micrologies: Walter Benjamin's artwork essay reconsidered', in Laura Marcus and Lynda Nead (eds), *The Actuality of Walter Benjamin* (London: Lawrence & Wishart, 1998).

The image of a well-ordered city: nineteenth-century Manchester theatre architecture and the urban spectator[1]

Viv Gardner

Provocations

> [Patrick Hughes] saw Fallon coming out of the Concert Hall bleeding from a wound on the head, and followed by a band of scuttlers headed by Beaty, who was taking off his waistcoat and shouting, 'Let's cut him up.' ... a rush was made in the direction of where he was standing. He [Hughes] ran, but was soon overtaken. He was kicked until he fell, and Beaty stabbed him on the head. Hewitt also stabbed him, and holding a knife covered with blood, over him, shouted, 'Shall I run it into him again?' The scuttlers however ran away, and the witness ... fainted and fell. Whilst lying on the ground he was stabbed in the shoulder by Norris. Beaty also rushed up, and was sitting on him with an open knife in his hand, when he was
>
> KNOCKED AWAY BY TWO GENTLEMEN
>
> *The Weekly Standard and Express*, 16 February 1895

In the first half of the 1890s there were a number of 'scuttling' incidents on Lower Mosley Street that originated inside the music hall known variously as the People's Concert Hall, the Casino, the Cass or 'Burton's Night School', and which spilled out onto the street itself. In May 1891, James Hillier, the notorious leader of the Deansgate Boys, was confronted in the gallery by the Bungall Boys, led by Tommy Callaghan, who had crossed the city from the area near London Road Station. The affray – with belts, an iron bar and knives – spread onto the street outside the Concert Inn opposite, and resulted in the hospitalisation of the two gang leaders and the imprisonment of three gang members for grievous bodily harm. Later that year, in August, Hillier

was involved in another fight in the gallery, this time with the Grey Mare
Boys from the Bradford area of Manchester, in which he stabbed the leader
of his rivals in the neck.[2] These incidents are not in themselves particularly
significant to the history of Manchester theatre – they were part of a decades-
long battle between rival gangs of scuttlers which traversed the city centre
from the 1870s to early 1900s – but neither were they unique; a 'scuttling
affray' was also reported at the St James's Theatre on Oxford Street in 1893
and another in 1895, again involving Tommy Callaghan and the Bungall
Boys, and once again, a 'most extraordinary scene of violence and lawlessness'
spilled onto the street.[3] In 1894, '50 youths, said to be from Owens College'
were 'unceremoniously' ejected from the pit of the Prince's Theatre during the
pantomime, by policemen wielding 'scuffle sticks' which were 'liberally used'.
'The whole gang [of students] were ultimately turned into the street, where
a great crowd was attracted by the commotion.[4] Though it is impossible to
know how typical and frequent these incidents were, the fact that Callaghan,
the 'King of the Scuttlers', was involved made the scuttling events newsworthy
beyond Manchester – reporting of the cases make it clear that the situation in
some of the city's theatres was sufficiently threatening to warrant concern and
regulation. In both the St James's Theatre incidents and that at the Prince's
Theatre, there was, as was common, policing inside the theatre; in 1895 St
James's employed 'a man named Hindley to keep order in the gallery' and at
least one other 'chucker-out'.[5] The level (in terms of number and leadership)
of policing at the Prince's on this occasion is, however, more remarkable and
perhaps suggests something of the importance to the theatre and city of the
'victims': 'for the comfort and protection [of those who endeavour to take an
intelligent interest in the pantomime] a strong body of detectives and plain
clothes policemen had been scattered about the pit, under the direction of
Chief-detective Caminada'.[6]

But how threatening were these incidents to those not involved? The
publicity surrounding outbreaks of gang violence in London produced a
'Hooligan Panic' in 1898. The *Echo* wrote of these that 'We steadily shut our
eyes to the submerged lawlessness of less fortunate districts until a series
of … Hooligan exploits, make us not only aware of what is going on, but
actually afraid for our lives.'[7] The 'scuttling' incidents may not have caused
a 'panic' but they were sufficiently worrying for an extraordinary meeting of
Manchester and Salford magistrates to be held in 1890, where, among other
depositions, Mr T.C. Horsfall reported that 'on one or two occasions the Art
Museum had been invaded by lads of this kind, carrying knives, and evidently
prepared for mischief; and he knew for a fact that many respectable people in
the neighbourhood went in terror of their lives'.[8] Manchester's reputation as
'the New Hades'[9] from earlier in the century had not been entirely eradicated

Figure 15: People's Concert Hall, Lower Mosley Street, 1897.

despite the many improvements made to the city's social and working conditions. Images of the industrial city and its almost uncivilised, savage population, were very powerful and pervasive, dominated by pictures of the slum areas adjacent to the city centre from which the scuttlers were drawn.[10] In the 1890s this image was still perpetuated in journalism and fiction. In Mrs Humphrey Ward's popular novel, *The History of David Grieve*, Ancoats was depicted as:

> that teeming, squalid quarter which lies but a stone's throw from the principal thoroughfares of Manchester ... there are innumerable low, red-brick streets where the poor live and work, which have none of the trim uniformity which belongs to the worker's quarters in the factory towns pure and simple ... Manchester in its worst streets is more squalid, more haphazard, more nakedly poor even than London ... mill-girls [could be seen] standing on the Ancoats pavements; the drunken lurryman [*sic*] tottering out from the public house under the biting sleet of February; the ragged barefoot boys and girls swarming and festering in the slums; the young men struggling all around him for subsistence and success ... [11]

In Margaret Harkness's melodramatic novel, *A Manchester Shirtmaker: A Realistic Story of Today*, in the district of Angel Meadow, also 'but a stone's throw from the principal thoroughfares of Manchester' and the fashionable

Figure 16: View of Lower Mosley Street, c.1897.

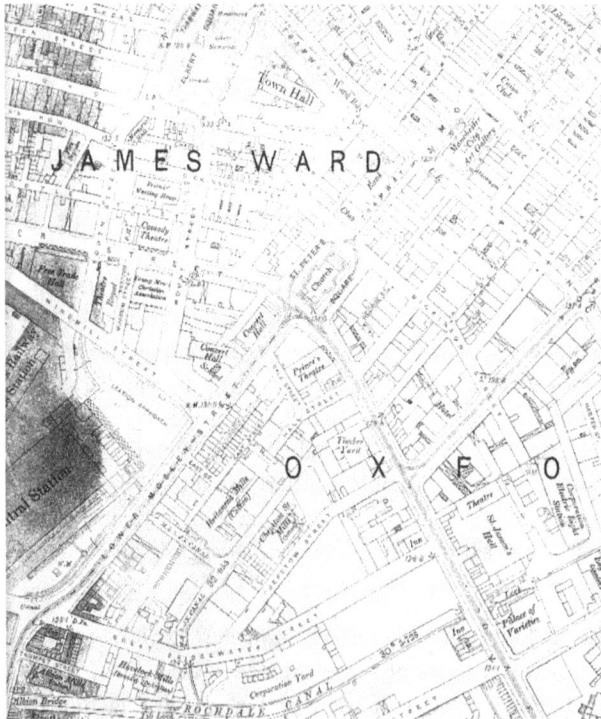

Figure 17: Ordinance Survey Map, 1893, showing theatres on Oxford Street, Peter Street and Lower Mosley Street.

shopping district around St Ann's Square, the heroine finds: 'Women with bloated features and matted hair, whose language none could understand except the initiated, men besotted with drink, who barely spoke at all ... two women were fighting with clogs, those weapons which are much worse than nails or fists.'[12] The terror of 'respectable people' may have been exaggerated by Horsfall, but there was almost certainly a degree of apprehension among those visiting central Manchester, particularly in the evenings in pursuit of entertainment.

In Andrew Davies's book, *The Gangs of Manchester*, the picture of the People's Concert Hall (Figure 15) is captioned thus: 'The ugly façade of the People's Concert Hall, popularly known as the Cass and frequented by bands of scuttlers ...'[13] which suggests that the apparent notoriety of the Cass was in some way projected onto the aesthetics of its façade. This begs the question: did it appear ugly to the passers-by? Or any more ugly than the Day and Sunday School next door? Or Platt's tripe shop or the Concert Inn opposite (Figure 16)? What Davies's account does not consider is the building's relationship to other buildings, especially theatre buildings, in the vicinity, and the 'vocabulary' of theatre architecture in the city. In 1891, the People's Concert Hall stood within a quarter of a mile of nine other performance venues (Figure 17).[14] Most significantly, adjacent to the People's Concert Hall, but with its 'face' on Peter's Street, was the Gentlemen's Concert Hall (Figure 18); the rear of the Gentlemen's Concert Hall lay against the side of People's with only a narrow alleyway dividing them. How far was the largely middle-class audience for Jenny Lind, Squire Bancroft's readings of 'Charles Dickens's "Christmas Carol" as arranged by himself' and the radical Independent Theatre Society's performances of Ibsen, George Moore and George Bernard Shaw at the Gentlemen's Concert Hall, intimidated by the proximity of the Cass with its 'ugly' façade, urban lower class audience, and threats of gang fights spilling onto the streets? If they were coming from the south Manchester suburbs or Cheshire by rail,[15] they needs must walk the short distance from Central Station (opened in 1880 for the Cheshire Lines Committee) up Lower Mosley Street past the 'Old Cass' to other performance venues; there was also a cab rank outside the Gentlemen's on Lower Mosley Street (see Figure 23). Were the 'Two Gentlemen' who assisted Patrick Hughes and 'knocked away' Richard Beaty, on their way to more 'gentlemanly' cultural events in the city centre? How can we evaluate the impact of these street incidents and this street architecture on the experience of theatregoers and urban spectators in Manchester at the end of the nineteenth century? How far was the demolition of both the People's Concert Hall and Gentlemen's Concert Hall in 1897–98 attributable to the late nineteenth-century city's civic agenda to challenge the city's reputation as crime-ridden and dangerous, and to develop a 'well-ordered city' in both image and fact?

THE CONCERT HALL, MANCHESTER.

Figure 18: Gentlemen's Concert Hall, facing St Peter's Square, 1865.

Any teleological narrative of progress and advancement would simplify the complex relationship of performance, performance sites and urban spectatorship within Manchester. Therefore this essay seeks, with caution, to suggest how theatre architecture might have been understood by the citizens and visitors who moved around the streets abutting sites of performance and how it might be seen to reflect the changing aspirations – commercial, civic and aesthetic – of the theatre owners and the city fathers towards the end of the century.

The city as a work of art

M. Christine Boyer argues that '[u]ntil the end of the nineteenth century, the city as a work of art carried a sense of moral order within its aesthetic forms, bringing the memory of a harmonious society to public view' and of the stage offering a 'perfected image of a well-ordered city'.[16] Evidence suggests that it was *by*, rather than *until*, the end of the nineteenth century that Manchester came close to creating a city that projected a public view of 'a harmonious society'. Boyer's thesis is largely dedicated to scenography and the internal architecture of the theatre and urban architecture, but it is possible to argue that it was not just the internal but external staging of the theatre that mirrored the aesthetic and civic agenda so clearly manifested through the architectural arrangements of the expanding Victorian city. As Manchester developed its entertainment industry, the geographical location of performance venues and the organisation of the outward, public face of theatre buildings maps the 'advancement' – or decline – of the theatre as a cultural force in the city.[17]

Joanne Robinson has written that 'layering social, cultural and economic data onto a basic spatial representation can help us to identify and sketch in the connections between that material so as to begin to build a sense of the social and cultural landscape through which the spectators of performance ... moved on their way to the theatre'.[18] However, those connections are often in tension, as Henri Lefebvre writes:

> urban space *is* concrete contradiction. The study of its logical and formal properties leads to a dialectical analysis of its contradictions. The urban center fills to saturation: it decays or explodes. From time to time, it reverses direction and surrounds itself with emptiness and scarcity. More often, it assumes and proposes the concentration of *everything* there is in the world ... the fruits of the earth, the products of industry, human works, objects and instruments, acts and situations, signs and symbols.[19]

Any study of late nineteenth-century Manchester performance sites must take into account connections *and* contradictions. Just as there was not one type of performance venue in Manchester (in 1891 Peter Street, Oxford Street and Lower Mosley Street housed music halls, a circus, concert halls, theatres of variety and dramatic theatres), one type of actor, theatre owner or builder, it is not possible to speak of 'the spectator' or even group of spectators, just as there is never one audience inside the theatre.

Jim Davis and Victor Emeljanow, in their study of Victorian audiences, sought to dismantle 'the myths and ideologically driven constructions through which the composition and behaviour of nineteenth-century audiences have been conveyed to us', and concluded that there was:

> no such thing as a Victorian audience, but rather a variety of audiences, embodying a range of perspectives. We can never be sure who exactly constituted these audiences, because even social demography can only suggest possibilities; it cannot provide definite answers. Yet, even if social demography cannot tell us exactly who attended London theatres in the nineteenth century, it can at least broaden or even redefine prior perspectives.[20]

Therefore to speak of 'an' or 'the' audience inside or outside the theatre suggests homogeneity, an audience rather than many audiences, one response rather than multiple or varied responses. And the audience for the theatre's architecture in the late nineteenth century was not just those 'on their way to the theatre', but those who passed by, the urban spectator, whether they were engaged in business, consumption, pleasure (in all its urban manifestations), flânerie or criminality.[21]

By the 1880s, most of the middle-class residential areas of the city centre had been replaced by civic, industrial and commercial buildings, leaving Manchester's working class living in districts close to the centre and their places of employment, often cheek by jowl with the unemployed and indigent. The 'civic' was increasingly inscribed onto the cityscape across a relatively small central area with the most important cultural buildings grouped along Cross Street and Upper Mosley Street. Patrick Joyce argues that the Royal Exchange (built 1874) on Cross Street, the cathedral (remodelled between 1864 and 1871), and the Town Hall (built 1867–77) 'throughout the century made up a trinity of "major" sites of the city. This trinity of commerce, religion and city government thus defined the city in these representations. These different elements were invariably placed in terms of an historical narrative of the town or city which itself emphasized progress and improvement.'[22] And it is within this 'trinity' that theatres sought to locate themselves throughout the nineteenth century.

In a speech in 1893, Herbert Beerbohm Tree, perhaps seeking to ingratiate himself with his Manchester audience, declared that 'We theatrical folk regard Manchester as the home of art', and the touring actor, 'Jack Rover', described Manchester 'as the cradle of histrionic genius' for its nurturing of Charles Calvert and Henry Irving.[23] Throughout its history, large sections of the theatre business have battled to attain the 'respectable' standing of the other 'arts', while other forms of performance have been more than content to attract the widest and most popular types of audience. The history of Manchester's nineteenth- and early twentieth-century 'respectable' theatre's aspiration to stand beside the other arts and cultural institutions is inscribed on the streets, as is the subversion of that ambition by less reputable theatre establishments.

Manchester, like many other British provincial cities and towns, has a rich performance history, professional and amateur, commercial and subsidised, popular and radical, street- and building-based, dating back to the mid-1700s.[24] The city's first permanent theatres were built between 1753 and 1845, scattered across what was then a town centre – the Marsden Street theatre (1743–75); the first Theatre Royal at the junction of York Street and Spring Gardens (1775–1869 under various names); the second Theatre Royal in Fountain Street (1807–44), the Olympic in Stevenson Square (1838–41) and Cooke's Circus (1844–50), renamed the City Theatre in December 1847.[25] The second Theatre Royal and the Portico Library (1802–6) shared an architect, Thomas Harrison, who was also responsible for the new Cotton Exchange (1806–8). In 1836, the Theatre Royal was linked, physically and ideologically, to other cultural monuments built in the period 1780–1810: the Assembly Rooms on Mosley Street (1792), with its ballroom, tea rooms and billiard room with separate entrance, and the Portico Library. These three buildings were connected by 'elaborately decorated temporary buildings … and the Theatre Royal transformed into a pink and white Persian Pavilion' to accommodate a great fancy dress ball as part of a Festival of Music.[26] However, the bourgeois ambition of the Theatre Royal project was, arguably, excessive or perhaps premature. In an attempt to reduce the theatre's capacity to a sustainable 2,000, the lobby, described by Mrs Linnaeus Banks as 'so capacious that a coach and four could have been driven from one end to the other', had in 1831 been converted into a warehouse by its manager, the elder Charles Macready.[27] Then, following refurbishment in 1842, and a number of more successful seasons, the theatre was destroyed by fire in 1844. With an insurance settlement of £15,700 the proprietor, John Knowles, decided to build his new theatre on Peter Street. Its location is important, as is its architecture. In building on Peter Street, John Knowles was moving – whether for commercial or space reasons[28] – away from the 'cultural centre' and Joyce's powerful 'trinity' of buildings – becoming part of what he describes as 'the marginal city … the new, unfamiliar, potentially dangerous city of pleasure and consumption … the city of the music halls, the theatres, the bars and brothels'.[29]

The 1840s saw development of the area to the west of the city centre; this would become known as Manchester's 'Theatreland', along the axis of Quay Street (northwards), Peter Street and Oxford Street, beginning with the building of the third Theatre Royal in 1845 (Figure 19). Designed by Francis Chester and 'a Mr Irwin' for Knowles, the theatre was built on the site of the Wellington Inn and Brogden's horse bazaar, which had been demolished to make space for the theatre enterprise.[30] Clare Hartwell has described this theatre as a 'splendid classical composition in stone; one of the best examples of theatre architecture surviving anywhere in England from the first half of the 19C … with its giant recessed portico with Corinthian columns and pilasters'.[31] She believes that its design was influenced by Charles Cockerell's Branch Bank of England being erected at the same time in nearby King Street, but one might equally argue that the theatre sought visual synergy with its recent neighbour, the Royal Manchester Institution on Mosley Street (Charles Barry, 1829–35), with its restrained classicism and Ionic columns, which was to house the city's art collection. The Theatre Royal's cultural credentials are further asserted through the copy of Peter Scheemakers's statue of Shakespeare in Westminster Abbey which still commands a central position in a pedimented niche in the frontage in its current incarnation as a night club.[32] The theatre then had

Figure 19: Theatre Royal, Peter Street, c.1885.

moved, if not to the periphery of the emergent city, at least to a position at some distance from the burgeoning commercial and administrative heart. It joined the Gentlemen's Concert Hall on Peter Street, also neo-classical in style, built by subscription in 1830, and designed by Richard Lane. What remained at the centre were the other architectural manifestations of Manchester's cultural development, the Portico Library, the Royal Manchester Institution and the Athenaeum Club on Princess Street (Charles Barry, 1836–39) – 'an institution for literary, political and scientific uses, [built] by a number of gentlemen who feel the desire to bring together in such a Club the class of superior mercantile servants and young men … to the news-room, the library, lectures etc.',[33] the 'institution which perhaps most clearly revealed the concern of Manchester's middle class with the cultural image of the city'.[34] So paradoxically, although the new Theatre Royal was visually in harmony with its fellow arts and cultural institutions with a shared classical vocabulary, its location was more geographically and culturally 'marginal'; closer not only to the bars and brothels, but also to the mills, industrial sites and working-class districts that were adjacent to the city centre, and also further from the advancing consumer heartlands north of Piccadilly Gardens.

Peter Street was a mixture of entertainment and educational or philanthropic institutions. To service both the daytime commercial, and the night-time

Figure 20: Free Trade Hall and Theatre Royal, Peter Street, n.d.

entertainment, activities, there were in 1900 on the east side four restaurants, a beer retailer and a tobacconist.[35] On the opposite side of the road, there were two more eating places including an 'Oyster Rooms and Stout House' and two shops. The chemist next to the Tivoli was reputedly 'beloved by theatricals for many a year. Sandersons the home of "Throat Specific" was patronised by all the famous artists', according to Joyce Knowlson. 'The Sandersons lived on the premises and let the touring artists use an upstairs room while the wives went looking for "digs". It became a sort of club for them to congregate in.'[36] Closer to the junction with Oxford Street were the Manchester and Salford Ragged School Union premises and the several Christian associations for the assistance of young working men.

On the opposite corner to the Theatre Royal in 1845 stood a substantial brick building, which became known in 1855 as the Free Trade Hall, erected in 1843 for the Anti-Corn Law League on St Peter's Field, site of the Peterloo Massacre of 1819. A stone-built building replaced it between 1853 and 1856 to celebrate the repeal of the Corn Laws, and provide a permanent monument to Manchester's moment of 'political triumph'[37] (Figure 20). Though the Free Trade Hall is most readily associated with the Hallé Orchestra, it was also a dramatic performance venue, thus combining both cultural and political populism within its walls. This theatrical 'trinity', the Free Trade Hall, Theatre Royal and Gentlemen's Concert Hall, provided an interesting juxtaposition of high art, classicism, radicalism and political martyrdom.[38] The Italianate frontage of the Free Trade Hall,[39] so different from the neo-classical concert hall and theatre, however, points to another of Manchester's mid-century industrial and civic projects. Edward Walters, the designer, was the foremost architect of Manchester's mid-century warehouses: he was responsible for the design of some fifteen and is also credited with transforming the city's architectural vocabulary in the 1840s. 'There was a freshness and purity about [his work] which quickly took hold of men's minds, and the building of Italian warehouses became almost a rage,' wrote the *Manchester Critic* in an obituary of Walters.[40] The palazzo warehouse – 'temples of commerce' or as Bradshaw's 1857 *Illustrated Guide to Manchester* put it 'structures fit for kings ... which many a monarch might well envy'[41] – dominated architectural design across the centre of Manchester into the twentieth century.[42] The scale of these warehouses – often five and six storeys in height – and the decorative boldness of the 'home trade warehouses', threatened to diminish existing buildings and challenge those built alongside them. Their influence can be seen in the design of most of the theatres built after 1850, including the Free Trade Hall. Theatre thus becomes part of a 'new Manchester', a temple of art and commerce.

The second half of the nineteenth century saw a boom in building along Peter Street, Oxford Street and the adjacent roads, including theatre building. The conversion of a Methodist chapel into the Alexandra Music Hall in 1865 was the first, and perhaps most symbolic of theatre's perceived 'godlessness', to be opened on Peter Street; the Gaiety Theatre of Varieties[43] in 1878, and the Grand Theatre or Pavilion of Varieties in 1883 followed, built within less than a quarter of a mile. On the first third of a mile of Oxford Street, which was dominated by commercial buildings (merchant and consular offices, small shops and eating houses), the Prince's Theatre was built in 1864, St James's Theatre in 1884 (inside the St James's Building) and the Palace Theatre of Varieties in 1891. Each of these theatres was substantially remodelled in the late nineteenth and early twentieth centuries to accommodate the changing tastes and size of their audiences, and advances in technical and safety resources – but did not lose their Italianate frontages until fashion dictated modernist design in the 1920s. A further two theatres were built in the first decade of the twentieth century on Oxford Street: the Midland Hotel Theatre (1903) and the Manchester Hippodrome (1904), and the 'Theatreland' axis was extended into Quay Street with the building of the New Theatre in 1912 (now the Opera House). In no other area of central Manchester was theatre building so extensive, although the only other city centre theatre, the Queen's on Bridge Street, was rebuilt in 1890 to accommodate 3,500 spectators. Beyond the city centre too, suburban theatre and music hall building boomed.

Although these post-1850 theatres – with the exception of the Manchester Hippodrome which was as tall as the adjacent buildings – do not match in

Figure 21: View of Oxford Street showing Prince's Theatre, n.d.

size the neighbouring buildings, they are assertive edifices, commercially and aesthetically. They no longer mimic the classical but imitate their merchant neighbours; and whilst the lines of their frontages are broken by necessary canopies and advertising hoardings, the elegantly windowed and decorated storeys of the 'palazzo' warehouses are there for all to admire (Figure 21). As with the earlier theatres there is a crossover amongst the architects between commerce and the commercial theatre. The Comedy Theatre (the rebuilt Gaiety Theatre, 1884) was designed and built by Alfred Darbyshire; the Prince's was designed originally by Edward Salomons and rebuilt by Darbyshire in 1869; the Palace was built by Darbyshire and Smith, whilst Frank Matcham was responsible for the 1898 remodelling of the Comedy Theatre and the design of the Manchester Hippodrome. Salomons and Darbyshire were both architects of commercial properties too, though in Darbyshire one sees the emergence of a theatre specialist alongside Matcham. Darbyshire was – in an extraordinary career – not only a theatre architect and developer of the Irving-Darbyshire Safety Theatre, but also an actor.[44]

There are exceptions to the grandiloquence of these theatre buildings, and it is perhaps significant that two of the more plain frontages are, as we have seen, the site of disturbances in the 1890s. The Casino, as the People's Concert Hall was originally known, was built in 1846 just behind the Gentlemen's Concert Hall. Its design was 'functional' as were many of the 'bread and butter' theatres built in Manchester's working-class suburbs by William Henry Broadhead at the turn of the century. However, it should be noted that it was one of the

Figure 22: St James's Theatre, Oxford Street, 1906.

earliest large-scale popular halls in Manchester, seating some 3,000 people, and drawing a lower-class audience away from the tavern singing saloons or penny gaffs.[45] The St James's Theatre and Opera House (1884) (Figure 22) on Oxford Street, had no frontage to speak of as it was set back behind the adjacent buildings and the far larger St James's Hall, with only a canopied passage to the street.[46] It was the least successful theatre on Oxford Street, perhaps because of its lack of 'front', and was, in 1908, the first theatre in Manchester to be converted to a cinema.

'A rapprochement of polite and popular culture': the urban spectator 1890–1900

The late Victorian middle-class spectator moving along Oxford Street and Peter Street would have experienced a symbiotic relationship between the theatres they visited and the coexistent street architecture that arguably reassured them. Whether they travelled to the theatre by train from the distant suburbs[47] – both Central Station and the Manchester South Junction 7 Altrincham Railway Station were within 50 metres of the main thoroughfare – or from the inner suburbs by tram and omnibus[48] the vista in Peter Street and Oxford Street was persuasively and harmoniously 'successful'. Though the experience was different for men and women – the predominance of commercial building was an indicator of an inherently masculine domain[49] – by 1900 the two streets were, in appearance, relatively secure. The new commercial buildings and the railways had displaced the early nineteenth-century slums and industrial areas from these streets,[50] though often only by a matter of a fraction of a mile. In 1870, the *Manchester Guardian* report, 'In the "slums" No. 4', had described Windmill Street, behind the Theatre Royal and Free Trade Hall, as 'a street occupied by such places that a local authority should forbid existing near places of public resort',[51] and little had changed by 1900. However, the public houses on Peter and Oxford Streets had been largely replaced by less threatening establishments for the respectable visitor to the city centre, such as restaurants, cafés and tea and coffee houses, though, again, the pubs remained within yards of the main thoroughfare on the side streets.[52] The frontages of the new buildings were ostentatiously wealthy, decorative and aesthetic, replicating the values embedded in suburban homes. The 'business side' of the premises, whether office, warehouse or theatre, was hidden behind ornamental façades, and where there were 'class co-minglings' the lower-class entrances to working or social areas were carefully separated from those of the middle classes. This is clearly seen with the theatres, where the decorative public frontage – with canopies and doorways for the monied classes – is very different from the utilitarian side walls – with the gallery entrance – which were most often covered with bill posters. The theatres had by the last decade of the nineteenth century achieved what Joyce describes as 'a *rapprochement* of polite and popular culture'[53] with music halls and variety theatres alongside the Calverts' Prince's Theatre productions of Shakespeare, the Theatre Royal's Number One tours (Beerbohm Tree as Svengali in *Trilby*, the first production of *La Bohème* in English attended by Puccini, and Dan Leno in pantomime) and the St James's Theatre's operas and melodramas.

Just how harmonious this '*rapprochement* of polite and popular culture' was may be assessed by a return to the events on Lower Mosley Street and at the St James's Theatre in the 1890s. While the fears of 'respectable people' – which would include members of the People's Concert Hall and St James's Theatre audience – were undoubtedly real, these people were rarely the target of violence though they may have been accidentally involved.[54] The threat of violence, and of 'contamination' by proximity to prostitution and other forms of criminality, was perceived to be more common in the city centre than the middle- or working-class suburbs.

The People's Concert Hall certainly had a reputation for 'liveliness'. One of its popular names, Burton's Night School, is attributed to its attraction for the 'young who ought to have been studying at the neighbouring evening school'.[55] In 1870, it was described as 'a dreadful place, a place which, under the guise of a concert hall, is the rendezvous of all the bad characters who make the night hideous with their revelry, or rather devilry; women drunk to madness are besieging men who are almost as drunken'.[56] Joe Toole (later an aspiring performer himself, and Labour MP for Salford) recalls in his autobiography how in the 1890s it was 'a rare treat' being taken by his uncle to the Cass: 'The programmes at the "Cass" were wonderful. All stars! The audience very rough and always ready for a disturbance.'[57] There were reports of netting being fixed over the orchestra pit to protect the musicians and performers from missiles thrown by the audience. There is a record of a disturbance which happened when a step-dancing competition was cancelled, and a large, disappointed audience threw seats into the pit, tore gas brackets from the walls and then, having been ejected, caused 'very great' disturbances on the street. 'Stones were thrown at the windows of the music hall and much injury was caused to the exterior of the building in the shape of broken lamps and panes of glass.'[58] And in 1895, a Mrs Merce was convicted of assault on 'a music-hall artist whose theatrical name [was] Miss Lawrence'. According to the court report, 'Whilst the latter was singing at the People's Concert Hall a quantity of tripe was thrown out of a side box and hit her in the face. This was followed by a shower of carrots. The occupants of the box had to be removed by the officials to protect them from the indignant pittites.'[59] Again, however, how typical or frequent these incidents were by the 1890s is impossible to quantify.

Audiences of the period, particularly at the music hall and melodrama, were, however, still far more visible and vocal than at the more middle-class variety and art theatres at the end of the century.[60] Audiences at the People's Concert Hall and St James's Theatre were undoubtedly more 'rough' than those of the Theatre Royal or Prince's, and many saw the influence of the popular theatre as deleterious, particularly for the working classes. However, the People's Concert Hall and the St James's theatres never appear to have had their licences threatened or revoked despite the *Manchester Guardian*'s finding it 'inexplicable' that 'some houses lost their licences, and some retained them [; how] is a matter of mystery to us',[61] and the protracted campaign for a liquor licence at the far more respectable Palace Theatre of Varieties through the 1890s and into the new century.[62] Indeed both the Concert Hall and St James's advertised their programme every week in *The Era*, alongside the Theatre Royal and the Prince's Theatre, until the closure of the Cass in 1897.

There is no doubt that the visual statements made by the architectural disposition of the fronts of the People's and the Gentlemen's Concert Halls

Figure 23: Side of the Gentlemen's Concert Hall on Lower Mosley Street, c.1897.

were very different – not least because the People's fronts the street directly, and the Gentlemen's is 'protected' by ornamental railings – but the side of the Gentlemen's Concert Hall is contiguous with, and as utilitarian as, the Cass's frontage (Figure 23). The audiences might also have been different, but the Gentlemen's was by no means exclusive after the 1860s. Charles Hallé, who continued to perform at the concert hall after his move to the Free Trade Hall in 1858, and the Independent Theatre Society which began performances there of the socially provocative 'New Drama' in 1891, were both committed to Manchester's 'free trade in art'. Hallé's concerts were the 'vogue with all classes, from the rich merchant and the manufacturer to the middle classes and bourgeois ... to the respectable, thrifty, albeit humbler, artisan'.[63]

We cannot know if the 'humbler artisan' also attended the Cass next door, but there must have been some co-mingling on Lower Mosley Street of both groups of urban spectator, and a brief comparison of the repertoire on a single night of these adjacent places of entertainment would seem to confirm this. The Independent Theatre Society staged its first production in Manchester, George Moore's *The Strike at Arlingford*, on 24 February 1893, at the Gentlemen's Concert Hall to an 'excellent house' which 'clapped very heartily at the slightest provocation'.[64] On the same night, the three principal theatres were all in the last weeks of their pantomime runs: *Little Red Riding Hood* at the Theatre

Royal, *Aladdin* at the Prince's and *Mother Goose* at the Comedy all claiming an increase in popularity. At the St James's Theatre, Miss Emma Rainbow[65] was 'seen to advantage' as the heroine in a new melodrama, *The Wheel of Time*.[66] The Palace Theatre of Varieties had a bill ranging from Harry Champion, the 'lively character comedian', a 'smart acrobatic troupe', Mdlle Jessica, 'a clever slack-wire performer' and the Fletchers skating act to a number of vocalists and singers. The Folly, a little lower down the social scale, offered a strongman, a 'big-boot dancer', and 'Miss Virginia Frances with her serpentine song and dance', while the old Grand Circus, which had only re-opened that week as the Temperance Theatre of Varieties, boasted an Irish comedian, a cornet player, a rope dancer and 'The Flying Dillons'. The People's Concert Hall offers no spectacular acts, but a large number of singers – inviting perhaps a greater degree of interaction between performer and audience – 'an acceptable Irish ballad vocalist', popular comedy duettists and dancers, 'clever Mr Charles Patterson, comic, topical and descriptive vocalist' and '"our" Beattie [doing] an excellent turn'.[67]

The audiences for the pantomimes at the Theatre Royal and the Prince's would have been mixed: predominantly, but not exclusively, middle class – a stage-struck Dodie Smith was most enamoured of the Theatre Royal's pantomimes, and was taken there as a child with her family.[68] The Comedy Theatre showed more popular fare but that does not preclude a wide class-based audience; that for the Independent Theatre Company at the Gentlemen's Concert Hall would have been the bourgeois intelligentsia, perhaps with members of the 'respectable, thrifty, albeit humbler, artisan' class that was later to be found at Miss Horniman's Gaiety Theatre after 1907.[69] The paths of these audiences would inevitably have crossed that of the People's Concert Hall.

Several commentators suggest that the greatest danger to a susceptible audience lay in the 'thrill which playgoers invariably appreciate and enjoy'[70] of melodrama. Charles Russell, writing in 1905 on 'Working Lads at the Music Hall' saw the 'moral harm' of the modern music hall as less than that of 'melodrama of the most deplorable kind' which familiarised young men 'with blood-curdling deeds … most violent passions – hatred, revenge, malice … which in the past led to so many instances of violence on the part of young men in the back streets of the city'.[71] At the St James's, the five acts of *The Wheel of Time*, 'fairly bristle[d] with incidents of the most startling kind', including murder, attempted seduction, disguise and a 'capitally realised' dynamite explosion.[72] Far from inciting mayhem, the play – as most melodramas do – presents a 'harmonious society to public view' in the end with the virtuous, orphaned heroines restored to their rightful place in society, unlike the Independent Theatre Society's dystopian, socialist, *Strike at Arlingford*.

Figure 24: The Midland Hotel, n.d.

While both plays feature strife between classes, the melodrama ends with the virtuous factory workers found to be 'aristocrats' in fact as well as nature, and the progressive drama with the 'Socialist labour leader' hero betraying his fiancée, his fellow workers and his faith, putting 'an end to himself, and the play, by taking poison'.[73] What the two dramas do have in common is their representation of virtue among the working and middle classes, and demonisation of the aristocracy and foreigners: the villain in Moore's play is Baron Steinbach, 'a foreign capitalist and a purely acquisitive animal or "economic man"', and in S. Barrington's melodrama, a rich baronet and member of a 'foreign political organisation'.[74] However, in the late Victorian industrial city, it is the popular dramatic stage which most unproblematically presented the 'perfected image of a well-ordered' society whatever subversion was occurring in the Gentlemen's Concert Hall, and given voice to in the comic topical songs of the People's Concert Hall.

The perfected image achieved?

Ironically, the fates of the concert halls were conjoined. In 1897 the Midland Railway Company bought both sites and the theatres were demolished to make way for the building of what is still the most decorative, most bourgeois, hotel in Manchester, the Midland (Figure 24). It was stipulated in the purchase agreement that the hotel should include a theatre. The ironies

Figure 25: The Grand Stair to the Midland Hotel Theatre.

Figure 26: Portico of the demolished Gentlemen's Concert Hall, 1898.

continued. This architectural 'work of art', and temple of consumption and good taste, in creating 'order' on the streets from Central Station into central Manchester, built a vision of a 'harmonious society on public view' very much in keeping with the city's civic and civilising agenda. In doing so it destroyed the social and visual contradictions and tensions between the Gentlemen's and People's Concert Halls. A theatre was built, but invisible, 'underground' in the basement of the hotel (Figure 25). The 'marble halls' of the Midland Hotel Theatre were placed well beyond the sight and reach of the scuttler and humble artisan, even of the majority of respectable middle classes. Rather than step-dancing competitions and comic songs, or even Jenny Lind and George Bernard Shaw, the theatre opened with the frivolous Pellisier's Follies[75] and the edifices – in both senses – of the popular, the radical[76] and 'high art' were all demolished along with the theatres (Figure 26), and their spectators 'exiled' from that place.

I would like to thank Victoria Garlick, David Huxley and the staff of the Manchester Room at the City Library, Manchester, for their direct and indirect help.

Notes

1 This essay develops research published as Viv Gardner, 'Documents of performance. Mapping performance culture 2: reading the street'. A detailed analysis of the 1900 Street Directory for Quay Street, Peter Street and Oxford Street is included with 'Documents of performance'.

2 For more details see Andrew Davies, *The Gangs of Manchester*, pp. 298–314, 320–3. Hillier and Callaghan both seem to have been known as the King of the Scuttlers in the 1890s.

3 *Lancaster Gazette*, 14 July 1893; *Manchester Times*, 29 March 1895 and Davies, *The Gangs of Manchester*, pp. 321–2.

4 *Lancaster Gazette*, 10 February 1894.

5 It was reported that Hindley had actually asked the defendant, Thomas (Tommy) Callaghan, 'known to the police as "The King of Scuttlers"', to assist him in keeping order which raises some questions about the 'private' policing of the theatre. *Manchester Times*, 29 March 1895.

6 *Lancaster Gazette*, 10 February 1894. Jerome Caminada (1844–1914), Manchester-born policeman and the city's first Detective Superintendent, known nationally for both his – at times eccentric – detective skills and reforming zeal.

7 The *Echo*, 11 August 1898, cited in Geoffrey Pearson, *Hooligan: A History of Respectable Fears*, p. 79. The link was made between '"Hooliganism" and the

Halls' in a letter from 'A Board School Manager' published in *The Times*, 26 September 1898, p. 11.

8 *Birmingham Daily Post*, 8 August 1890.

9 Alexis de Toqueville, *Journeys to England and Ireland*, cited in Tristram Hunt, *Building Jerusalem: The Rise and Fall of the Victorian City*, pp. 25–6.

10 Most obviously: de Tocqueville, *Journeys to England and Ireland*, Friedrich Engels, *The Condition of the Working Class in England* and the novels of Elizabeth Gaskell.

11 Mrs [Mary] Humphrey Ward, *The History of David Grieve*, pp. 412, 408, quoted in Trefor Thomas, 'Ancoats and the Manchester slums in two late Victorian novels'.

12 Margaret Harkness [John Law], *A Manchester Shirtmaker: A Realistic Story of Today*, p. 67, quoted in Thomas, 'Ancoats and the Manchester slums'.

13 Davies, *The Gangs of Manchester*, facing p. 256. This is the only image in the book to be given such a value-laden adjective.

14 The Grand Circus/Grand Pavilion, Folly Theatre, Comedy Theatre, Free Trade Hall, Theatre Royal, Gentlemen's Concert Hall, all on Peter Street; Prince's Theatre, St James's Theatre, Palace Theatre of Varieties on Oxford Street.

15 As is suggested by the mid-century removal of the middle classes from the city centre to the suburbs and beyond. See: H.B. Rogers, 'The suburban growth of Victorian Manchester'.

16 M. Christine Boyer, *The City of Collective Memory: Its Historical Imagery and Architectural Entertainments*, p. 74.

17 N. Burton argues that the development of the entertainment industry in Manchester was largely commercially driven. I would not disagree with that but would suggest that there are other factors and effects at work. See N. Burton, 'Leisure in the city: the entertainment sector in the Manchester Central Business District, 1770–1930'.

18 Joanne Robinson, 'Mapping performance culture: locating the spectator in theatre history', p. 4.

19 Henri Lefebvre, *The Urban Revolution*, p. 39.

20 Jim Davis and Victor Emeljanow, *Reflecting the Audience: London Theatregoing, 1840–1880*, pp. 227–9.

21 For a discussion of the urban spectator in relation to Manchester and other Victorian cities, see Patrick Joyce, *The Rule of Freedom: Liberalism and the Modern City*.

22 *Ibid.*, p. 198.

23 *Stage*, 13 September 1894; 'Jack Rover', 'The Tale of a Tour', *Stage*, 24 March 1892, p. 15.

24 As yet, there have only been two publications on Manchester theatre as a whole, both detailed handlists: Joyce Knowlson, *Red Plush and Gilt: The Heyday of Manchester Theatre During the Victorian and Edwardian Periods*; T. Wyke and N. Rudyard, *Manchester Theatres*. Studies of individuals and their contribution to Manchester theatre include Richard Foulkes, *The*

Calverts: Actors of Some Importance; Rex Pogson, *Miss Horniman and the Gaiety Theatre Manchester*; Sheila Gooddie, *Annie Horniman: A Pioneer in the Theatre*. Surprisingly there is no sustained exploration of Manchester's theatre as a social and cultural phenomenon. An independent scholar, David Huxley, has a history of Manchester theatre in preparation. The music hall and street performance are considered in a number of wider studies of Manchester history or working class culture, but not the commercial theatre with its mixed or predominantly educated or middle-class spectatorship. Most notably: Andrew Davies, *Leisure, Gender and Poverty: Working Class Culture in Salford and Manchester*; Alan Kidd, *Manchester* has index entries for 'music halls' and 'cinema' but not 'theatres'. As Kidd observes in his introduction to *City, Class and Culture: Studies of Social Policy and Cultural Production in Victorian Manchester*, 'the Victorian middle class has received remarkably little attention from social historians compared to the treatment accorded working class history' in the Victorian city. However, in his project to develop both 'the history of the middle class and of cultural production in the nineteenth century city' – and subsequent studies – the theatre plays little or no part: Alan J.Kidd and K.W. Roberts (eds), *City, Class and Culture*, p. 1. Two chapters in Peter Bailey (ed.), *Music Hall: The Business of Pleasure* deal with aspects of the Manchester music hall: Dagmar Höher, 'The composition of music hall audiences 1860–1885', pp. 73–92; Chris Waters, 'Manchester Morality and London capital: the battle over the Palace of Varieties', pp. 141–61.

25 See Knowlson, *Red Plush and Gilt*, and Wyke and Rudyard, *Manchester Theatres*.

26 For more detail see Ann Brooks and Bryan Haworth, *Boomtown Manchester, 1800–1850: The Portico Connection*, pp. 93–5; John J. Parkinson-Bailey, *Manchester: An Architectural History*, pp. 10–13. The Cotton Exchange was replaced by the present Royal Exchange in 1869–74 (St Ann's Square/Exchange Street), and now coincidentally houses a theatre.

27 Brooks and Haworth, *Boomtown Manchester*, pp. 97–8; Wyke and Rudyard, *Manchester Theatres*, pp. 56–7.

28 Burton argues that these streets 'had available space, and many of the new buildings required large plots. In the older part of the town, space was limited and costs may well have been too high, particularly since leisure would have to compete with commercial land-uses on central streets like Market Street and King Street.' This analysis does not, however, take into account contiguous developments in London or Birmingham. Burton, 'Leisure in the city', p. 25.

29 Joyce, *The Rule of Freedom*, pp. 204–5.

30 Parkinson-Bailey, *Manchester*, p. 13.

31 Clare Hartwell, *Manchester*, pp. 184–5.

32 *Ibid*.

33 James Wheeler, *Manchester: Its Political, Social and Commercial History*, cited in Parkinson-Bailey, *Manchester*, p. 67.

34 Michael E. Rose, 'Culture, philanthropy and the Manchester middle classes',

p. 111. See also Kidd, *Manchester*, pp. 69, 73; Hartwell, *Manchester*, p. 91 who remarks on the 'impressive' lecture theatre built into the attic in 1871 which was also used for readings.

35 It may be this tobacconist referred to by a *Manchester Guardian* report of 'a cigar shop in Peter Street' where behind the shop was 'a small parlour and behind the parlour a bedroom or two' which were occupied by: 'four females … well dressed, and alas one [was] good looking; but the vile, foul ribaldry and impious blasphemy which reek[ed] from their lips [was] beyond anything heard in Charter Street, and this for the amusement and delectation of a couple of young men, who would be considered swells – clerks in warehouses, they undoubtedly were.' 'In the "slums" No. 4', *Manchester Guardian*, 10 March 1870, p. 6.

36 Knowlson, *Red Plush and Gilt*.

37 Hartwell, *Manchester*, p. 92.

38 Nor was this the only link between the Peterloo Massacre (19 August 1819) and the Theatre Royal. Earlier in 1818, on 23 January, a fight had taken place in the Theatre Royal between the Constitutionalists and Reformers. 'Officers of the 7th Light Dragoons, led by the Earl of Uxbridge, came down into the Pit with drawn swords and asked ['Orator'] Hunt to leave. Scuffles broke out, and Hunt was knocked down. The theatre was closed.' *The Annals of Manchester*, cited in Brooks and Haworth, *Boomtown Manchester*, p. 79.

39 Ironically, there is a link here to the second Theatre Royal. The warehouse 'invaded' the social space of the Free Trade Hall too when the auditorium was raised by ten feet to enable the basement to be rented out as commercial storage. Terry Wyke, *A Hall for All Seasons: A History of the Free Trade Hall*.

40 Parkinson-Bailey, *Manchester*, p. 73.

41 *Bradshaw's Illustrated Guide to Manchester 1857* cited in Kidd, *Manchester*, p. 105.

42 See Simon Taylor, *Manchester: The Warehouse Legacy*.

43 'Of Variety' or 'Varieties' as a description of a theatre mid-century is usually synonymous with music hall, but increasingly comes to signal a more respectable form of mixed-act entertainment.

44 See Alfred Darbyshire, *An Architect's Experiences: Professional, Artistic and Theatrical* and Parkinson-Bailey, *Manchester*, pp. 123–5.

45 The first purpose-built music hall was Charles Morton's Canterbury Hall in Lambeth, which opened in 1852 and seated a modest 700 people. For a description of a Deansgate singing saloon in 1870, see 'In the "slums" No. 4'.

46 Knowlson, *Red Plush and Gilt*; Wyke and Rudyard, *Manchester Theatres*, p. 53.

47 See Kidd, *Manchester*, pp. 143–6; R.N. Dore, 'Manchester's discovery of Cheshire: excursionism and commuting in the 19th century'.

48 From the 1880s theatres began to supply information about transport to the city centre. See, for example, Theatre Royal programme for 1881 which gives details of train times, tram-cars, omnibuses and cab fares. Reproduced in Wyke and Rudyard, *Manchester Theatres*, p. 91.

49 The more woman-friendly retail areas were/are to the east of the Oxford Street/Peter Street axis along Market Street, upper Deansgate and around St Ann's Square. See Viv Gardner, 'The invisible spectatrice: gender, geography and theatrical space' for a discussion of gender and the experience of theatrical space in London's West End. And Gardner, 'Documents of performance' for a detailed analysis of the 1900 Street Directory for Quay Street, Peter Street and Oxford Street.

50 'Offices and shops replaced dwelling houses, and commercial occupations escalated, reflecting the greater complexity of business life. Between 1871 and 1914 the number of firms [in the centre of Manchester] increased by 41%.' Kidd, *Manchester*, p. 103.

51 'In the "slums" No. 4'.

52 See Chapter 7, 'Living in Victorian Manchester' in Kidd, *Manchester*, pp. 118–41, for an overview of social developments in Manchester before 1914.

53 Borrowed from Joyce, *The Rule of Freedom*, pp. 204–5.

54 See Andrew Davies, 'Masculinity and violence in late Victorian Manchester and Salford', pp. 351, 353, 359.

55 Wyke and Rudyard, *Manchester Theatres*, p. 47.

56 'In the "slums" No. 4'.

57 Joe Toole, *Fighting Through Life*, p. 2.

58 *Manchester Guardian*, 21 November 1891.

59 *Sheffield and Rotherham Independent*, 2 March 1895.

60 For more on music hall audiences, see Höher, 'The composition of music hall audiences'; Peter Bailey, 'Conspiracies of meaning: music-hall and the knowingness of popular culture'; Peter Bailey, *Leisure and Class in Victorian England: Rational Recreation and the Contest for Control, 1830–1885*; Patrick Joyce, *Visions of the People: Industrial England and the Question of Class, 1848–1914*, especially Chapter 13, 'Stages of class: popular theatre and the geography of belonging', pp. 305–28. On the silencing of middle-class audiences, see Richard Sennett, *The Fall of Public Man*.

61 'In the "slums" No. 4'.

62 See Waters, 'Manchester morality and London capital'.

63 *Musical World*, 1860 cited in Simon Gunn, 'The sublime and the vulgar: the Hallé concerts and the constitution of "high culture" in Manchester c.1850–1880', p. 213.

64 *Manchester Guardian*, 25 February 1893; *Manchester Courier*, 25 February 1893.

65 With her own company, Emma was a member of the long-established Rainbow family who ran the Theatre Royal, West Bromwich.

66 Sidney Barrington, *The Wheel of Time*. Premiered Theatre Royal, West Bromwich, 26 December 1892.

67 *Era*, 25 February 1893.

68 Dodie Smith, *Look Back With Love: A Manchester Childhood*.

69 We know something of this audience from caricatures of them as an audience

of 'nut-eating Fabian freaks [and] soulfully spoofing spiritualists' (*Gaiety Theatre Annual*, 1911, p. 24) and Bolton mill-girl Alice Foley's account of her Clarion Club visits to the Gaiety: Alice Foley, *A Bolton Childhood*, p. 66. I do think it would have been more comfortable for Foley to go to the democratically redesigned Gaiety Theatre (the old Comedy) than the intimidating Gentlemen's Concert Hall, or the Midland Hotel Theatre where Horniman's first season took place.

70 *Manchester Courier*, 25 February 1893.
71 Charles Russell, *Manchester Guardian*, 4 April 1905, p. 12.
72 *Era,* 31 December 1982.
73 *Manchester Courier,* 25 February 1893; George Moore, *The Strike at Arlingford.*
74 *Manchester Guardian,* 25 February 1893.
75 Barbara Frost, *Memories of the Midland.*
76 I can find no reaction to the end of the People's Concert Hall, but the *Manchester Guardian* commented: 'The [Gentlemen's] Concert Hall, the scene of the Manchester Independent Theatre, is to disappear, and the Committee intimate that the performance of yesterday evening is likely to be the last they can promote. We hope this is not so: that the mechanical or financial difficulty of finding a fit stage of operations will not be fatal; that the Manchester public will in future have the chance more than ever to encourage the presenting of plays that are for some reason unusual or adventurous.' *Manchester Guardian,* 15 March 1898.

Bibliography

Bailey, Peter, *Leisure and Class in Victorian England: Rational Recreation and the Contest for Control, 1830–1885* (London: Methuen, 1978).

Bailey, Peter (ed.), *Music Hall: The Business of Pleasure* (Milton Keynes and Minnesota: Open University Press, 1986).

Bailey, Peter, 'Conspiracies of meaning: music-hall and the knowingness of popular culture', *Past and Present*, 144 (1994), pp. 138–70.

Barrington, Sidney, *The Wheel of Time* (Unpublished. Lord Chamberlain's Plays, British Library).

Boyer, M. Christine, *The City of Collective Memory: Its Historical Imagery and Architectural Entertainments* (Cambridge, Mass. and London: The MIT Press, 2001).

Brooks, Ann and Bryan Haworth, *Boomtown Manchester, 1800–1850: The Portico Connection* (Manchester: The Portico Library, 1993).

Bullock, Thomas Austin, *Bradshaw's Illustrated Guide to Manchester* (London: W.J. Adams; Manchester: Bradshaw & Blacklock, 1857).

Burton, N., 'Leisure in the city: the entertainment sector in the Manchester Central Business District, 1770–1930', *The Manchester Geographer* (1987), pp. 15–32.

Darbyshire, Alfred, *An Architect's Experiences: Professional, Artistic and Theatrical* (Manchester: J.E. Cornish, 1897).

Davies, Andrew, *Leisure, Gender and Poverty: Working Class Culture in Salford and Manchester* (Buckingham and Philadelphia: Open University Press, 1992).

Davies, Andrew, 'Masculinity and violence in late Victorian Manchester and Salford', *Journal of Social History*, 32:2 (1998), pp. 349–69.

Davies, Andrew, *The Gangs of Manchester: The Story of the Scuttlers, Britain's First Youth Cult* (Preston: Milo Books, 2009).

Davis, Jim and Victor Emeljanow, *Reflecting the Audience: London Theatregoing, 1840–1880* (Iowa City: University of Iowa Press, 2001).

de Toqueville, Alexis, *Journeys to England and Ireland*, ed. J.P. Mayer, trans. George Lawrence and K.P. Mayer (London: Faber and Faber, 1958 [1835]).

Dore, R.N., 'Manchester's discovery of Cheshire: excursionism and commuting in the 19th century', *Transactions of the Lancashire and Cheshire Antiquarian Society*, 82 (1983), pp. 1–21.

Engels, Friedrich, *The Condition of the Working Class in England*, ed. David McLellan (Oxford: Oxford University Press, 1993 [1844]).

Foley, Alice, *A Bolton Childhood* (Manchester: Manchester University and WEA, 1973).

Foulkes, Richard, *The Calverts: Actors of Some Importance* (London: The Society for Theatre Research, 1992).

Frost, Barbara, *Memories of the Midland* (Stockport: Stockport Printing Company, n.d.).

Gardner, Viv, 'The invisible spectatrice: gender, geography and theatrical space', in Maggie B. Gale and Viv Gardner (eds), *Women, Theatre and Performance: New Histories, New Historiographies* (Manchester: Manchester University Press, 2001).

Gardner, Viv, 'Documents of performance. Mapping performance culture 2: reading the street', *Nineteenth Century Theatre and Film*, 31:1 (2004), pp. 59–80.

Gooddie, Sheila, *Annie Horniman: A Pioneer in the Theatre* (London: Methuen, 1990).

Gunn, Simon, 'The sublime and the vulgar: the Hallé concerts and the constitution of "high culture" in Manchester c.1850–1880', *Journal of Victorian Culture*, 2:2 (1997), pp. 208–28.

Harkness, Margaret [John Law], *A Manchester Shirtmaker: A Realistic Story of Today* (London: Authors' Co-operative Publishing Company, 1890).

Hartwell, Clare, *Manchester* (New Haven and London: Yale University Press, 2001).

Höher, Dagmar, 'The composition of music hall audiences 1860–1885', in Bailey (ed.), *Music Hall*, pp. 73–92.

Hunt, Tristram, *Building Jerusalem: The Rise and Fall of the Victorian City* (London: Phoenix, 2005).

Joyce, Patrick, *Visions of the People: Industrial England and the Question of Class, 1848–1914* (Cambridge: Cambridge University Press, 1991).

Joyce, Patrick, *The Rule of Freedom: Liberalism and the Modern City* (London: Verso, 2003).

Kidd, Alan, *Manchester* (Edinburgh: Edinburgh University Press, 2002).

Kidd, Alan J. and K.W. Roberts eds., *City, Class and Culture: Studies of Social Policy and Cultural Production in Victorian Manchester* (Manchester: Manchester University Press, 1985).

Knowlson, Joyce, *Red Plush and Gilt: The Heyday of Manchester Theatre During the Victorian and Edwardian Periods* (Manchester: J. Knowlson, c.1984).

Lefebvre, Henri, *The Urban Revolution*, trans. R. Bononno (Minneapolis and London: University of Minnesota Press, 2003).

Moore, George, *The Strike at Arlingford* (London: Walter Scott, 1893).

Parkinson-Bailey, John J., *Manchester: An Architectural History* (Manchester: Manchester University Press, 2000).

Pearson, Geoffrey, *Hooligan: A History of Respectable Fears* (London: Macmillan Press, 1983).

Pogson, Rex, *Miss Horniman and the Gaiety Theatre Manchester* (London: Rockliff, 1952).

Robinson, Joanne, 'Mapping performance culture: locating the spectator in theatre history', *Nineteenth Century Theatre and Film*, 31:1 (2004), pp. 3–17.

Rogers, H.B., 'The suburban growth of Victorian Manchester', *Journal of Manchester Geographical Society* (1962), pp. 1–12.

Rose, Michael E., 'Culture, philanthropy and the Manchester middle classes', in Kidd and Roberts (eds), *City, Class and Culture*.

Sennett, Richard, *The Fall of Public Man* (London: Faber and Faber, 1986).

Smith, Dodie, *Look Back With Love: A Manchester Childhood* (London: Heinemann, 1974).

Taylor, Simon, *Manchester: The Warehouse Legacy* (London: English Heritage, 2002).

Thomas, Trefor, 'Ancoats and the Manchester slums in two late Victorian novels': www.mcrh.mmu.ac.uk/pubs/pdf/mrhr_07_thomas.pdf, pp. 85–92 (accessed 10 September 2012).

Toole, Joe, *Fighting Through Life* (London: Rich and Cowan, 1935).

Ward, Mrs [Mary] Humphrey, *The History of David Grieve* (Toronto: Copp, Clarke Co.; New York: Macmillan & Co., 1892).

Waters, Chris, 'Manchester morality and London capital: the battle over the Palace of Varieties', in Bailey (ed.), *Music Hall*.

Wheeler, James, *Manchester: Its Political, Social and Commercial History* (London: Whittaker and Co.; Manchester: Love and Barton/J. Wheeler, 1842).

Wyke, Terry, *A Hall for All Seasons: A History of the Free Trade Hall* (Manchester: Charles Hallé Foundation, 1996).

Wyke, T. and N. Rudyard, *Manchester Theatres* (Manchester: Bibliography of North West England, 1994).

'He saw the city and wept': the Manchester and Salford Methodist Mission, 1910–60

Angela Connelly

Introduction

The title for this article is taken from the Gospel of St Luke (19:41–2). As Jesus Christ approached Jerusalem from Bethany: 'he saw the city and wept over it' because it rejected salvation.[1] Often invoked in sermons given at the Methodist Central Mission, it still resonates in contemporary mission work.[2] A superficial reading may suggest that religion mourned for the city believing it to be a place of inevitable sin and vice predicated on materialism and self-interest. Certainly, many scholars consider secularisation to be rooted in the nineteenth century, therefore implying that religion and its moral teachings were incompatible with the modern city.[3]

This essay will add to a growing body of literature that demonstrates this to be too simplistic a view.[4] It concerns the Manchester and Salford Methodist Mission (MSM) with a focus on one of their buildings: the Albert Hall and Aston Institute (1910).[5] Initiated by the Wesleyan Methodists, the MSM was part of a wider movement in the denomination to reach out to the poorer working classes in Britain's towns and cities through public worship, charitable works and associational and temperance activities. The programme resulted in the construction of around 100 'Central Halls' that took their design cues from the secular world with theatre-like interiors and activity rooms. Manchester was the first and the most extensive of the provincial Methodist Central Missions. In 1927, it had nine places of worship and four active centres of social work across the city centre and its immediate vicinity in Ancoats, Ardwick and Hulme.[6] Collectively, their buildings provided teetotal social and spiritual spaces. Volunteers and church members received training and spiritual sustenance to go out into the city streets of Manchester

Figure 27: The Albert Hall and Aston Institute, Peter Street, Manchester.

to win converts. While their activities aimed to persuade people to follow the Christian life and to accept moral tenets that frowned upon drinking and gambling, they contributed to the cultural life of the city and became a highly regarded institution.[7]

Religious change

Until recently, historians and sociologists argued that religion and modern life were incompatible.[8] Using the model of 'secularisation', the decline in church attendance during the nineteenth and twentieth centuries was thought to be indicative of institutional Christianity's peripheral nature. The seeds of secularisation were sown in the nineteenth century as a consequence of the move to industrial society, which broke the social connections of a pastoral village environment in which religion thrived. Religion in the city, it was argued, was a middle-class phenomenon to which the working classes were indifferent.[9]

Doubts are cast over the efficacy of the statistical evidence base for secularisation, but the debate remains lively. Hugh McLeod looked to oral history and illuminated the complex ways that social class, status and religion were related. He consequently pointed out that urbanisation processes alone could not explain Christianity's decline.[10] Steve Bruce concedes that there are multiple processes behind religious change – including urbanisation – but maintains that these can be called, for conciseness, 'modernisation'.[11] The argument has recently centred on the timing of secularisation.[12] Callum Brown's seminal contribution, *The Death of Christian Britain*, argues that prior to the 1960s, Britons largely accepted Christian moral tenets evidenced by the significant numbers of people who were baptised, married and given a funeral by the Christian churches.[13] Taking a comparative perspective, Grace Davie points to the peculiarities of a British case that has given so much sustenance to the wider secularisation thesis since many other nations continue to engage in high levels of religious observance.[14]

Others have chosen to define religion more widely than Sunday attendance or formal membership by considering how, outside of institutional confines, it maintained relevance in everyday life.[15] Robin Gill looks beyond church attendance to the material provision of churches and seating. He persuasively argues that an enormous burst of asset-building in the nineteenth century left subsequent generations with the burden of onerous debts and maintenance that turned their concerns from evangelising towards internal issues of maintaining existing structures.[16] However, these observations still occur within the terms of the secularisation debate.[17] This essay will not contribute directly to that debate. However, it provides context to the neglect of religion more generally in social and cultural history.[18] This has overlooked the material manifestations of the twentieth-century church, the spaces that it provided and how it interacted with processes of urban development.

Manchester's Whit walks are important in this regard. During the annual Whit weekend, the city centre was given over to religious celebrations with processions undertaken by Catholics on the Friday and the Protestant denominations on the Monday. These peaked in importance during the inter-war period and 'caused the city centre to become increasingly important as a stage for the performance of an episodic and public form of shared religious identity'.[19] Charlotte Wildman suggests that the Catholic community reasserted its collective identity in response to slum clearances that dispersed the population to new towns and council estates. Callum Brown alluded to the links between population movement and religious change in his early work but did not follow through, choosing instead to focus upon the changing cultural roles of women.[20]

Excepting Wildman, much of the literature that considers religion and philanthropy in Manchester concentrates upon the Victorian and Edwardian period. Here, philanthropic agencies were hard at work. Audrey Kay describes Charles Rowley's Ancoats Recreation Movement and its attempt to infuse high culture in the slums of Manchester. She believes that it did little to penetrate the community in which low wages were the main problem.[21] Michael Harrison notes that T.C. Horsfall's Ancoats Art Museum fared better with a broader array of recreational activities, although art exhibitions tended to attract a narrow crowd.[22] The Salvation Army established corps in Ancoats, attracting support from across the social and political spectrum. Although their historian generally considered them to be successful, he notes that the socially mixed Chorlton-upon-Medlock was more receptive than the deprived population in Ancoats.[23] Simon Gunn focuses on the culture of the nonconformist ministry in the middle-class suburbs but is dismissive of a 'civilizing mission' that did more to constitute middle-class identity in the city than it did to touch the working classes.[24] This echoes the views of J.H.S. Kent, who argued that religious institutions purveyed a suburban view of religious behaviour that was incompatible with working-class leisure practices.[25]

Framed in this context, the following will discuss the MSM, from its heyday in 1910 to the beginnings of severe contraction in 1960. By the twentieth century, the MSM did not frown upon all working-class leisure pursuits. Its main concern as a religion that, since its founding, has always emphasised social justice, was to evangelise the poor.[26] Part of its programme included offering wholesome alternatives to the public house and music hall. Equally, as Peter Bailey has noted, class identity was not fixed and unchanging.[27] This essay will show that the MSM remained a significant social and cultural institution in Manchester up until the 1950s, holding wide appeal outside of Sunday worship, and attracting many classes and types of people. Neglect by scholars is particularly surprising given the plaudits that it received from contemporaries. The *Manchester Guardian* commented in 1910 that 'it is unequalled by any similar organisation in the scope of its work and the extent of its operations. It is the oldest Free Church Mission of its kind; and it stands for the "best for all" in civic and national life.'[28]

Origins

One of Methodism's defining features is its organisational system. The Annual Conference acts as a strong, centralised decision-making body. Power is diffused through subdivisions into circuits, which are local groupings of one or more churches (or 'societies'), to channel resources fairly between the richer and poorer districts. In a similar vein, ministers are traditionally itinerant, moving between circuits after a period of three years.

The origins of the MSM lay in the discovery of the Victorian 'slum' by middle-class observers.[29] The Wesleyans responded belatedly to this agenda and were afforded an opportunity caused by the removal of their wealthy middle-class constituents to Manchester's suburbs. This left them with a conundrum of empty chapels, particularly one located on Oldham Street in the centre of the city. They were reluctant to leave the central district for a number of reasons: this was a prime piece of real estate and, symbolically, to retreat from city centre to suburb did not sit well with their collective image as a denomination of religious and civic importance.[30] This mirrored a crisis in the national body regarding their inability to make headway with urban congregations. By 1885, the Annual Conference pronounced that city work required a dedicated team of ministers, supported ably by deaconesses, who were not required to be itinerant. The Central Missions were permitted to become detached from the circuit system and allowed to operate on their own, free from commitments to the wider Methodist community.[31] City centre sites were to be retained where possible and their activities 'should be adapted to meet the requirements of the people [and] ... more practical interest should be shown in the domestic and social well-being of the people'.[32] What 'adapted to meet the requirements of the people' meant was left unspecified. Presumably, even the authoritarian Wesleyan Conference believed that particular solutions should emerge from local circumstances.

The MSM had its headquarters at Central Hall on Oldham Street.[33] This building provided the blueprint for a movement that resulted in 'Central Halls' in many major British towns and cities between 1886 and 1945.[34] These halls are the material form of a theology that asserted the relevance of religion to everyday life. Designed to contrast with typical Gothic churches, their buildings had no spires, no church bells and certainly no identifying markers such as a cross. The public hall, the theatre and similar civic and cultural buildings were their main architectural influences. They expressed urban modernity in stone by confidently appropriating the contemporary vernacular. Internally, they contained a large auditorium to seat upwards of 1,000 people with a platform and 'tip-up' seats more common in theatres than churches. A myriad of rooms provided for the administrative and social functions of these churches that were open for a wide variety of uses seven days a week.

When the MSM was officially founded in 1885, Samuel Collier, a relatively unknown minister from Cheshire, was appointed as its superintendent minister ahead of Wesleyan preachers of greater renown.[35] In the later Victorian period, the tactics of religious charitable organisations evolved to place more emphasis on providing material assistance rather than moral counsel as a means to changing behaviour.[36] This was clearly the task for the MSM. Given a free rein to decide on the Mission's tactics, Collier realised that in order to provide spiritual help, bodily needs must be met first.[37] Soon the mission was operating an extensive programme of social work, district visitation and religious services. To cater for the demand, the Free Trade Hall was hired in 1889 for Sunday evening services at which Collier preached to 3,000 people for almost twenty-five years.[38] By 1908, he estimated that around 16,000 people came to Sunday services in all of the MSM's premises combined.[39]

The Albert Hall and Aston Institute (1910) was the pinnacle of Collier's achievements. The Peter Street site, purchased from the Manchester Corporation in 1903, formerly contained the spinning and weaving branch of the Manchester Technical School. Location was important: this was Manchester's entertainment district, close to the Free Trade Hall and the Tivoli and Gaiety theatres. Compelling funding appeals were surely designed to appeal to supporters of the temperance cause. One brochure pleaded that:

> There is a great need of a centre of aggressive work on the Oxford Street side of the City. Within a distance of 500 yards from Oxford Road Station, along Oxford Street into Peter Street (where we have secured a site) there are ten places of amusement, nine of which are theatres or music halls seating nearly 25,000 people, and bringing greater crowds – perhaps the largest crowds in the city – on one thoroughfare at night between the hours of seven and eleven. There are 22 licensed places in the immediate vicinity.[40]

When the wealthy philanthropist Edward Aston died, leaving the mission a substantial bequest, it had the financial clout to make a grand statement. William J. Morley, an architect from Bradford and a practising Wesleyan, designed the premises under the watchful eye of a building committee. The main hall contained 2,000 tip-up seats with a horseshoe gallery to the second floor. Mosaic and marble flooring lined both entrances and their hallways. Floor to ceiling was tiled; Samuel Collier was among a deputation who chose the tiles based upon surveys of similar materials in the John Rylands Library and the Whitworth Hall at Owens College.[41] Partly because of its location and its intended multiple uses, the Albert Hall was designed to compete with the glamour and appeal of nearby theatres as well as the most civic of Manchester's great Victorian buildings. As a building, it forged a new, hybrid space: one both public *and* sacred.

The basement contained a large social club for boys and a reading room adjoining the same with a girls' club of similar proportions. Ample kitchens had a service lift to upper floors, and lavatories were provided on all floors.[42] To the first floor was the main hall along with offices for the ministerial team and two vestries for the minister and choir. Located on the second floor was the main hall gallery along with more rooms for weekly devotional and social activities. Larger rooms could be subdivided using partitions made by the

North of England School Furnishing Co. Ltd, meaning that these flexible premises could house many activities at the same time.[43]

Such a building was not only for religious purposes. Renting out the buildings and providing a weekly programme of entertainment helped to pay for the expensive upkeep of the building fabric and the mission work. As with other nonconformist denominations, Methodist buildings are undedicated. Sanctity is found in the corporate body of worshippers.[44] Bricks and mortar merely facilitate the act of public worship and symbolically give stability to the religious community.

Business acumen and sanctity went hand in hand.[45] When Reverend Thomas Bowman Stephenson, founder of 'the Children's Home' in 1869,[46] put pen to paper on four occasions to consider the relationship between music and Methodism for the *Wesleyan-Methodist Magazine*, he puzzled over the practice of church buildings closing their doors during the week. Stephenson believed that this was 'a very insufficient return for the outlay'.[47] In setting out the permitted activities in Wesleyan places of worship, he was careful to avoid encouraging: 'what some call the secularizing of places of worship', going on to suggest that 'within the limits of propriety and reverence, there are very many uses to which they might well be put and many of these uses are closely associated with music'.[48]

Music

While Stephenson illustrated his argument with a description of a fine choral performance at Berne Cathedral, Samuel Collier was experimenting with 'popular' entertainment at the Lever Street Sunday School while the Central Hall on Oldham Street was under construction.[49] This involved ballads and tunes chosen because they were widely sung by the non-churchgoers that Collier wished to reach. Rather than remonstrating against vice, religion had to offer a plausible alternative. The 'gospel temperance concerts' became the leitmotif of the MSM at all of its various branches through the city. A refreshment bar was provided in the hallway so that patrons did not have cause to leave the premises to seek alcoholic refreshment.[50]

As the MSM grew, Collier delegated many of his responsibilities to a growing team of junior ministers, lay preachers and deaconesses. However, he retained full charge over what he considered to be the most important elements of the programme: the concerts and preaching to the largest congregation at the Free Trade Hall.[51] Soon renamed as 'the People's Concerts' to remove any sacred connotations, the concerts were the central platform for temperance work with music, recitations and lantern lectures.[52] Songs were chosen if they were believed to be decent and were interspersed with moral anecdotes.

In the early days, the mission made innovative use of the cinema so that an evening programme would provide two hours of music with one hour of films. The *Manchester Guardian* contains a story recounting that the mission was one of the first places to show films in Manchester. The reporter looked at a programme from 1898 which listed eighteen items including 'Arrival and Departure of Train' and 'Steamboat on Lake'.[53] With an average attendance of 1,600, another observer was keen to note that:

> A study of the types of humanity gathered at this 'feast of the soul' would provide the philanthropist with a great deal of food for profitable reflection. While by no means confined to the poorest classes of the community, the audience included a large number of men and women, neatly though coarsely dressed … and one watched with pleasure the look of deep attention and the smile that frequently lit up these seared and careworn faces. The applause was uproarious, the laughter loud and long; and every 'catchy' chorus was enthusiastically taken up by the audience.[54]

However, a series of accidents with flammable film meant that many local authorities tightened their regulations, requiring fireproof construction for the operating chamber.[55] In 1930, the mission officials took the decision not to comply with stricter Corporation regulations on cinematic equipment, and to concentrate on providing only concerts instead.[56]

One undated advertisement for a recital featuring the pianist George Hadjinikos exists at the Greater Manchester County Records Office (Figure 28).[57] It possibly dates from the 1960s and may indicate the changing nature of the concerts as the years progressed. Tickets could be purchased from the Central Hall on Oldham Street or at the Hallé Concerts Society Box Office on St Peters Square with all proceeds from the five-shilling ticket going towards the mission fund, to be reinvested back into social work. It was at the Albert (as it was affectionately known) that the concerts had the grand theatrical backdrop to complement them. There is one pre-1945 programme at GMCRO, dating from 1928. The concert price on this night was nine pence and a programme cost two pence. The entertainment comprised variety performances in which operatic favourites were meshed with hymns, popular ballads and a 'humorous turn'.[58] Proceedings began at 7p.m. with the hymn 'God Bless Our Native Land' and a prayer. The chorus 'Bird songs at eventide' and a recital entitled 'An Irishman's love for his child' followed this. After the interval, the large mahogany encased organ, built by Wadsworth in 1910, was employed during a solo featuring Guilmant's *Marche aux Flambeaux* in F major. Even the violin solo, Brahms's *Hungarian Dances* Nos. 1 and 2, was designed to be uplifting. Three hours later, the audience departed, having joined in the singing with fortifying ballads such as 'From Oberon in Fairyland' and 'When Allen-a dale

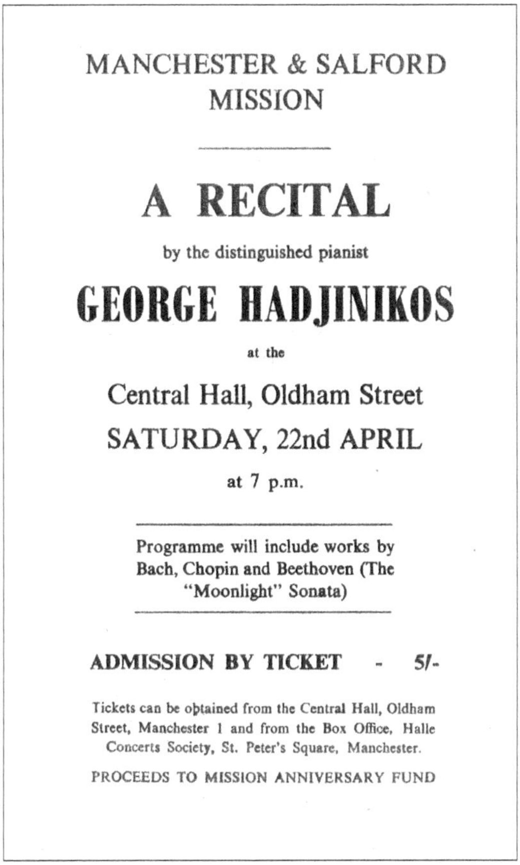

MANCHESTER & SALFORD
MISSION

A RECITAL

by the distinguished pianist

GEORGE HADJINIKOS

at the

Central Hall, Oldham Street

SATURDAY, 22nd APRIL

at 7 p.m.

Programme will include works by
Bach, Chopin and Beethoven (The
"Moonlight" Sonata)

ADMISSION BY TICKET   -   5/-

Tickets can be obtained from the Central Hall, Oldham
Street, Manchester 1 and from the Box Office, Halle
Concerts Society, St. Peter's Square, Manchester.

PROCEEDS TO MISSION ANNIVERSARY FUND

Figure 28: Advertisement for a recital by George Hadjinikos at the Central Hall, Oldham Street, n.d.

went a-hunting'.[59] Of course, Handel's *Messiah* was the perennial favourite and performed at least once a year.

In the nineteenth century, the middle classes sought musical excellence in the choirs and orchestras in their chapels. James Obelkevich suggests that the vitality of religious music explained why the English excelled at oratorios rather than opera,[60] and by the twentieth century, the oratorio may have held appeal to a wider number of people. A favourite with the MSM was Dame Isobel Baillie. She was born in Hawick in the Scottish borders but raised in Manchester and began performing at Sunday Schools and in church halls. She recalled that although her performances mostly consisted of ballads, she perfected her virtuosity at the oratorio on the occasions that she was accompanied by a local orchestra or amateur choral society.[61] Even when she achieved national fame, Baillie continued to perform at both the Central and Albert Halls. She implies that the clientele were slightly more respectable than those attending the Cooperative Halls, where a similar programme of wholesome family entertainment to attract the working classes was offered.[62] She says that 'A broader spectrum of humanity ... could be discovered in the then flourishing halls of the Cooperative Society where I also sang, though I obtained the biggest thrills from appearances in such venues as the city's Albert and Central Halls.'[63]

When the Free Trade Hall was bombed in 1941, the peripatetic Hallé orchestra soon found suitable temporary premises at the Albert Hall. The Hallé's Saturday night spectacular took place at the King's Hall in Belle Vue Gardens but the highlight of the 1944 winter season was Wednesday nights at the Albert Hall playing, in chronological order, the seven symphonies of Sibelius. Again, this was not high culture for a narrow range of people: the box office was so crowded for midweek tickets, it was estimated that the Albert Hall's 2,000-seat capacity could have been filled twice over. While this led to accusations that the Hallé was dumbing down, Sir John Barbirolli was keen to stress otherwise, maintaining that the programme made 'no doubtful concession to the crowd'.[64]

The Anniversary meetings

Every year, each of Methodism's Central Missions held an Anniversary, typically commemorating the date that their premises opened. This served three purposes. Firstly, although the mission raised most of its finance from within, there was always a shortfall in the funds to be redressed through the Anniversary proceeds. Secondly, representatives and members of the surrounding circuits made a point of supporting the mission at its annual event to show the relationship of mission work to Methodist witness in the outlying areas of the city.[65] Lastly, a sub-committee oversaw the organisation of the Anniversary events. For many converts and members, this was a real chance at sharing responsibility.

Prominent preachers provided the entertainment for evening services and a series of events aimed to attract Methodists from across the district. Bazaars and sales of work could last up to six days and showcased the work of the various clubs as well as the work of those accessing the social work facilities or resident in the homes, such as sewing or woodwork. The Lord Mayor or other civic dignitaries attended and assumed a place on the platform along with the ministerial staff. The Anniversary meetings also provided the basis for developing ecumenism; representatives of the Church of England or the other Free Churches also provided speeches.[66]

Up until the 1930s, the Anniversary day consisted of three services at the Free Trade Hall. It quickly reached capacity so 'overflow' meetings were held at the Albert Hall and the addresses relayed there via loudspeakers.[67] Even in 1968, only three years before the Albert Hall closed, Manchester's Lord Mayor, Harry Stockdale, attended the Anniversary celebrations that were still held at the Free Trade Hall.[68]

Children

The initial years of success with conversions, increasing members and facilities began to stagnate by the 1920s. Writing in the report to commemorate the diamond jubilee of the MSM, the Reverend W. Russell Shearer admitted that the policy in the inter-war years had been to consolidate.[69] Attaining full membership of the Methodist Church was voluntary and open to those over the age of fifteen. The focus shifted from gaining converts amongst the unchurched to the children of existing members or 'the outsiders within the gates'.[70]

By this time, the MSM was proud of its work, and the diamond jubilee offered the chance to tell the story in its own words. Particularly referring to youth work, Shearer wrote that 'unaided by lavish public grants and often compelled to manage with inadequate apparatus, loyal and energetic leaders – most of them voluntary – gave their time and strength to the training of large companies of lads and girls'.[71]

Clubs were numerous and covered a range of activities including swimming, cycling and hockey (for both sexes); sewing and baking (for girls) and woodwork (for boys). Each club met weekly with more regularity over winter. During the summer, the fruits of their efforts would be shown to the wider congregation through sales of work. The Albert Hall, with its extensive institutional spaces, ran a full programme with rooms in simultaneous use for these social clubs.

The MSM also had annual competitions that pitted each of the various branches against one another for prizes. One lady, who spent her early life in Moss Side near the city centre, made particular mention of the swimming gala held at the Victoria Baths on Hathersage Road.[72] Whilst spirited, there was always an atmosphere of mutual support. One particular hall, with notoriety for always coming last, soon found itself on the winner's podium when the other contenders elected to give them a head start.

Outdoor preaching

The MSM regarded its mission as 'many-sided' in a direct attempt to influence all aspects of city life, saying that 'if men and women will not come to Church or Chapel, then bring them to the theatre or the music-hall or the street corner – anywhere and everywhere so long as they have the Gospel preached unto them'.[73] It could not be confined only to church buildings. Concerts and social clubs were only one part of their armoury, and a major element of the mission was continuous publicity through advertising, which had two aims: to raise funds, and to highlight the work in an attempt to attract people to the premises.

With enough room and plenty of willing volunteers who wanted to learn how to play an instrument, the MSM had its own brass band. After some food and prayers, they went onto the city streets in the evening in order to advertise an evening service at 11p.m. in the Central Hall. Alongside the band marched 'button-holers' armed with literature and leaflets to distribute along the route.[74] This seemed to be a feature of the early work of the MSM and was probably dispensed with as congregations grew.

More sustained attention was given to outdoor preaching. Stevenson Square in Manchester, located to the north of Piccadilly Gardens, was one of the city's key public forums and believed to attract some 3,000 to 4,000 hearers.[75] Central Hall on Oldham Street was conveniently located close by. Lay preachers would set up a box outside and begin preaching, often inciting heckling from both Communists and Fascists.[76]

The preaching tradition continued after the Second World War when the Reverend Bill Gowland, one of Methodism's famed preachers, came to the Albert Hall. He expressed some reservations as he began his ministry there in 1948 because the Albert Hall's congregations had substantially dropped during the Second World War and had not entirely recovered. Moreover, according to his biographers, he considered the building to be 'scarcely conducive to public worship and suggested the architects had drawn their inspiration from a swimming pool and a football ground.'[77] Gowland, therefore, continually grasped opportunities to take his message beyond the confines of a place of worship.

Gowland was a clever and impassioned speaker who was not afraid to remain true to his own conscience even when this conflicted with the authorities of the mission. On Saturday evenings he could be found in Piccadilly Gardens conversing with prostitutes, if not trying to convert them.[78] He also set up a folding stand on a blitzed bombsite between St Mary's Gate and Deansgate. He chose the location believing that the street peddlers, performers and political organisations who also spoke there were a 'spectacle … being as close as any he had seen to the secular setting of the Church in Corinth'.[79] The MSM's literature estimated that Gowland could attract between 400 and 600 people to his regular Thursday lunchtime slot between 12.30p.m. and 2p.m.[80]

At these outdoor events, Gowland insisted on having no collections and no hymns; it was to be an evangelistic forum in which to voice the social implications of the Gospel and allow people to ask questions. Gowland reported that:

> In the crowd you will find shop-stewards and directors, town councillors and crooks, clerks and bookies, and the Communists have never missed a meeting. It is a complete cross-section of society. Thinking of the size of some morning congregations, and the reasons some Church members give for not being at church in the winter months, it is a salutary rebuke that the crowd at this open-air meeting has stayed for an hour in a heavy snowstorm and then accused me of stopping five minutes earlier than usual![81]

In 1953, one of the doyens of London's own Speakers Corner, Reverend Donald Soper, came to address the 'hats, caps, bare heads, berets, and shopping baskets' from a rostrum on the Deansgate bomb site. Dressed in a leather-belted black cassock, Soper answered hecklers with the good humour required of an outdoor preacher, at one point being asked whether he was an incarnation of Jesus Christ.[82]

Gowland went on to pioneer Methodism's 'Industrial Mission' in Luton in 1954.[83] It built upon practices that he established in Manchester where his charisma and reputation attracted theology students from the Hartley Victoria College in Whalley Range, who assisted with Gowland's work at the Albert Hall. For three years, they made monthly visits to 10,000 houses. They contacted hostels and visited public houses. Gowland persuaded factory managers to allow him to establish a 'Padre's Hour' at several unnamed factories or works in the city, allowing him to reach an estimated 10,000 people.[84] His rationale was that 'We have Harvest Festivals and it is just as important to remind the community that coal, steel and other products are as much the gifts of the Creator as apples and grapes.'[85]

The Albert Hall also targeted specific groups: there was the Manchester, Salford and District Butchers' and Meat Traders' Association service; an annual sportsmen's rally; a professional men's service; and a police service. An annual report indicated that on these occasions the Albert Hall would be near capacity,[86] and between fifty and one hundred representatives would share the platform with the ministerial team. One photograph in Manchester's Local Studies collection indicates that this was not hyperbole, showing an almost full Albert Hall during a service in which sportsmen reaffirmed their faith, at which Bert Whalley of Manchester United shared the platform (Figure 29).

It is difficult to tell if such actions did influence the workers. What it should show, along with the outdoor preaching, was that the appearance of Christianity in such mundane places as the street and the workplace was not deemed incongruous or inappropriate by either party.

Figure 29: A sportsmen's service at the Albert Hall, c.1949. Bert Whalley, Manchester United Football Coach, is sitting immediately behind the speaker, Reverend Bill Gowland.

Urban change

As early as 1909, a lay preacher attributed a slight fall in attendance at Sunday evening worship to:

> fewer people coming in to the city on Sunday evenings to parade up and down and those that do come in later than before so making it harder to reach them for the services. Also effected [*sic*] by the exodus of people to the suburbs, which has been facilitated by the excellence of electric trams. A great many of our members now live 2½ to 4 miles away. Passing through a period of bad trade has told upon the giving powers of our people and many have absented themselves from public worship who would most certainly have been present had their clothes been more presentable (in their judgement), and their powers of giving greater.[87]

Manchester began piecemeal programmes of slum clearance and rehousing in new developments in the late Victorian period. Initially these were on the periphery of the city centre, for example the Corporation of Manchester's labourers' dwellings on Oldham Road (1895).[88] Slum clearance was stimulated by the 1919 Addison Housing Act which popularly aimed to provide 'homes for heroes' returning from the First World War. In Manchester, sites were bought up for development, some from the estate of Lord Tatton.[89] These included the development of the Wilbraham Estate near Fallowfield as well as the Corporation of Manchester's most audacious experiment: a new town based upon the principles of the Garden City, located at Wythenshawe.[90]

Rowland Nicholas's *City of Manchester Plan*, published in 1945, largely disparaged the unplanned and unregulated Victorian city and recommended comprehensive redevelopment.[91] This continued slum clearance but also provided motorways, car parking and new modern developments. Manchester's Victorian environment, with its connotations of dirt, overcrowding and unplanned developments, would be erased. Nicholas believed that around half of the population needed to be relocated in order to raise the standard of living. Moreover, the 1945 plan acknowledged that inter-war housing estates lacked amenities, community facilities and meeting places. The overriding idea to be taken through was solving the housing problem, relieving the city centre of congestion and zoning areas of the city to accommodate particular activities. Nicholas confidently prophesied that: 'We are entering upon a new age: it is for us to choose whether it shall be an age of self-indulgent drift along the pre-war road towards depopulation, economic decline, cultural apathy and social dissolution, or whether we shall make it a nobler, braver age in which the human race will be master of its fate.'[92] The solution was to be found in the creation of 'district centres' for every 40,000 of the population in designated localities such as Longsight and Moss Side that would provide for all amenities.

In 1938, the superintendent minister of the MSM, Herbert Cooper, complained to the Annual Conference that 'the removal of poor people from slum areas to distant housing estates has already depleted some of our congregations, and affected week-night activities … The matter is being closely watched, but until some of these new schemes are more advanced, it will not be possible to decide on a policy.'[93] The Department for Chapel Affairs, who controlled Methodism's physical assets, had already decided on their policy. A sub-committee on planning and design was set up in 1942 composed of members from the Department for Chapel Affairs and architects from within the laity. These consultations led to the eventual publication of *The Methodist Church Builds Again* (1946).[94] In a reversal of the policy of remaining on prominent sites as set out at the 1885 Conference, the Department for Chapel Affairs claimed that 'the future of our Methodist Church depends upon the extent to which we are to develop Methodism in the new towns and areas being replanned'.[95]

The visionary 1945 City of Manchester Plan was never entirely realised because of the shortages in labour and materials. Moreover, the Town and

Country Planning Act (1947) had initially nationalised the right to develop land. An owner had to obtain the formal consent of the local planning authority to develop land and pay a charge to the Central Land Board. The Conservative government abolished these charges in 1954 to inject greater competitiveness into the property market.[96] The Town and Country Planning Act (1959) went one step further and denationalised development values, giving city centre redevelopment fresh impetus. With regulation removed, land prices soared in central Manchester and thus led to increased speculation in the centre of the city, particularly around the areas of Market Street and Deansgate up to Shudehill and down to Quay Street.[97]

The traffic around Stevenson Square began to increase when it became a bus interchange. As noted above, religious and political speakers made use of a blitzed site at the corner of Deansgate and St Mary's Gate. However, having lain derelict for fifteen years, the site was purchased by Manchester City Council and then sold for redevelopment. The National Secular Society, the Communist Party, the Roman Catholics and the Methodists were, for once, united in opposition. They demanded that the General Parliamentary and Standards Committee of the Corporation provide an alternative site for regular public speaking.[98] Their request was declined. The Corporation argued that other public sites existed, naming Platt Fields and Alexandra Park, both on the southern outskirts of the city. To the aggrieved orators these were a poor substitute since those places only attracted crowds of people during the summer.

Between 1951 and 1971, Manchester lost 23 per cent of its population.[99] The building of motorways and a greater level of personal car ownership facilitated the dispersal of population, and the planned decentralisation added to the natural process of suburbanisation.[100] Along with Methodism's other Central Missions, Manchester suffered a very sharp contraction in its congregations after 1959. At the Albert Hall and Aston Institute, congregations plummeted from an average of 1,000 in 1960 to 200 in 1969.[101] Sixty-one years after opening, the Methodist society took the decision to put it on the property market and the Albert Hall and Aston Institute ceased to be a place of Methodist worship.

It still stands on the Peter Street site protected by Grade II listing. It makes up a remarkable trio of buildings in that area along with the Free Trade Hall and the Young Men's Christian Association building (another of Manchester's neglected religious institutions). The Methodists put it up for sale in 1971, where it remained for sixteen years. The covenants placed on the building to restrict certain activities at odds with Methodist teaching were eventually circumvented when the building changed hands between numerous property development companies and it ultimately became a public house.

Conclusion

As S.J.D. Green points out, social and cultural historians of twentieth-century England are surprisingly silent on religion and its significance, despite the animated debates in academic ecclesiastical history.[102] Though there can be no definitive explanation for religious change, the example of the Manchester and Salford Mission shows the way in which religion and culture interact.

In the years after the Albert Hall closed its doors, the MSM scaled back its activities further and sold the majority of its premises. Any new initiatives took place in the suburbs or on new housing estates. In one hundred years, the MSM suffered a reversal of fortune that may make it hard for contemporary Mancunians to understand the importance and the influence that the mission made to their city's cultural life.

A small snapshot of that story has been shown above. There are four main points to note. Firstly, there was little discord between the sacred and secular from the point of view of the MSM. Its aims were more subtle than merely appropriating secular practices in the face of decline and unbelief. Religion – or the Methodist word of *fellowship* – was at the forefront of its activities, seen in the prayers and hymns which interspersed proceedings. The MSM drew on popular culture; yet in other ways it sought to redirect it. Secondly, the size and versatility of MSM premises meant that they were likely to be more widely used than a typical Methodist Church. The Albert Hall is indicative of the varied features of institutional religious buildings. Thirdly, the mission retained a highly public role up until the 1960s. The only testaments to its former strengths are in archives and the physical remains of its buildings. Lastly, part of the explanation of its decline resides with material change and urban redevelopment that fundamentally changed the relationship that people had to the city and how they used it, with consequences for its cultural institutions.

Notes

1 *The New Testament of our Lord and Saviour Jesus Christ, Translated out of the Greek: Being the Version Set Forth A.D. 1611 Compared with the Most Ancient Authorities and Revised A.D. 1881*, pp. 130–1.

2 Alison Maddocks, 'City centre chaplaincy'.

3 For example, Kenneth S. Inglis, *Churches and the Working Classes in Victorian England*; E.R. Wickham, *Church and People in an Industrial City* and Alan D. Gilbert, *Religion and Society in Industrial England: Church, Chapel, and Social Change, 1740–1914*.

4 David Nash, 'Reconnecting religion with social and cultural history: secularisation's failure as a master narrative'.

5 The Manchester and Salford Mission (hereafter MSM) was initiated by the

Wesleyan Methodists. However, references to 'Wesleyan' were frequently dropped because their work aimed to reach out to people regardless of their denominations. In 1932, the Wesleyans joined together with the Primitive Methodist and United Methodist Churches to become the Methodist Church of Great Britain.

6 H. Cooper, 'A plain unvarnished tale'.

7 The research was funded under the AHRC/ESRC *Religion and Society* programme. It was a collaboration between the Methodist Church Property Office and the Manchester Architectural Research Centre. Research Grant Award: CDA 07/288.

8 For example, Bryan Wilson, *Religion in a Secular Society: A Sociological Comment* and Robert Currie, Alan D. Gilbert and Lee Horsley, *Churches and Churchgoers: Patterns of Church Growth in the British Isles since 1700*.

9 See note 3.

10 Hugh McLeod, *Piety and Poverty: Working-class Religion in Berlin, London and New York, 1870–1914*. His body of work is discussed in Callum G. Brown and Michael Snape (eds), *Secularisation in the Christian World*.

11 Steve Bruce, *Secularization: In Defence of an Unfashionable Theory*, p. 57.

12 Steve Bruce and Anthony Glendinning, 'When was secularisation?'

13 Callum G. Brown, *The Death of Christian Britain: Understanding Secularisation 1800–2000*.

14 Grace Davie, *The Sociology of Religion*.

15 For example, Jeffrey Cox, *The English Churches in a Secular Society: Lambeth, 1870–1930*; Sarah Williams, *Religious Belief and Popular Culture in Southwark, c.1880–1939*; Dorothy Entwhistle, '"Hope, colour, and comradeship": loyalty and opportunism in early twentieth-century church attendance among the working class in North West England'.

16 Robin Gill, *The Empty Church Revisited*.

17 Nash, 'Reconnecting religion', p. 303.

18 S.J.D. Green, *The Passing of Protestant England: Secularisation and Social Change, c.1920–1960*, p. 7.

19 Charlotte Wildman, 'Religious selfhoods and the city in inter-war Manchester', pp. 104–5.

20 Compare Callum G. Brown, 'Religious growth in urban societies', with Brown, *The Death of Christian Britain*.

21 Audrey Kay, 'Charles Rowley and the Ancoats Recreation Movement, 1876–1914'.

22 Michael Harrison, 'Art and social regeneration: the Ancoats Art Museum'.

23 Glenn K. Horridge, '"Invading Manchester": responses to the Salvation Army 1878–1900'.

24 Simon Gunn, 'The ministry, the middle class and the "civilizing mission" in Manchester, 1850–80'.

25 J.H.S. Kent, 'The role of religion in the cultural structure of the later Victorian city'.

26 Richard P. Heitzenrater (ed.), *The Poor and the People Called Methodists*.

27 Peter Bailey, '"Will the real Bill Banks please stand up?" Towards a role analysis of mid-Victorian working-class respectability'.

28 'An ever-open door: Mr Collier's work at the Central Hall', *Manchester Guardian*, 14 November 1910, p. 9.

29 See Gertrude Himmelfarb, *Poverty and Compassion: The Moral Imagination of the Late Victorians* and H.L. Platt, 'From Hygeia to Garden City: bodies, houses and the rediscovery of the slum in Manchester 1875–1910'.

30 See Angela Connelly, '"A pool of Bethesda": Wesleyan Methodist Central Hall, 1886–2010'.

31 The Wesleyan Methodist Church, *Minutes of Conference* (1884), p. 251.

32 The Wesleyan Methodist Church, *Minutes of Conference* (1885), p. 265.

33 Connelly, '"A pool of Bethesda"'.

34 Angela Connelly, 'Methodist Central Halls as public sacred space'.

35 George Jackson, *Collier of Manchester: A Friend's Tribute*, p. 44.

36 Martin Hewitt, 'The travails of domestic visiting, Manchester: 1830–1870'.

37 Jackson, *Collier of Manchester*, p. 51.

38 William Henry Crawford, *The Church in the Slum: A Study of English Wesleyan Mission Halls*, p. 43.

39 *Ibid.*, p. 38.

40 A. Brookes and S. Barker, 'A city's need, a church's extremity and a great opportunity'.

41 'The Peter Street Building Committee', 18 November 1909, Greater Manchester County Records Office (hereafter GMCRO), GB127.M196/8/1/1/1.

42 The Wesleyan Chapel Committee, *The Thirty-Second Annual Report of the Wesleyan Chapel Committee, 1909*, p. 212.

43 'The Albert Hall and Aston Institute', p. 102.

44 George W. Dolbey, *The Architectural Expression of Methodism*.

45 David Jeremy, *Capitalists and Christians: Business Leaders and the Churches in Britain, 1900–1960*.

46 The Children's Home later became the National Children's Home and exists today as Action for Children (2008).

47 T.B. Stephenson, 'Missions and music', p. 291.

48 *Ibid.*

49 MSM, *The First Annual Report of the Manchester and Salford Wesleyan Methodist Mission*, p. 22.

50 H.E.C., 'The missions and music', *Manchester Evening Chronicle*, 14 January 1901, p. 8.

51 MSM, *The Sixth Annual Report of the Manchester and Salford Wesleyan Methodist Mission*, p. 13.

52 MSM, *The Twelfth Report of the Manchester and Salford Wesleyan Methodist Mission*, p. 124.

53 Staff Correspondent, 'When the pictures began', *Manchester Guardian*, 4 July 1930, p. 13.

54 H.E.C., 'The missions and music', p. 8.
55 'Paisley cinema disaster: a new regulation, notice to local authorities', *The Times*, 12 July 1930, p. 9.
56 Staff Correspondent, 'Kinema licences refused', *Manchester Guardian*, 19 February 1930, p. 9.
57 'A recital by George Hadjinikos at the Central Hall, Oldham Street', GMCRO, GB127.Broadsides/FND.282.
58 The Albert Hall, 'Programme for the People's Concert', 8 September 1928, GMCRO, GB127.M196/8/2/7/1.
59 *Ibid.*
60 James Obelkevich, 'Music and religion in the nineteenth century'.
61 Isobel Baillie and Bryan Crimp, *Never Sing Louder Than Lovely*, pp. 17–19.
62 See Peter Gurney, *Cooperative Culture and the Politics of Consumption in England, 1870–1930*, pp. 58–87.
63 Baillie and Crimp, *Never Sing Louder Than Lovely*, p. 19.
64 Observer Correspondent, 'Hallé society plans a notable new season', *The Observer*, 10 September 1944, p. 5.
65 P. Bartlett-Lang, 'Rallies and their relevance today', pp. 6–7.
66 *Ibid.*
67 MSM, Anniversary of the Manchester and Salford Mission, advertising booklet, n.d. GMRCO, GB127.Broadsides/FND.409.
68 MSM, *The Record*, 10 (October 1968), p. 13.
69 W. Russell Shearer, *These Sixty Years: Commemorating the Diamond Jubilee of the Manchester & Salford Methodist Mission*.
70 *Ibid.*, p. 22
71 *Ibid.*, p. 7.
72 Interview with the author, 26 June 2009.
73 F.E. Hamer, *After Twenty Five Years [1886–1911]: The Story of Evangelism and Social Reform, In Connection with the Manchester and Salford Mission*, p. 25.
74 MSM, *The First Annual Report of the Manchester and Salford Wesleyan Methodist Mission*, pp. 14–16.
75 Andrew Davies, *Leisure, Gender and Poverty: Working-Class Culture in Salford and Manchester, 1900–1939*, p. 137.
76 Manchester and Salford Methodist District, *Tell It How It Was: The Story of 200 Years in Oldham Street as Seen Through the Eyes of Those Who Have Shared the Experience*, p. 30.
77 D.A. Gowland and S.R. Roebuck, *Never Call Retreat: A Biography of Bill Gowland*, p. 77.
78 William Gowland, *Militant and Triumphant*, pp. 50–7.
79 Gowland and Roebuck, *Never Call Retreat*, p. 78.
80 The Albert Hall Society, *Outward Bound: 41st Anniversary and Annual Report*, p. 8.
81 Gowland, *Militant and Triumphant*, p. 60.

82 'A bit of Tower Hill descends on Deansgate', *Manchester Guardian*, 17 November 1953, p. 5.

83 Elaine McFarland and Ronnie Johnston, 'Faith in the factory: the Church of Scotland's industrial mission, 1942–58'.

84 Gowland, *Militant and Triumphant*, p. 33.

85 *Ibid.*, pp. 39–40.

86 The Albert Hall Society, *Outward Bound*, p. 4.

87 MSM, *The Twenty-First Annual Report of the Manchester and Salford Wesleyan Mission, 1907–8*, p. 117.

88 'Labourer's dwellings, Oldham Road, Manchester', *The Building News*, 13 December 1895, p. 188.

89 City Planning Office, *Manchester, 50 Years of Change: Post-War Planning in Manchester*.

90 Peter Shapely, Duncan Tanner and Andrew Walling, 'Civic culture and housing policy in Manchester, 1945–1979'.

91 Rowland Nicholas, *City of Manchester Plan: Prepared for the City Council*.

92 *Ibid.*, p. 205.

93 'Representative Session: Manchester and Salford Mission', *Methodist Conference Agenda* (London, 1938), p. 195.

94 E. Benson Perkins and Albert Hearn, *The Methodist Church Builds Again*.

95 Department for Chapel Affairs, *Problems of Town and Country Planning Today*, p. 17.

96 Oliver Marriot, *The Property Boom*, pp. 324–6.

97 John J. Parkinson-Bailey, *Manchester: An Architectural History*, pp. 170–1.

98 Our own reporter, 'Seeking ground for debate: city forum in peril', *Manchester Guardian*, 30 November 1957, p. 12.

99 Paul Lawless and Frank Brown, *Urban Growth and Change: An Introduction*, p. 95.

100 Brian Robson, *Those Inner Cities: Reconciling the Economic and Social Aims of Urban Policy*.

101 Figures from 'Records of home mission and evangelism', Methodist Archives Research Centre, John Rylands University Library, MA 9863, Box 1.

102 Green, *The Passing of Protestant England*, p. 7.

Bibliography

'The Albert Hall and Aston Institute', *Modern Buildings Record*, 3 (1912), p. 102.

The Albert Hall Society, *Outward Bound: 41st Anniversary and Annual Report* (1951)

Bailey, Peter, '"Will the real Bill Banks please stand up?" Towards a role analysis of mid-Victorian working-class respectability', *Journal of Social History*, 12:3 (1979), pp. 336–53.

Baillie, Isobel and Bryan Crimp, *Never Sing Louder Than Lovely* (London: Hutchison & Co., 1982).

Bartlett-Lang, P., 'Rallies and their relevance today' in *Laymen Speak with Laymen* (London: Methodist Home Mission, n.d).

Benson Perkins, E. and Albert Hearn, *The Methodist Church Builds Again* (London: Epworth Press, 1946).

Brookes, A. and S. Barker, 'A city's need, a church's extremity and a great opportunity', brochure for appeal for donations to the Albert Hall building scheme, 1907, Greater Manchester County Records Office, GB127.M196/8/1/9/1, 4.

Brown, Callum G., 'Religious growth in urban societies', in Hugh McLeod (ed.), *European Religion in the Age of Great Cities, 1830–1930* (London and New York: Routledge, 1995).

Brown, Callum G., *The Death of Christian Britain: Understanding Secularisation 1800–2000*, 2nd edition (London: Routledge, 2009).

Brown, Callum G. and Michael Snape (eds), *Secularisation in the Christian World* (Farnham: Ashgate, 2010).

Bruce, Steve, *Secularization: In Defence of an Unfashionable Theory* (Oxford: Oxford University Press, 2011).

Bruce, Steve and Anthony Glendinning, 'When was secularisation?', *British Journal of Sociology*, 61:1 (2010), pp. 107–26.

City Planning Office, *Manchester, 50 Years of Change: Post-War Planning in Manchester* (London: HMSO, 1995).

Connelly, Angela, 'Methodist Central Halls as public sacred space', PhD thesis, University of Manchester, 2010.

Connelly, Angela, '"A pool of Bethesda": Manchester's First Wesleyan Methodist Central Hall', *Bulletin of the John Rylands University Library of Manchester*, 89:1 (2012/13) pp. 105–25.

Cooper, H., 'A plain unvarnished tale', *Annual Report of the Manchester and Salford Mission* (Manchester: Foulkes, Hall & Walker, 1927).

Cox, Jeffrey, *The English Churches in a Secular Society: Lambeth, 1870–1930* (Oxford: Oxford University Press, 1982).

Crawford, William Henry, *The Church in the Slum: A Study of English Wesleyan Mission Halls* (New York: Eaton & Mains, 1908).

Currie, Robert, Alan D. Gilbert and Lee Horsley, *Churches and Churchgoers: Patterns of Church Growth in the British Isles since 1700* (Oxford: Clarendon Press, 1977).

Davie, Grace, *The Sociology of Religion* (London: SAGE, 2007).

Davies, Andrew, *Leisure, Gender and Poverty: Working-Class Culture in Salford and Manchester, 1900–1939* (Buckingham: Open University Press, 1992).

Department for Chapel Affairs, *Problems of Town and Country Planning Today* (Manchester: Manchester Central Buildings, 1948).

Dolbey, George W., *The Architectural Expression of Methodism* (London: Epworth Press, 1964).

Entwistle, Dorothy, '"Hope, colour, and comradeship": loyalty and opportunism in early twentieth-century church attendance among the working class in North West England', *The Journal of Religious History*, 25:1 (2001), pp. 20–38.

Gilbert, Alan D., *Religion and Society in Industrial England: Church, Chapel, and Social Change, 1740–1914* (London: Longman, 1976).

Gill, Robin, *The Empty Church Revisited* (Aldershot: Ashgate Publishing Company, 2003).

Green, S.J.D., *The Passing of Protestant England: Secularisation and Social Change, c.1920–1960* (Cambridge: Cambridge University Press, 2010).

Gowland, D.A. and S.R. Roebuck, *Never Call Retreat: A Biography of Bill Gowland* (London: Chester House, 1990).

Gowland, William, *Militant and Triumphant* (London: Epworth Press, 1954).

Gunn, Simon, 'The ministry, the middle class and the "civilizing mission" in Manchester, 1850–80', *Social History*, 21:1 (1996), pp. 22–36.

Gurney, Peter, *Cooperative Culture and the Politics of Consumption in England, 1870–1930* (Manchester: Manchester University Press, 1996).

Hamer, F.E., *After Twenty Five Years [1886–1911]: The Story of Evangelism and Social Reform, In Connection with the Manchester and Salford Mission* (Manchester: Foulkes, Hall & Walker, 1911).

Harrison, Michael, 'Art and social regeneration: the Ancoats Art Museum', *Manchester Region History Review*, 7 (1993), pp. 63–82.

Heitzenrater, Richard P. (ed.), *The Poor and the People Called Methodists* (Nashville: Kingwood Books, 2002).

Hewitt, Martin, 'The travails of domestic visiting, Manchester: 1830–1870', *Historical Research*, 71:175 (1998), pp. 196–228.

Himmelfarb, Gertrude, *Poverty and Compassion: The Moral Imagination of the Late Victorians* (New York: Alfred A. Knopf, 1991).

Horridge, Glenn K., '"Invading Manchester": responses to the Salvation Army 1878–1900', *Manchester Region History Review*, 6 (1992), pp. 16–29.

Inglis, Kenneth S., *Churches and the Working Classes in Victorian England* (London: Routledge and Kegan Paul, 1963).

Jackson, George, *Collier of Manchester: A Friend's Tribute* (London: Hodder and Stoughton, 1923).

Jeremy, David, *Capitalists and Christians: Business Leaders and the Churches in Britain, 1900–1960* (Oxford: Clarendon Press, 1990).

Kay, Audrey, 'Charles Rowley and the Ancoats Recreation Movement, 1876–1914', *Manchester Region History Review*, 7 (1993), pp. 45–54.

Kent, J.H.S., 'The role of religion in the cultural structure of the later Victorian city', *Transactions of the Royal Historical Society (Fifth Series)*, 23 (1973), pp. 153–73.

Lawless, Paul and Frank Brown, *Urban Growth and Change: An Introduction* (London: Harper & Row, 1986).

McFarland, Elaine and Ronnie Johnston, 'Faith in the factory: the Church of Scotland's industrial mission, 1942–58', *Historical Research*, 83 (2010), pp. 539–64.

McLeod, Hugh, *Piety and Poverty: Working-class Religion in Berlin, London and New York, 1870–1914* (New York and London: Holmes & Meier, 1996).

Maddocks, Alison, 'City centre chaplaincy', *Methodist Diaconal Order: Faith and Work* (2009): www.methodist.org.uk/downloads/FandW_G1.pdf (accessed 11 July 2010).

Manchester and Salford Methodist District, *Tell It How It Was: The Story of 200 Years in Oldham Street as Seen Through the Eyes of Those Who Have Shared the Experience* (Manchester: Manchester and Salford Methodist Mission, 1981).

Marriot, Oliver, *The Property Boom* (London: Hamilton, 1967).

MSM, *The First Annual Report of the Manchester and Salford Wesleyan Methodist Mission* (Manchester: Foulkes, Hall & Walker, 1888).

MSM, *The Sixth Annual Report of the Manchester and Salford Wesleyan Methodist Mission* (1893).

MSM, *The Twelfth Report of the Manchester and Salford Wesleyan Methodist Mission* (Manchester: Hall & Son, 1899).

MSM, *The Twenty-First Annual Report of the Manchester and Salford Wesleyan Mission, 1907–8* (Manchester: Foulkes, Hall & Walker, 1908).

Nash, David, 'Reconnecting religion with social and cultural history: secularisation's failure as a master narrative', *Cultural and Social History*, 1 (2004), pp. 302–25.

The New Testament of our Lord and Saviour Jesus Christ, Translated out of the Greek: Being the Version Set Forth A.D. 1611 Compared with the Most Ancient Authorities and Revised A.D. 1881, English Revised Version (Oxford: The University Press, 1881).

Nicholas, Rowland, *City of Manchester Plan: Prepared for the City Council* (Norwich and London: Jarrold & Sons, Ltd., 1945).

Obelkevich, James, 'Music and religion in the nineteenth century', in J. Obelkevich, L. Roper and R. Samuel (eds), *Disciplines of Faith: Studies in Religion, Politics and Patriarchy* (London: Routledge & Kegan Paul, 1987).

Parkinson-Bailey, John J., *Manchester: An Architectural History* (Manchester: Manchester University Press, 2000).

Platt, H.L., 'From Hygeia to Garden City: bodies, houses and the rediscovery of the slum in Manchester 1875–1910', *Journal of Urban History*, 33:5 (2007), pp. 756–72.

Robson, Brian, *Those Inner Cities: Reconciling the Economic and Social Aims of Urban Policy* (Oxford: Clarendon Press, 1988).

Shapely, Peter, Duncan Tanner and Andrew Walling, 'Civic culture and housing policy in Manchester, 1945–1979', *Twentieth Century British History*, 15:4 (2004), pp. 410–34.

Shearer, W. Russell, *These Sixty Years: Commemorating the Diamond Jubilee of the Manchester & Salford Methodist Mission* (Manchester: Hotspur Press, 1946).

Stephenson, T.B., 'Missions and music', *Wesleyan-Methodist Magazine* (April 1889).

The Wesleyan Chapel Committee, *The Thirty-Second Annual Report of the Wesleyan Chapel Committee, 1909* (London: Hayman Brothers & Lilly, 1909).

The Wesleyan Methodist Church, *Minutes of Conference* (London: City Road, 1884).

The Wesleyan Methodist Church, *Minutes of Conference* (London: City Road, 1885).

Wickham, E.R., *Church and People in an Industrial City* (London: Lutterworth Press, 1964).

Wildman, Charlotte, 'Religious selfhoods and the city in inter-war Manchester', *Urban History*, 38 (2011), pp. 103–23.

Williams, Sarah, *Religious Belief and Popular Culture in Southwark, c.1880–1939* (Oxford: Oxford University Press, 1999).

Wilson, Bryan, *Religion in a Secular Society: A Sociological Comment* (London: Watts, 1966).

A case of cosmopolitanism:
the Manchester International Club

Bill Williams

The liberal elite which came to dominate Manchester politics after Peterloo was excessively proud of its tolerance towards people of all origins, nationalities and religions. Its mouthpiece, the *Manchester Guardian*, bounced Manchester's liberality off reports of prejudice, and particularly of anti-Semitism, practised by other people in other places. Such 'archaic' intolerance, it reiterated, was out of place in modern Manchester. It gave its support to Jewish emancipation in Britain and to those nationalist revolutionaries fighting the oppression of the Ottoman, the Austro-Hungarian and the Czarist empires. It opened its doors to some of those whose aspirations for liberty and nationhood had been crushed by repressive regimes. As time went on, the very presence of so many foreigners in Manchester was paraded as proof of Manchester's 'cosmopolitan views'. 'We welcome men from all parts of the world,' Louis Hayes wrote in 1905: 'Manchester makes no distinction as to creed or race'.[1] Certainly the Manchester of 1905 housed substantial and growing communities of Jews, Germans, Greeks and Italians, as well as significant numbers of Moroccans, Syrians, Armenians, Africans and Chinese. This was still a cause of pride at the time of the British Empire Exhibition in Wembley in 1930, when the lyrics of a song composed on the streets of Gorton advised people to be content with what they had at home: 'Italy Grand' in Ancoats, 'China and Japan' on Upper Brook Street, 'Alabam' in Greengate and, 'if you have to travel still', 'Palestine' on Cheetham Hill. Much of this was window-dressing. The tolerance of which the *Manchester Guardian* boasted was notoriously withheld from the Irish. Hayes himself wrote (in the same book) of the 'swarm' of 'dirty, unkempt' Jews and be-wigged women bringing 'degeneration' to a Manchester suburb.[2] The African residents of Salford's 'Alabam', like the Jews who dared to seek a home in Robert Roberts's 'classic slum',[3] faced daily violence and abuse.

The Manchester International Club represented the first time that anyone had thought to give Manchester's tradition of tolerance a local, practical and institutional form. This article explores the founders' objects and assesses their achievements. Did the club represent, as one of them claimed, Manchester's 'true self' any more than the Manchester of the liberal imagination?

The club's founders were drawn from those reservoirs of pacifism and liberal internationalism which had been building up throughout Britain since the First World War, as much in response to the carnage on the Western Front as in reaction to the aggression of the new dictatorships. In Manchester these ideals were particularly strong, not simply amongst the Quakers, in whose concerns the origins of the club were rooted, but amongst the radical Christians and enlightened liberals who formed the core of the strong Manchester branches of the Peace Pledge Union, the Fellowship of Reconciliation, the Federal Union, the League of Nations Union, the International Friendship League, the International Student Service and the Women's International League for Peace and Freedom.

The club was frequently described in terms of Manchester's traditional internationalism. Wright Robinson, a Manchester Labour alderman who was amongst the club's early patrons and latterly its president, saw Manchester as 'one of the great international cities of the world … sending out both ideas and goods to the ends of the earth': in such a city, an International Club was 'an asset of the highest possible importance'. Without it, he came to believe, Manchester 'could not be its true self'.[4] The founders of the International Club were either pacifists or internationalists, or both, all of them Utopians, all committed to the belief that, in spite of a disappointing past and a precarious present, world harmony might still be achieved by the promotion of mutual understanding between the peoples of the world. The International Club was their contribution to the achievement of this goal.

In March 1939, W.M. Phillips identified that the need for some kind of institutional provision for Manchester's 'overseas population' had been 'felt for many years'.[5] According to a retrospective account written in 1940 by members of the International Service Committee (ISC) in 1929, two Christian groups, the (Manchester) 'Young Friends' and 'the SCM Auxiliary' in Manchester came together to set up an 'International Group … to give those interested in international fellowship an opportunity to meet together'.[6] Its immediate inspiration is uncertain. One former member traces it to the return from China of two unmarried Quaker missionaries, the Baker sisters, Mary Eleanor and Hilda Margaret, who first invited Chinese students living in Manchester to their home at 254 Rye Bank Road, Chorlton-cum-Hardy, and subsequently extended invitations to other foreign students to what became regular meetings.[7] It was from some of these students that the call came in 1929 for a more formally constituted group. The group then evolved as a form of international fellowship which complemented the policy making and casework remit of the ISC, to which it owed allegiance and which monitored its progress. Benia Hesford,[8] the representative of the ISC on the group's committee, presented regular reports of its activities. From the start, its programme included monthly rambles, discussion groups and social gatherings, to which people were invited from a mailing list kept by the group.[9] It also held occasional get-togethers for overseas students and other foreigners new to Manchester.[10] There were no fees for joining; the group was financed by collections taken at its meetings.[11]

According to a Quaker account, the International Club 'sprang out of the Group'.[12] This is perhaps an overstatement. The idea of an International Club in Manchester was certainly first mooted by members of the Quaker group who, at some time in 1935, are said to have 'realised that more frequent meetings were necessary' in order to promote 'a real understanding of international affairs' and to acquire a 'real understanding of other peoples'.[13] But in a special committee which was then set up 'to see what kind of club was wanted by overseas students', to 'look at international clubs elsewhere' and to seek out possible premises,[14] the Quakers were joined by internationalists from a variety of other backgrounds, including, according to one account, members of 'peace societies, religious bodies [and] local foreign communities and some of Manchester's [foreign] consuls'.[15] Although the precise composition of this steering group is unknown, it certainly included the young peace campaigner, Herbert Phillips, his 'pretty young wife', Mary, a 'Cambridge graduate' and a Quaker whom he is said to have met when both were members of a 'peace-promoting organisation'. It is likely to have included also T.M. ('Tom') Hudson, the son of a Manchester textile manufacturer, and a Liberal Party activist who was later to emerge as a key figure in the movement to create a club.

Following discussions with 'prominent citizens associated with international affairs', a scheme for a club was 'brought to the notice of the public' and an approach made to societies in Manchester likely to be interested. Representatives of these societies were then invited to a meeting held in May 1937 to discuss 'the possibility of starting an International Club in Manchester'.[16] The first reference to the club in the Quaker records is in the minutes of a meeting of the ISC, probably in May 1937, at which it delegated two of its members, Robert Thornton Smith, himself a former China missionary, and Benia Hesford, to attend such a meeting.[17] Smith and Hesford reported back to a meeting of the ISC on 17 June that a small committee had been set up in the city (later called the 'International Club Inquiry Committee') 'to study the details of this scheme'. The ISC expressed its general sympathy for the idea but declared that it could 'offer no practical help at the moment', perhaps because of its preoccupation with the catastrophic train of events in China, Spain and Germany, though in fact they later supported it.

During 1938 these various strands were gradually brought together. Promises of financial support to carry the club through its initial year were made by a variety of 'interested organisations'.[18] On 20 January 1938 Kate Croft[19] reported that the Inquiry Committee was preparing to approach 'wealthy people for substantial subscriptions with a three-year guarantee'. 'Suitable premises' had been found but 'no definite plans [had] yet been formulated'. The ISC decided to guarantee five pounds a year for three years and suggested that 'other similar bodies' be asked to do the same. Shoran S. Singha, the Warden of the Indian Student Hostel in London, was brought to Manchester to whip up popular support. On 25 March 1938 he spoke to a meeting of some 200 people in Manchester, announcing, inter alia, the issue of a leaflet 'which challenged Manchester, in its centenary year, to come into line with London, Glasgow, Newcastle and Cambridge in providing a recognised meeting place for visitors from overseas'.[20] On 22 September 1938 the ISC expressed its full support for the constitution adopted by the International Club and delegated Benia Hesford to represent it on the club's committee. In December 1938, when the registered membership stood at 152, a general meeting of supporters approved a recommendation of the Inquiry Committee that two rooms identified by Herbert Phillips at the Manchester Athenaeum, 68 George Street – 'central and self-contained, but available at a reasonable rent' – be acquired as the club's premises.[21] There, on 4 February 1939 the club held its 'inaugural social'.[22] It was attended, according to a report in the *Manchester City News*, by 'over 200 members and potential members of at least a dozen nationalities', the treasurer, a 'Mrs. A. Wormald of Worsley', estimating that the membership would reach 300 'before the evening was out'. It was something, the reporter added, of which Mancunians 'ought to be very proud', creating, as it did, a way of 'bringing together Manchester people and foreign visitors'.[23]

Although the original constitution has been lost, it is possible to deduce something of the high hopes nursed by the club's promoters from an article announcing its foundation which appeared in the *Manchester and Salford Woman Citizen*, under the name 'W.M. Phillips' (almost certainly Herbert Phillips's wife), in March 1939.[24] It would be, according to Phillips, 'a social centre in the widest sense of the word, the place to which all foreign visitors will ask to be directed immediately on arrival' not only in the city but in 'that wider region of which Manchester and Salford are the hub'. It would be 'the natural answer to the policeman's problem when confronted with a gesticulating foreigner'. It would promote 'better understanding … peace and friendship', not only between its members but also between the nations to which they belonged. 'Citizens of all countries' would meet 'on a basis of equality'. '"Arab meets Jew, Germans meet Frenchmen, Chinese meet Japanese" in a friendly atmosphere, and what forces for promoting international understanding can be released!' In addition to the existing facilities of the Athenaeum, which now became available to the club's members – reading and writing rooms, lounges, a library and a restaurant – there would be a new 'international lounge' supplied with foreign newspapers and, 'in time, a foreign library'. 'Cultural groups' would be formed for the study of the languages, literature, arts and music of the nations represented at the club. 'What had been done in Glasgow, Newcastle and Cambridge', Phillips added, could surely be achieved in Manchester 'which is more accustomed to lead than to follow'.[25]

The club would be an entirely independent organisation, its government 'democratic', its funds raised from a membership fee of one pound and 'small donations' from other sources.[26] It was not, however, to be freely open to all. Applicants were called upon to appear before a membership committee, which judged their suitability: largely, it would seem, in terms of the tolerance of their outlook, their 'respectability' and the likelihood of their interest in the kind of educational and cultural activities the club had in mind. Applications from those who showed a hint of national, religious or racial prejudice were invariably rejected. As well as foreigners from any nation, membership was open to those native Mancunians who could show that they had a commitment to international understanding and a genuine interest in foreign ways of life, and it is the recollection of one former secretary that at any one time 'Britishers' made up something like half the total membership.[27]

The club was governed by a General Committee, elected by universal suffrage at its Annual General Meeting, which then elected from amongst its members a president, chairman, secretary and treasurer, and set up the sub-committees[28] which organised the club's routine activities and events. A former secretary of the club remembers that the constitution made it possible for up to one hundred members to participate in the running of the club, all voluntarily, at any one time.[29] This was the club's formal 'democracy': the nature of its events and the criteria by which it selected its members both suggest a club membership which, however diverse in its national origins, was relatively narrow in its social composition. By and large it was made up of educated men and women from middle-class families.

It might be thought that such a structure was particularly attractive to refugees with a recent experience of a totalitarian regime and a majority of whom were from just the kind of background to which the club appealed. In the Jewish case, however, the fact that, in the interests of harmony and equality, there were to be no concessions to the religious taboos of any of the members, and no partisan politics, limited its appeal to Jews, either refugee or native, who were orthodox in their observance or active in the Zionist cause. Kosher food was not available in the club canteen; the meetings committee took no account of the Jewish Sabbath or Holy Days; political propaganda for any cause was unacceptable. Fred Arlsberg, himself of Jewish origin, who joined the club in 1941, believes that the membership included only a handful of observant Jews and Zionists. Amongst refugees, although the club attracted some orthodox Jews, like the Polish refugee Rejika Monat, who found the Jewish clubs of north Manchester too 'snobbish' for her liking,[30] the appeal was chiefly to non-Jews and to those Jews, like Arlsberg, who came from liberal or secular backgrounds. It provided them with a safe landing in Manchester, with ready-made leisure in a relatively unthreatening setting and with a respite from their bleak lives in hostels, bed-sits and in the kind of menial work to which they were initially condemned by British alien legislation. For many it was the source of their first friendships in Manchester.

A key organiser was the Channel Islander H.J. Fleure, a geographer, anthropologist and folklorist, a popular public speaker active in local philanthropic, internationalist and egalitarian causes, and since 1930 Professor of the newly-established Department of Geography at Manchester University. Formerly incumbent of the Gregynog Chair in Geography and Anthropology at Aberystwyth, he had undertaken the research into the geography of Welsh physical types which was to form the basis of his perception of human and cultural change and to underlie a commitment to physical and cultural diversity which was to earn him renown as a 'biological socialist'.[31] Fundamental to his thinking was a belief that physical intermixing, the free interchange of ideas and cultural diversity had not only been central to the evolution of human societies in the past but were the means by which humanity and civilisation were to be enriched in the present. Even before Hitler's ascent to power Fleure had rejected Nazi claims of the purity and superiority of the 'Nordic Race'.[32]

Thereafter he launched a sustained attack on the 'fantastic nonsense' that 'blond people ... are ... the creators and distributors of modern civilisation', that there could be superior races of 'pure descent' and that there existed inferior peoples worthy only of extinction.[33] The free intermingling of ideas was equally important to the health of civilisation. 'Authoritarian repression' was another target of Fleure's scorn: 'any group that tries to claim for itself complete truth or knowledge really forfeits its status and title as a contributor to civilisation'.[34]

Fleure was particularly alert to the dangers faced by a 'so-called Jewish race' as mythical, in his view, as the 'Aryans' of the Nazi imagination. These were the inventions of hate and self-promotion. The 'Jewish tradition', on the other hand, had:

contributed and can contribute to enrich our European civilisation. To try to suppress it in the interests of a supposed unity is to impoverish Europe as well as to act on a false principle. All the European people of diverse heritage live side by side in the same street, and our problem is to build up an overriding harmony which will permit enriching diversities within the group to contribute of their best to the commonwealth.[35]

All present attempts to evaluate human types as superior or inferior are 'based on prejudice ... wherever through intercourse there have been opportunities for diverse stocks to supplement one another's efforts a focus of civilisation has been developed'.[36]

Within academic circles Fleure was 'an important [and influential] figure in the radical humanist tradition of geography': from 1917 he was secretary and honorary editor of the Geographical Association; in 1936 he became the first geographer to be elected to a Fellowship of the Royal Society.[37] In the city and the region he was sought after as a speaker by local societies and as a governor by local schools, all of which became platforms for the spread of his ideas.[38] In the face of the 'rheumatic' conformity preached by Nazism, he told one audience, he stood for the social and religious diversity generated by 'the ceaseless change which is the essence of life'.[39] The International Club epitomised his attack on the 'static' cultures and racial arrogance of the totalitarian dictatorships. It stood, in his view, for 'free choices between alternatives openly offered freely to all', for the promotion of 'mutual knowledge and understanding' and for a 'large freedom of expression and criticism in public affairs'.[40]

The club's treasurer, Godfrey William Armitage,[41] was a Quaker. Managing Director of his family's long-standing and successful firm of cotton manufacturers, Armitage and Rigby, and from 1933 a director of the Manchester Chamber of Commerce, he was also well known in the city as a Liberal Party[42] activist and as an advocate of structural changes in Lancashire's cotton trade which he believed, by reducing its costs and recovering its markets, would survive the slump of 1929. He made his case in a series of speeches, pamphlets, articles and poems, some of which were accorded prominent space by his ally in the press, the *Manchester Guardian*. A man valued by his peers for his 'singular dignity', 'Olympic' eloquence, 'majestic intelligence', 'sagacity', 'probity' and 'immense modesty', he was sought after as a fund-raiser, not least by his alma mater, Manchester Grammar School.[43] Less is known of the club's two other officers. Tom Hudson, the chairman, was heir to Richard Hudson and Son, a successful firm of cotton manufacturers and merchants established in Manchester since the 1890s,[44] a resident of the Monton district of Eccles and a Liberal who had been active in the affairs of the party and of the League of

Nations Union (LNU) in which he had served as secretary and chairman of the Eccles branch. The secretary was Herbert Phillips about whom little is known other than that he was a peace campaigner.

The only paid employee was a warden, appointed in January 1940, whose primary task was apparently to watch over the personal welfare of the club's members. This was Mrs Vera Barson, the widow of a Christian missionary to the East,[45] a 'benevolent lady', according to the young Viennese Jewish refugee Hanna Siederer, who in the late summer of 1940 organised free holidays at her own house in Manchester and at a Quaker Home in North Wales for Hanna and her friend Evi, also a Viennese Jewish refugee, both of them then hard-worked probationer nurses at the County Mental Hospital in Prestwich.[46] Some members, including Arlsberg, came to see her caring presence as an essential ingredient in the club's success. The Labour alderman, Wright Robinson, who was later to become Fleure's successor as president of the club, also counted Mrs Barson's 'great personal friendliness and resource' as central to the achievements of a group of workers which, in his view, 'deserved more public ... recognition than it [had] received': if the club owed its survival to Phillips's 'devoted services', Mrs Barson was 'the real ministering angel who gave [the club] a soul'.[47]

Perhaps it was because the club's 'international' remit was open to misinterpretation as evidence of a subversive political intent, whether pacifist or Communist, that the committee also surrounded itself with a cordon of 'patrons' of high social standing and impeccable patriotic repute. To the Lord Mayor, the Lord Bishop and the University Vice-Chancellor, as ex-officio members, was added an impressive body of prominent citizens which included a local aristocrat (Lord Stamford of Dunham Massey Hall), two leading nonconformist clergymen and six businessmen active in local philanthropy and civic affairs and well known for their liberal inclinations: Sir Frederick West, Sir Robert Noton Barclay, Alfred P. Simon, Sir Christopher Needham, C.G. Renold and Sir Ernest Simon. They were men whose status lent weight to the club's periodic public appeals for funds.[48]

From the beginning the club was seen by refugees, Jewish and non-Jewish, as offering a comfortable social haven in an otherwise strange and perhaps intimidating city. Gerhard and Alice Zadek, who arrived in Manchester together as refugees from Berlin in 1939, and resided for their first six weeks in the Kershaw House Hostel of the Manchester Jewish Refugees Committee, found the club 'particularly welcoming'. Quite apart from enabling them 'to cope with their isolation', it opened up to them a more 'colourful spectacle' than any they had experienced in Berlin's Jewish Quarter. At the club, Alice Zadek remembers, 'one would meet daughters of ordinary Canadian farmers or wood cutters, Indian students from the highest castes, even two brothers from the Ivory Coast, Adi and Tunga, who were members of a very ancient royal house'. As escapees from Nazism, the Zadeks were 'much in demand' in club discussions on conditions in Hitler's Germany.[49] Hanna Behrend, a young Jewish refugee from Vienna, who in late 1939 took up residence in a Quaker boarding house in Manchester, found that the club 'provided aliens from all parts of the world with a home from home'; at the club's tea parties, talks and Sunday outings she met some of her best friends.[50]

For some Jewish refugees, the club very soon served as an unintended pathway to nonconformity. On 22 October 1940 a 20-year-old German-Jewish refugee domestic servant, Johanna Blanca Sarah Hopp, who had arrived in Manchester from Berlin at the beginning of August 1939, appeared in the Manchester City Police Court on a charge of absenting herself (as an alien) for two nights from her 'registered place of residence' in Cheetham Hill. According to the evidence reported in the *Manchester Guardian*, Hopp had been before the court on earlier occasions for similar offences and had already been 'repeatedly warned' that such behaviour might lead to her internment. On this last occasion, when the warning was again repeated, she is said to have met an Indian mechanical engineering student at the International Club and, after dancing and going to the cinema with him, to have stayed the night at his lodgings in Fallowfield.[51]

It may be that the club also served in its earliest days as a potentially soft target of Communist propagandists, both native and refugee. Early Communist members included the German International Brigader, Hans Bauer. It was after meeting refugees at the club in the spring of 1939 that a local 'comrade', the industrial chemist, Harold Teel, put together a Salford Committee for Refugees from Czechoslovakia. The committee, in turn, with help from members of the clandestine Manchester branch of the German Communist Party (the KPD), created a hostel in Salford which, amongst other things, became a local cell of German refugee Communists. It was probably only the firm insistence of the club's leading founder-members that prevented it from falling, as the Free German League of Culture (created by and for German refugees) had done, under the domination of skilled Communist activists. It served more obviously as a kind of information exchange for refugees unfamiliar with the city and perhaps with the English language; within it news of need travelled fast to volunteers in a position to offer it. Paula Rosner remembers that when forced by circumstances to leave her accommodation, through the club her plight very rapidly came to the notice of workers ready to help her find an alternative.[52] It was primarily for refugees (although it was available to 'all foreign residents') that in April 1941 the club opened an 'advice and information bureau' at its clubroom to deal with 'any enquiry relating to a cultural, educational or social need'. The bureau was open every Wednesday evening, Herbert Phillips informed the public, but if this proved inconvenient, assistance was available 'by appointment or letter'.[53]

It was at the very moment of its consolidation as an independent and popular social, cultural and information centre for foreigners in Manchester that the International Club attracted the attention of what, in all but name, was an agency of the British state. The 'British Council for Relationships with Other Countries' (otherwise, the British Council) was founded in November 1934 on the initiative of a British Foreign Office 'roused to action', it was said, by the need to counteract the anti-British propaganda of Fascist Italy and Nazi Germany.[54] Accusations of 'decadence, incapacity and self-interest' were now to be answered by a sustained educational and cultural counter-offensive which would promote a 'friendly knowledge' of British life and so safeguard British interests overseas and create a more 'sympathetic appreciation of British foreign policy'.[55] It was a top-heavy organisation, run by an Executive Committee of government nominees, supported by an annual parliamentary grant and 'carried on under the supervision of the Foreign Office'.[56] It would abstain, however, 'from all political propaganda' and from any attempt to impose British ideas on the 'outside world'; its 'ultimate object', rather, was 'to create friendship and understanding' by encouraging 'closer cultural relations between the United Kingdom and other countries'.[57] One of its many strategies for achieving these purposes was the establishment of cultural 'institutes' and so-called 'Anglo-phil' societies throughout the globe.[58]

On the outbreak of war, however, the British Council persuaded itself that the foreigners then effectively locked in Britain, most of them refugees, lay 'well-within' its province. They would, after all, it was argued, be returning to their homelands with impressions, good and bad, of the British way of life.[59] With the arrival of thousands of war refugees during the summer of 1940, however, and thereafter of allied and dominion troops, merchant seamen of every nationality, and technicians and apprentices from India, the West Indies and elsewhere in the Empire, it expanded its activities.[60] At the same time, in 1940, as the German advance drastically curtailed the opportunities for overseas institutes, at least in Europe, the British Council was forced back on a reconsideration of what it had always seen as its secondary 'resident foreigners department'. The discussions which followed between the British Council and the Foreign Office, War Office and Board of Education culminated in November 1940 in what the *Manchester Guardian* saw as the 'diversion of its interests' to the 'educational and cultural needs' of the substantial body of civilian war refugees, merchant seamen and allied troops who had taken refuge in Britain following the successive fall of Norway, the Low Countries, France and Poland. Beginning in that month with the establishment of a Polish Centre (the so-called 'Polish Hearth') in London and the organisation of classes in English for Poles throughout the country, the change of emphasis was officially announced on 5 December, together with the appointment of three regional officers to 'place the resources of the Council at the disposal of foreigners in their areas'. The 'Northern Region', comprising Lancashire, Yorkshire and Cheshire, became the responsibility of Professor T.S. Simey, a former member of the British Council's 'resident foreigners department', who now set up his headquarters at Liverpool University, where before the war he had been Professor of Social Sciences.[61] His brief, like that of the other regional officers, was, 'in co-operation with local educational authorities', to generate educational services and cultural facilities either by the creation of new centres or by the adaptation of existing bodies to serve the British Council's purposes.[62]

When, in February 1941, the extent of the government grant to the British Council came in for some criticism from the floor of the House of Commons, Eleanor Rathbone intervened in its defence: the British Council, she believed, 'should make known that part of our culture which had a bearing on our war effort, our sense of freedom, and our ideas of democracy'.[63] In reality, there is unlikely to have been anything quite so politically innocent about a body subservient to government control and closely identified with the British Foreign Office. The realpolitik of the British Council was the maintenance of that 'spirit of friendship and co-operation' between Britain and her allies vital to the effective conduct of the war at its most crucial stage and potentially useful to any post-war settlement.[64] Through its contacts beyond Europe – contacts said to have stretched in June 1941 'from China to Peru … and from the Near East to Latin America' – the British Council was able to counter the political as well as the cultural influence of the Axis powers.[65] In that month it was reported to be seeking means of countering clandestine Italian and German efforts to woo Arab support in Palestine and Iraq.[66]

The British Council's first major foray into the provinces was the creation in April 1941 of an Allied Centre in Liverpool, an impressive social, cultural and educational club for Merseyside foreigners which was to become the prototype for similar centres in other towns. From the spring of 1941 Manchester was brought within the British Council's orbit. A lecture delivered by R.H. Bruce Lockhart, the British government's representative to the Czech government-in-exile, to a joint meeting of the city's three Czech societies on 18 April 1941 was described in a *Manchester Guardian* report as 'the first meeting to be arranged by the British Council in Manchester.'[67] Early the following month, the British Council was providing speakers for a series of lectures on English literature and 'political topics' mounted by the (as yet homeless) Manchester Czech Centre at All Saints Parish Church.[68] In July, an audience of 300 was attracted to a British Council-sponsored talk at the Manchester College of

Technology by Commandant Simone, an officer from Charles de Gaulle's London headquarters, on 'The Advance of Free France'.[69] It seems likely that by this time the British Council's officers were seeking some means of establishing a permanent centre in Manchester on the Liverpool model.

In Manchester, however, there existed a ready-made operation, the objects of which at least approximated to those of the British Council and which might readily be transformed to serve its wider purposes. It was with this object that during August of 1941 the British Council opened negotiations with the managers of the International Club. The aim, according to Hudson, was to have the club open its doors 'to members of allied armed forces and merchant navies … for whom … there is little accommodation in the city apart from cinemas and public houses'.[70] The timely incentive was the promise of 'a substantial grant' from the British Council towards the provision of the larger premises that would be necessary, provided only that the club made a contribution to the rent. The offer was particularly attractive at a time when the club was itself facing difficulties in coping with the demands not only from foreign (now including American) troops but from a regular membership which had now reached 250.[71]

By early September relations between the club and the British Council were sufficiently close to make possible a joint garden party in Fallowfield, 'with guests of many nationalities', and entertainment that was 'international in character': 'there were English folk dances … Morris, sword and country … a Royal Dutch cabaret, music and dances from Central Europe and music from the band of the Royal Dutch Army, as well as games, competitions and side-shows'.[72] A fortnight later came an official announcement by the club's managers of its formal alliance with the British Council.[73] The wording of their letter to the *Manchester Guardian* through which the announcement was made, in part a reiteration of the British Council's rationale, reflected clearly enough its superior bargaining power. 'To our Allies', they wrote:

> Great Britain is a foreign land whose inhabitants speak a language which many [foreigners] have difficulty understanding, and in Manchester there is a great need for suitable premises where they can meet each other and their British friends, and where they can read newspapers and periodicals printed in their own native languages and pass their leisure time in comfort. This need the International Club, aided by the British Council, is prepared to meet.[74]

To embrace 'Allied troops and seamen' would also be of future benefit to the nation: 'among the many distinguished refugees in our midst are probably many future leaders of Europe … It is in the national interest that our guests should have contact with the best British traditions of democratic liberty and that we and they should learn to co-operate with a view to European reconstruction'.[75] The letter appealed to the public for regular subscriptions and for 'offers to guarantee a portion of the possible deficit' during the period of the club's expansion.[76]

In a special leader, the *Manchester Guardian* applauded the deal. During its two years of 'inconspicuous life' the club had already done 'admirable service'. Now, with the British Council's help and with the citizens of Manchester playing their part (as 'surely they will'), it would 'improve on the job'.[77] The benefits of the new arrangements were certainly clear enough to the club's officers and volunteers. British Council grants made it possible to add a reading room, library and restaurant to the club's facilities[78] and apparently to take over neighbouring premises at 64 George Street. Lecture programmes now drew upon the British Council's contacts and resources. Weight was added to public appeals for funds such as that initiated by Armitage in November 1941 to cover 'a large increase of its premises' and 'the increasing demands upon it'. 'We want to make a success of the club,' Armitage wrote. 'We want the friendliness and liberality of Manchester to shine out of it.'[79]

The exact relationship between the British Council and the club is more difficult to fathom. What was happening, after all, was some form of alliance between a club dedicated to a mutual understanding between nations and a government agency, which held the purse strings, committed to the propagation of 'the British Way'. Fred Arlsberg describes the relationship as having been one of co-operation between two bodies, each of which retained its separate identity and pursued its distinctive aims. The club's General Committee, while occasionally collaborating with the British Council's authorities on joint enterprises, and lending its premises to British Council events, remained, as Arlsberg remembers it, independent of British Council control. Relations between the two were 'managed', and with great diplomatic tact, by Herbert Phillips, who, while remaining secretary of the club, now became a paid official of the British Council as its 'representative' in Manchester.[80] In practical terms the constituents of both used the same premises and shared the same facilities, the British Council now paying for the running of the club canteen. Each pursued its own aims, the British Council countering Fascist 'derision' of British culture by 'explaining Great Britain, its institutions, art, science, and recreation to the rest of the world'; the club promoting mutual respect between the homelands of its members. What they shared was a positive response to the 'pestilential political doctrines' emanating from Italy and Germany.[81]

It does not seem likely that British Council control made much impact on the routine activities of most of the club's ordinary members. On the eve of the alliance with the British Council, half of the club's 250 members were native British 'friends' of Manchester's foreign nationals. Of the rest, most were either young students, chiefly under thirty, from the university and the College of Technology, or equally young refugees from Central Europe. They were engaged in what had become the club's staple activities: musical evenings, lectures on subjects of 'general interest', 'discussions on life in other countries … opened by natives', 'occasional dances', table tennis and rambles.[82] These were largely untouched by the link with the British Council; what changed from the autumn of 1941 was the presence at the club in increasing numbers of the allied troops whose 'education' had now become the British Council's province and whose friendship and partnership in marriage now became available to its members.

The development of the club during 1940 and 1941 coincided with a demographic explosion which created a city probably more cosmopolitan in its population and variegated in its cultural expression than at any time in its earlier history. Thirty Chinese students at the University of Manchester were stranded in the city by the Sino-Japanese War. On 9 May 1942 the International Club offered space, and the British Council funds, to a Manchester China Institute, the third of its kind in Britain, to provide a meeting place for Chinese students to enable them 'to learn the English language' and 'to help them generally until they can "stand on their own feet"'.[83] The initiative was apparently taken by the Manchester branch of the Universities China Committee which, drawing on the Boxer Indemnity, had been promoting Chinese studies and funding student exchanges with China since 1932. The Institute was intended as a means by which British people could meet Chinese students and learn from them something of 'the great and deep cultural heritage of China'.[84] The link was reinforced by the establishment of a Sino-British Society, with the institute as its base, that December.[85] By 1943, the International Club had come to serve also as a venue in Manchester for meetings between delegations from Republican China and Chinese students at the university.[86] In February 1944 the China Institute and the Sino-British society were the joint sponsors of a lecture in Manchester on 'Chinese Drama' by S.I. Hsiung, the author of *Lady Precious Stream*.[87]

African sailors from an expanding wartime merchant fleet were finding their way to the city from the Port of Manchester on the Ship Canal, a port visited in the early years of the war by an estimated 100,000 seamen every year.[88] It was for them that in July 1940 the port's Mission to Seamen opened 'The Flying Angel Lascar Club' on Trafford Road in Salford, opposite the dock gates.[89]

During the winter of 1940–41 officials from the Ministry of Labour and the Colonial Office, concerned at the shortage of munitions workers at a crucial stage in the war, came together to devise a scheme for the recruitment of volunteers from the West Indies and British Honduras. They were to be young men of 'good education and mechanical skill', who, after attending government training centres in the north-west, were to be dispersed for specialist work in the armaments factories of Manchester, south Lancashire and Merseyside.[90] Following a massive response in the West Indies, the first 188 of these 'colonial trainees', most of them Jamaicans, arrived in Manchester in February 1941, to be followed by further batches, each of up to 200 persons, during the following two years.[91] The *Manchester Guardian* of 4 November 1942 reported the presence in Manchester of 17 Bahamians and 20 British Hondurans, who had survived the torpedoing of their ship, and noted the arrival of sixteen Barbadians and forty-nine Jamaicans, forty-three of whom were housed in a hostel established for that purpose in Bolton ('Colonial House', with its own 'coloured warden'), the rest in two converted YMCA hostels (West India House and Saxon House) in Manchester's Whalley Range.[92] Although the scheme was 'imperfectly planned', the recruits often lacked relevant skills (those arriving in Manchester in November 1942 included clerks, journalists, policemen, sign painters, linotype operators and a grocer) and there were initial problems with both employers and unions, it was adjudged by Learie Constantine, the Trinidadian cricketer and trainee lawyer who from the autumn of 1941 acted as the welfare officer to recruits reaching the north-west, to have been a 'great success'.[93]

Another Ministry of Labour scheme, which apparently came into operation in the spring of 1941, brought to Manchester 'trainee technicians' from India for six months' training in engineering and workshop management, before returning them to play their part in building up an Indian munitions industry. The first thirty arrived in May 1941, and a second group of fifty that autumn, when they were said to be being initiated into 'British methods of mass-production'.[94] They were able to make links with a Manchester Indian Association, a vehicle of Indian nationalist aspirations, certainly in existence by the December of 1941, when it was said to have organised the celebration of 'the Muslim festivals' at the Koh-i-Noor on Oxford Road, a restaurant then owned by the Syrian merchant and vocal anti-Zionist, Saleh M. Haffar.[95]

The American servicemen who, following Pearl Harbor, began to arrive in Manchester during the summer of 1942, included black GIs, who in August of that year were challenged to a game of 'indoor baseball' on Platt Fields by a Canadian army team.[96] An American Servicemen's Club was opened by the American Red Cross in December 1942 in the former premises of the Manchester Constitutional Club, where, on Christmas Day, 400 GIs sat down to dinner; a second club, for black troops (described in the *British Council's Guide to Manchester and Salford for the US Armed Forces* as 'negro staffed'), was opened in Lever Street soon afterwards, so perpetuating in Manchester the friction that existed in the United States between white American troops and the black comrades-in-arms whom they considered their inferiors, itself a reflection of the racial divide in American society.[97]

Whatever the other facilities open to them, it seems likely that men and women from every element of Manchester's vast and growing floating population of 'foreigners' found their way to the club. During 1942, apart from the overseas students, refugees and native Jews identified in the oral testimony, its membership was said to include 'trainees from India, Barbados and British Honduras, American soldiers and technicians, Finnish seamen involved in factory work and allied convalescent soldiers'.[98] The widening sources of the club's membership, as much as the British Council's concept of its mission, are reflected in the gradually increasing breadth of the club's activities beyond the regular round of socials, dances, talks and rambles.

From the government's perspective, the British Council, by its 'alliance' with the International Club, had forged an effective mechanism for sweetening the sojourn in Manchester of those foreign nationals whose friendship, morale and 'appreciation' of things British were vital to the war effort and the partnership of whose nations in the defence of shared democratic values seemed likely to prove reciprocally advantageous in the remaking of Europe. Part of this strategy was a plan, devised (probably by the British Council) during 1942, to create at the club, on the Liverpool model, 'special rooms for each nationality'. Whether the true intent was ever to provide dedicated space for all the allied nationalities represented at the club, the reality was an emphasis on two nations, China and Czechoslovakia, whose future as democratic republics seemed most likely to serve as a bulwark against Communist domination. In the pursuit of the Czech cause, nationalism and idealism were neatly intertwined. On the one side, it accorded with the primarily nationalist concerns of the International Club's British Council masters. It would promote amongst Czechs a respect for things British which it was hoped they would take back to their liberated nation. On the other, it reflected the iconic place of Czechoslovakia in the minds of internationalists like Hudson and Fleure, as the sacrificial victim to Fascist aggression, to whom was owed a special debt for the debacle at Munich. Before the war, Hudson, as chairman of the Eccles branch of the LNU, had engineered a 'peace link' with Dvur Kralove, a Czech textile town (in common parlance, 'the Manchester of Czechoslovakia'), from where some twenty-four refugees had since taken refuge in Britain, at least three of them in Manchester.[99] It seems likely that Hudson was now the go-between in negotiations between the British Council, the International Club and Czech émigré associations in Manchester, and, in particular, with the so-called Czech Centre, of which the president, Dr Pavel Krug, was a native of Dvur Kralove, and which up to this point had held its meetings in private accommodation, including a room provided by a generous 'English lady'.

In January 1942 the *Manchester Guardian* reported that the British Council had offered rooms at its premises in George Street to the Masaryk Society, another local Czech émigré organisation, 'for the purposes of a club and meeting place'.[100] It was only when the offer was (for reasons unknown) not taken up, that the British Council turned to one of its two main competitors, the Manchester Czech Centre, which by then, under the presidency of the Manchester Labour alderman, Wright Robinson, had begun to mount public events at the International Club. Although details of the discussions which followed are now lost, on 4 December 1942 Dr Edouard Benes, President of the Czech Republic in Exile, visited Manchester, in part to open the 'Czechoslovak Room' in British Council House at 64 George Street, as the Czech Centre's headquarters. In a speech which must have warmed the hearts of the British Council's officers, Benes spoke of the necessity of a 'close relationship' between the British and Czech peoples; 'bonds of sympathy' between Czechoslovakia and Lancashire symbolised by the room were 'a vital factor in helping to restore a free Czechoslovakia to a free Europe'.[101] The *Manchester Guardian* believed that, in the circumstances of war, the British Council had 'charmingly' exchanged its original function of familiarising other nations with the British way of life for the lauding of the cultural achievements of Britain's allies.[102]

Lily Neustadt, a Czech Jewish refugee who arrived in Britain from Prague in July 1939, and in Manchester a few months later, and who had been a member of the Czech Centre since its foundation, remembers it as having been made up in its beginnings largely of Jews and Sudeten Social Democrats. Immediately after the German invasion of Russia, however, it rapidly acquired, although apparently only temporarily, an additional 150 members. A 'Jew by birth, not by observance', Lily felt very much at home in the club; it was there that she met her husband, Franz Krug, also a 'non-practising' Czech Jewish refugee, whom she married in Manchester in March 1942. During the war, the International Club offered Lily the only social life beyond a circle otherwise made up entirely of Czechs and other Central European refugees.[103]

With a permanent home at the International Club, and the promotional support of the British Council, the Czech Centre now overtook its main rival, the Masaryk Society, to become, by the autumn of 1943, the only Czech émigré body in the city.[104] These were the climactic months of Britain's guilt-ridden love affair with Czechoslovakia. The twenty-fifth anniversary of Czech independence was celebrated in Manchester in October 1943 by a special service at Manchester Cathedral, a Hallé Concert made up of music by Czech composers conducted by John Barbirolli and a reception at the Czech Centre attended by Sir William Jowitt, Minister without Portfolio in the Coalition Government, Dr K. Skalicky, Minister Plenipotentiary for Czechoslovakia, and local dignitaries who included the Anglican Dean of Manchester, the

Communal Rabbi, Wright Robinson and John Coatman, Director of the Northern Region of the BBC. The new and substantially strategic dalliance with the Soviet Union was symbolised in November 1943 by the celebration at the Czech Centre of the anniversary of the Russian Revolution;[105] further Czech 'understandings' with the Soviet regime were rendered necessary in May 1944 as the advancing Russian army neared the border of Czechoslovakia.

By the beginning of 1943 the International Club had become a recognised part of the institutional furniture of the city, as a social centre for foreigners and their English friends, as a venue for local societies as various as the Astronomical Society, the Esperanto Society, Women for Westminster and the Women's International League for Peace and Freedom, and as the place where foreign delegations to Manchester were typically entertained.[106] The club has left no records which explain the inner workings of its committees during what was its heyday in the last two years of war, when it boasted over 500 members, drawn from thirty-five nations.[107] Nor is it possible to distinguish, either from press reports or from the British Council's annual reports, the roles played by the club's General Committee and by their British Council paymasters. Herbert Phillips, in his dual role, tactfully negotiated the relationship between them.[108] What reports and notices in the press suggest is an eclectic programme which reflected the priorities of both: the club's concern to promote international understanding, the British Council's to impress upon foreigners images of the British way of life; the interest of both, if for different reasons, in the education and well-being of allied troops stationed in or near the city.

The allied forces, their members passing through Manchester at a rate of at least 30,000 a month by 1945,[109] constituted a major focus of attention. During 1943–44 at least 600 other troops visited the club: Poles, Czechs, Norwegians, Belgians, Hungarians and, Arlsberg remembers, Jamaican recruits to the RAF like Archie Downey, whom he befriended and who remained in Manchester after the war.[110] The British Council was particularly concerned for the image of Britain which might be taken home by her allies from the United States, with which Britain sought to maintain a 'special relationship' in a post-war world. Alone and in combination with the North Western District of the Workers Educational Association (WEA) and the Manchester Regional Committee for Education in the Forces, the British Council mounted a series of study courses for Americans and Canadians in the university and the city. The British Council's guide to the city was only the first of a series of pamphlets produced during 1943–44 introducing Manchester and Salford to US troops.[111]

Some of the many public exhibitions mounted at the club between 1943 and 1945 were designed to publicise more generally what the British Council saw as the 'British way.' One, 'Britain in Pictures', in November 1944, was made up of a selection of the photographs which had been 'sent abroad by the British Council ... to make Britain better known and understood by other peoples'.[112] Another, 'Artists of Today and Tomorrow', put on for ten days in January 1945 by the club's cultural sub-committee, and described by the *Manchester Guardian* as the club's first showcase for British contemporary art, included work by Jacob Epstein and Frances Hodgkins as well as 'local talent'.[113] Other exhibitions were more obviously an earnest expression of the club committee's continuing attachment to democratic values and an internationalist intent. These included, for a week in September 1943, 'From the Four Corners', an exhibition made up, it was said, of materials provided by club members as well as foreign embassies and consulates, and accompanied by film shows and lectures on each of the nations represented.[114] Arlsberg remembers many more minor exhibitions, all open to the public, each focusing on a different country and made up of 'bits and pieces' from citizens who were members of the club.[115]

From July 1944, perhaps as a consequence of the conference, the club began a series of social evenings, to which Manchester schools were invited to send delegates 'to meet [foreign] people now in this city ... in an effort to increase international understanding and co-operation'.[116] At a conference at the club in March 1945 the plan was extended to include monthly meetings of delegates from schools and youth organisations at which 'speakers from overseas' would each speak about their own countries, beginning on 21 April 1945 with speakers from India and China.[117] At an international brains trust at the club in March 1945 on 'Trades Unions', the speakers included a former Austrian trade unionist and a German Social Democrat.[118]

The post-war role of refugees in British society remained a paramount concern. In June 1942, the club had provided the venue for a conference organised by the Foreign Scientists Committee of the Association of Scientific Workers aimed at finding ways in which refugee scientists might more readily contribute to the British war effort. Although, according to the committee's secretary, E. Kornreich, the government had been slow to take advantage of the skills of *all* scientific workers, refugees faced the additional obstacle of 'prejudice against foreigners'.[119] In March 1944 David Goldblatt, secretary of the Refugee Industries Committee, a body set up in London to assert the right of refugee industrialists to remain in Britain when the war ended and to participate as equals in the post-war reconstruction of the British economy, was invited to address the club on 'The Contribution of Immigrants Throughout the Ages to the Economic and Cultural Life of Great Britain'.[120] In August 1944 Tom Hudson was one of the signatories of a memo to Sir Ernest Bevin on 'The Export Trade', which again highlighted the actual and potential contribution of refugee industrialists to Britain's economic recovery.[121] At some time during 1943–44 the club organised a conference, the purposes of which are unclear, but in which the concern for refugees is obvious, for 'refugee workers in outlying districts'.[122]

The most obvious expression of the club's determination to remain true to its utopian ideals, as well as the clearest indication of its integration, in only the fifth year of its existence, into the mainstream institutional life of the city, was the election, in May 1944, of the Manchester alderman and trade union official, Wright Robinson, as president in succession to Fleure who, then on the verge of retirement from his university post, was due to leave that autumn on an extended lecture tour of the United States.[123] In recognition of Fleure's services, the club initiated a 'Fleure Prize', to be awarded annually for the best essay on international understanding.[124] His last lecture to the club, in June 1944, on 'Peasant Life and its Renovation', was yet another appreciation of the simple rural life in danger of submergence by urban materialism.[125] He left without doubting the efficacy of the club's mission: 'the ideals for which the club stood were of the utmost importance to the immediate and post-war future'.[126]

Wright Robinson was known to share these ideals. A man of humble Lancashire origins and little education, he had risen through the ranks of local Labour Party politics and the trade union bureaucracy to become a highly respected public servant, philanthropist and champion of radical, including refugee, causes.[127] First elected as a Manchester City Councillor for Beswick Ward in 1919, he had made a name for himself particularly as 'a keen educationalist' who, as a leading member (and chairman during 1929–32) of the Education Committee had helped launch a local programme for the extension of secondary and higher education, an interest said to arise from his own lack of educational opportunities as a child. Before his election to the presidency of the club, of which he had been one of the earliest patrons, his single-minded energies on behalf of the city had already brought him honour, position and respect. A JP since 1934, an alderman since 1935, Lord Mayor during 1941–42, he was also, amongst other things, a member of the Court and Council of the University, active on the Boards of Governors of the Manchester Municipal College of Technology (as chairman from 1930), Manchester Grammar School, John Rylands Library and the Hulme Trust and Estates, a member of the central executive of the WEA, and the holder of an honorary Manchester MA.[128] A morale-boosting mayoralty during the Manchester Blitz had cemented his reputation as 'a quiet man ... even tempered, shrewd ... with a keen sense of humour',[129] disrespectful of authority, class and hierarchy, ready to work with men and women of every party and social position, and with an abundance of compassion for the suffering.

Since 1939 a leading figure in the support of Czech refugees, Robinson was already closely associated with the International Club, not only as one of its patrons, but as the president of the Czech Centre to which it had accorded hospitality at the end of 1942. He now accepted the club's presidency because, in his own words, 'international fraternity [was] part of my creed' and central to Manchester's traditions. As an international trading centre, Manchester had always felt a 'special obligation to provide a place where men and women from other countries overseas could meet and find a welcome'.[130] It was also said of him in 1943 that he was 'particularly keen that Manchester should take advantage of the presence of refugees from the overrun countries' to strengthen international harmony and 'friendship between the Allied Nations'.[131] He was then, according to the same source, chairman of the Friends of Czechoslovakia, the Friends of Austria, Manchester's Anglo-Russian Friendship Committee and of the Manchester and District Committee of the Free Austria Movement.

The roots of his interest in refugees, already evident in 1937, when he joined the Manchester Committee supporting the Basque children at Watermillock,[132] is less easy to detect. It was perhaps rooted in his sense of himself, for all his civic prestige, as a perennial outsider: born in 1876 into a working-class Burnley family living on the verge of abject poverty; a half-timer in a cotton mill while at elementary school; a young man living from hand to mouth without a fixed trade; an early member of the Fabian Society and the Independent Labour Party, whose local paper, *Liverpool Forward* he had edited; a trade union official since 1917; a conscientious objector, on political grounds, during the First World War, when he was forced to abandon his place on Liverpool City Council and flee to Manchester, where he became, at first, an assistant porter (his tasks, he was to remember, were made up of 'boots, coal, lawn and windows') at the Quaker student hostel, Dalton Hall. Always a moderate within the Labour movement, his preference for 'co-operation' – between workers and employers, between the otherwise competing towns and cities of south Lancashire, between councillors and their constituents, between countries, between old and young, between men and women of different faiths and political persuasions – inclined him towards the support of foreigners seeking acceptance by the British state and by Manchester society.[133] There is no doubt of his particular empathy with those foreigners who had been forced into flight. 'When we use words like Refugee,' he wrote in his diary in 1940, 'it is so easy to forget that the term covers people much like ourselves, coming from homes which they loved, and where they lived unsuspicious of exile and disaster.'[134] It was this 'formidable fighter for his ideals'[135] who now steered the International Club through the final year of war.[136]

To what extent had the International Club reflected Manchester's 'true self'? It was certainly the first time that Manchester's cherished self-image as a cosmopolitan city, an image which had found purchase in the first decades of the nineteenth century, had been given institutional shape. That shape, however, had been designed by a liberal and humanitarian elite which had earlier paraded Manchester's multinational population as proof of the city's tolerance towards people of every nation and religion. However, this was never more than partially the case. There were times when sections of the city had veered into fierce anti-Semitism and xenophobia. Hayes himself had followed his account of Manchester's tolerance with an attack on the 'swarm' of Jews who were then supposedly undermining the welfare of a city suburb. In a sense the International Club, however valuable it became as a haven for refugees and for Manchester's 'foreign' population in wartime, was the fragile product of liberal rhetoric. The club's managers found little difficulty in incorporating the cultural nationalism of the British Council.

The nature of the club's core activities, combined with its insistence on the respectability and political silence of its entrants, were also most likely to produce a middle-class liberal clientele, both native and foreign. For the working-class segments of Manchester's population – Chinese laundrymen scattered throughout Manchester's working-class districts and the black seamen settled in Salford's Greengate and beginning to move towards Moss Side – the club would have had no appeal. Members of the club, banned from 'political debate', were ill-equipped to participate in the post-war protest movements by which other internationalists – the Communists, the Indian nationalists and the Pan-Africans – sought a more harmonious society. It played no part in the Pan-African Congress of October 1945 which initiated post-war struggle against colonial oppression.

Notes

1 Louis M. Hayes, *Reminiscences of Manchester and Some of its Surroundings from the Year 1840*, p. 286.
2 *Ibid.*, pp. 102–3.
3 Robert Roberts, *The Classic Slum: Salford Life in the First Quarter of the Twentieth Century*.
4 Undated (1945–46?) letter from Wright Robinson to the City Council objecting to a proposed increase in the rental of the club's premises, Wright Robinson Papers (hereafter WRP).
5 W.M. Phillips, 'The International Club in Manchester', pp. 7–8.
6 A brief history is included in *From Idea to Ideal: The International Club, Manchester, England, 10th Anniversary Brochure, 1948*; the minutes of a meeting of the International Service Committee of the Manchester Society of Friends (hereafter ISC) on 4 April 1940 includes an account of how the group was set up and of its organisation and activities.
7 Interview of Lisa Wolfe by Bill Williams.

8 Benia Hesford was a professional teacher of the hearing impaired.
9 ISC, 4 April 1940.
10 ISC, 24 October 1935.
11 ISC, 4 April 1940.
12 *Ibid.*
13 *From Idea to Ideal.*
14 ISC, 4 April 1940. In 1937 there were international clubs in Glasgow, Newcastle and Cambridge.
15 Phillips, 'The International Club'.
16 *From Idea to Ideal.*
17 ISC, undated (May 1937?) meeting.
18 Phillips, 'The International Club', p. 7.
19 Kate Croft was a specialist teacher of the deaf, like her companion, May Elliott, with whom she lived in Ashton-on-Mersey.
20 *From Idea to Ideal.*
21 *Ibid.* and Phillips, 'The International Club', p. 7.
22 *From Idea to Ideal.*
23 *Manchester City News*, 11 February 1939 in its regular 'Round and About Manchester' column.
24 Phillips, 'The International Club'.
25 *Ibid.*
26 *Ibid.*
27 Taped interview of Fred Arlsberg by Bill Williams, 14 February 2006. Arlsberg, a German refugee of Jewish origin, joined the club in July 1941 and was for a time its chairman and secretary in its post-war years.
28 A house committee was responsible for domestic matters; a meetings committee arranged the programmes of talks; a membership committee considered applications for membership; a cultural committee arranged exhibitions, plays, readings and musical events; and a social committee arranged outings and dances.
29 Interview with Arlsberg.
30 Interview of Rejika Fruhman (née Monat) by Rosalyn Livshin, May 2002. Monat followed her parents from Cracow to Manchester in February 1939. Soon afterwards, the family rented a house in Heywood Street, Cheetham. There she found the nearby Waterpark Club 'very snobbish' and preferred either the Maccabi Club or the International Club, which she found 'a very nice intellectual club'.
31 *Oxford Dictionary of National Biography*, 'Herbert John Fleure 1877–1969'. His collaborator in the research was his colleague, T.C. James.
32 H.J. Fleure, *The Geographical Background of Modern Problems*, pp. 1, 34.
33 H.J. Fleure, *Race and its Meaning in Europe*, p. 10
34 *Ibid.*, pp. 22–3.
35 *Ibid.*, p. 16.
36 *Ibid.* Although there was no 'Jewish race', Fleure believed that there were

physical characteristics which occur frequently among Jews. Other references to Jews in history are on pp. 12–15.

37 *Ibid.* For an account of Fleure's place in the development of 'race science', see Tony Kushner, 'H.J. Fleure: a paradigm for inter-war race thinking in Britain'.

38 He was a governor, and one-time Chairman of Governors, of the Manchester High School for Girls, as sought after by the Manchester middle classes for the education of their daughters as Manchester Grammar School was for their sons.

39 In a speech delivered to the 'summer gathering' of Abbotsholme School in Derbyshire, *Manchester Guardian*, 22 June 1942.

40 *From Idea to Ideal.*

41 He followed short-lived tenures of the office by Mrs Wormald and a 'Miss Hartley'. This latter may well have been the 'Mabel Hartley, a religious pacifist' whom Hanna Seiderer met at the club. See Sir Jacob Behrens's autobiography, *Sir Jacob Behrens 1806–1889*, p. 71.

42 In 1945 he was chairman of the Withington Divisional Liberal Association (*Manchester City News*, 23 February 1945).

43 Godfrey William Armitage, *Scrapbook of Articles, Letters etc*, in Manchester Central Library (hereafter MCL), very probably put together by his widow, the art historian, Margaret Armitage, herself a patron of the International Club. It includes letters, cuttings of published articles and poems, company brochures, a centenary history of Armitage and Rigby, and obituaries. Armitage retired from business in 1950 and died on 17 January 1958. The firm Armitage and Rigby was founded in Ancoats in 1836 by William Armitage and by the late 1930s had evolved into a major company of cotton spinners, manufacturers and merchants with mills in Ancoats and a factory in Warrington. Armitage became treasurer of Manchester Grammar School in 1940.

44 The firm appears in a Manchester Trade Directory of 1938 as 'manufacturer and merchants of cotton goods, grey and white calicoes, shirtings and flannelettes etc' at 40 Newton Street and 10 Stevenson Square.

45 She would talk constantly of 'her time in Penang', according to Fred Arlsberg.

46 Hanna Behrend, 'A political refugee in Manchester', p. 31.

47 WRP.

48 The list is taken from a letter from the Club committee to the *Manchester Guardian*, 20 September 1941.

49 Alice and Gerhard Zadek, *Mit dem Letzen Zug nach England*, p. 236.

50 Behrend, 'A political refugee', p. 31.

51 *Manchester Guardian*, 23 October 1940.

52 Paul Bitzberg, e-mail correspondence with Lynne Jesky.

53 *Manchester Guardian*, 29 April 1941.

54 The British Council (hereafter BC) Annual Report for 1940–41, pp. 13–14.

55 *Ibid.*, pp. 15, 20–1.

56 *Ibid.*, pp. 9–13.

57 *Ibid.*, pp. 10–11, 15, 21.

58 *Ibid.*, pp. 22–3.
59 Frances Donaldson, *The British Council: The First Fifty Years*, pp. 112–13. The proposition came in September 1939 from S.H. Wood, who represented the Board of Education on the British Council's Executive Committee.
60 Donaldson, *The British Council*, pp. 112–19.
61 *Manchester Guardian*, 5 and 7 December 1940.
62 *Manchester Guardian*, 5 December 1940.
63 *Manchester Guardian*, 19 February 1941.
64 This aim is stated at its plainest in the *Manchester Guardian*'s account of the opening of the British Council's Czech Institute in London in January 1941, *Manchester Guardian*, 16 January 1941.
65 *Manchester Guardian*, 14 June 1941.
66 *Ibid.*
67 *Manchester Guardian*, 18 April 1941.
68 *Manchester Guardian*, 3 May 1941.
69 *Manchester Guardian*, 24 July 1941.
70 Article by T.M. Hudson, chairman of the Manchester International Club, *Manchester and Salford Woman Citizen*, No. 273 (February 1942), p. 2.
71 *Ibid.*
72 *Manchester Guardian*, 1 September 1941.
73 In a letter to the *Manchester Guardian* written on 17 September and signed by Hudson, Herbert Phillips and Armitage, *Manchester Guardian*, 20 September 1941. Phrases like 'the International Club, aided by the British Council' suggest, wrongly, that the club retained a degree of autonomy.
74 *Ibid.*
75 *Ibid.*
76 *Ibid.*
77 *Manchester Guardian*, 20 September 1941.
78 For example, BC Annual Report for 1942–43.
79 *Manchester Guardian*, 29 November 1941.
80 Interview with Arlsberg.
81 Speech by Sir Malcolm Robertson MP, Chairman of the British Council, to the Manchester Luncheon Club, quoted in the *Manchester Guardian*, 22 October 1943. See also the leader on 'The British Council' in *Manchester Guardian*, 30 June 1943.
82 Article by Hudson, p. 2.
83 *Manchester City News*, 8 and 15 May 1942.
84 *Manchester Guardian*, 11 May 1942. The same committee funded a Readership in Chinese at Manchester University.
85 *Manchester Guardian*, 19 December 1942.
86 *Manchester Guardian*, 22 December 1943.
87 *Manchester Guardian*, 4 February 1944.
88 *Manchester Guardian*, 22 July 1941.
89 *Manchester Guardian*, 20, 23 and 25 July 1940.

90 *Manchester Guardian*, 27 December 1941.

91 *Ibid.*

92 *Manchester Guardian*, 3 October and 4 November 1942. The Bahamians were said to have all been former pupils at the Eastern Senior School in Nassau.

93 Learie Constantine, *Colour Bar*, pp. 146–8; *Manchester Guardian*, 4 November 1942.

94 *Manchester Guardian*, 1 August and 18 October 1941. Their sponsors in Manchester were the North-West Regional Board of the Production Executive and the Regional Advisory Committee in Training, both chaired by Sir Frederick West.

95 *Manchester Guardian*, 29 December 1941. The Manchester Indian Association was represented at Manchester meetings of the India League.

96 *Manchester Guardian*, 17 August 1942.

97 *Manchester Guardian*, 23 and 31 December 1942. *A British Council's Guide to Manchester for American Troops*, published in 1943, notes two clubs run by the American Red Cross, one for blacks only. For friction between white and black American troops in Britain, see Sonya O. Rose, *Which People's War? National Identity and Citizenship in Wartime Britain 1939–1945*, pp. 248–52.

98 BC Annual Report for 1942–43, pp. 69–70.

99 *Manchester Guardian*, 22 and 25 January 1943.

100 *Manchester Guardian*, 19 January 1942. Since August 1940 the Masaryk Society had been hoping to rent a house, part of which would be devoted to social and cultural events for Czechs 'and their English friends' and part reserved as living accommodation for some of its members, *Manchester Guardian*, 21 August 1940. Nothing came of the idea.

101 *Manchester Guardian*, 21 November, 4 and 5 December 1942.

102 *Manchester Guardian*, 5 May 1942.

103 Taped interview of Mrs Lily Crewe by Rosalyn Livshin. Lily remembers that the 'elite' of the Czech Centre was made up of Pavel Krug and his two brothers. Its secretary was Vera Foldes.

104 The last reference to the Masaryk Society in the Manchester press is in the *Manchester Guardian*, 22 August 1943; the last reference to the Czech Circle is in the *Manchester Guardian*, 13 July 1943.

105 *Manchester Guardian*, 5 November 1943.

106 For example, *Manchester Guardian*, 8 February, 21 June 1944, 19 April 1945.

107 *Manchester Guardian*, 24 May 1944 gives the total membership as 550.

108 Interview with Arlsberg.

109 *Manchester Guardian*, 7 March 1945 estimated that 29,581 allied troops had stayed in the YMCA alone during February 1945.

110 Interview with Arlsberg.

111 *Manchester Guardian*, 3 April 1944.

112 *Manchester Guardian*, 14 November 1944.

113 *Manchester Guardian*, 9 January 1945.

114 *Manchester Guardian*, 21 September 1943.

115 Interview with Arlsberg.
116 *Manchester Guardian*, 19 March 1945.
117 *Ibid.*
118 *Manchester Guardian*, 10 March 1945.
119 *Manchester Guardian*, 16 and 20 June 1942.
120 Manchester Jewish Refugees Committee (hereafter MJRC) Memorandum from Werner Treuhertz to the North West Regional Refugee Industries Committee, 3 March 1944.
121 MJRC Minutes of the Executive Committee of the North West Regional Refugee Industries Association, 24 August 1944.
122 BC Annual Report for 1943–44, p. 95.
123 *Manchester Guardian*, 24 May 1944.
124 *Ibid.*
125 *Manchester Guardian*, 26 June 1944.
126 *Manchester Guardian*, 24 May 1944.
127 In 1911 Robinson was elected to Blackburn Town Council. He left for Liverpool in 1913 to become Independent Labour Party organiser and editor of its local newsletter. In 1917 he moved to Manchester as a trade union organiser, securing election to the City Council for Beswick Ward in 1919. He was elevated to the aldermanic bench in 1935.
128 For biographical details, *Manchester Review: The Quarterly Journal of the Libraries Committee*, Vol. 3 (Spring 1943) pp. 127–8; report of the conferment of the Freedom of the City, *Manchester Guardian*, 6 April 1956; Programme for the Presentation of the Freedom of the City, 5 April 1956 (MCL MSC 920/R); obituary in *Manchester Guardian*, 18 June 1960; leading article, 'A pioneer', *Manchester Guardian*, 22 June 1960; funeral oration by Lady Simon of Wythenshawe (MCL MSC 920/R).
129 Obituary in *Manchester Guardian*, 18 June 1960.
130 Draft autobiography, WRP, Box 12.
131 *Manchester Review.*
132 Watermillock was a house near Bolton loaned by its owner to the Basque Children's Committee to house some of the children from the Basque country, then under threat from Franco's forces, allowed temporary residence in Britain.
133 He saw himself essentially as a mediator: as Lord Mayor, for example, he instituted meetings for Manchester senior schoolchildren in the Council Chamber, where senior city officials spoke about their work, and for juniors in the Central Library, where he himself described the government of the city (*Manchester Review*). His own trip abroad was a few months spent recuperating in the USA and Canada as a young man following a fall from a roof.
134 'Gossiping commentary on the year 1940', WRP, Box 7, p. 2.
135 Funeral oration by Lady Simon.
136 The club continued, with a diminished membership, a more limited programme of events and a series of financial crises, until 1972, when the collapse of the club's roof, and its inability to pay for its repair, brought its disappearance.

Bibliography

Behrend, Hanna, 'A political refugee in Manchester', *North West Labour History: Journal of the North West Labour History Group*, 18 (1993–94), pp. 27–43.

Behrens, Sir Jacob, *Sir Jacob Behrens 1806–1889* (London: Percy Lund, Humphries and Co Ltd, n.d.).

Constantine, Learie, *Colour Bar* (London: St Paul, 1954).

Donaldson, Frances, *The British Council: The First Fifty Years* (London: Cape, 1984).

Fleure, H.J., *The Geographical Background of Modern Problems* (London: Longmans, 1932).

Fleure, H.J., *Race and its Meaning in Europe* (Manchester: John Rylands Library, 1940; reprinted from the *Bulletin of John Rylands Library*, 24:2 (October 1940)).

Hayes, Louis M., *Reminiscences of Manchester and Some of its Surroundings from the Year 1840* (London and Manchester: Sherratt and Hughes, 1906).

Kushner, Tony, 'H.J. Fleure: a paradigm for inter-war race thinking in Britain', *Patterns of Prejudice*, 42:2, 2008, pp. 151–66.

Phillips, W.M., 'The International Club in Manchester', *Manchester and Salford Woman Citizen*, No. 245 (March 1939), pp. 7–8

Roberts, Robert, *The Classic Slum: Salford Life in the First Quarter of the Twentieth Century* (Harmondsworth: Penguin, 1973).

Rose, Sonja O., *Which People's War? National Identity and Citizenship in Wartime Britain 1939–1945* (Oxford: Oxford University Press, 2004).

Zadek, Alice and Gerhard, *Mit dem Letzen Zug nach England* (Berlin: Dietz, 1992).

Culture, participation and identity in contemporary Manchester

Andrew Miles

Introduction

Manchester's cultural institutions have historically played a pivotal role in shaping the city's public spaces, civic identity and international profile. Both the mid-Victorian reconstruction of the city and the narratives underpinning its late twentieth-century regeneration were fundamentally 'culture-led'.[1] The image of contemporary Manchester is one of a city lifted out of industrial decline and transformed by a new 'spirit of place' founded on cultural investment and creative industries development. In turn, the roots of its success as England's leading provincial 'creative city', which has continued with the BBC's recent relocation to Mediacity on Salford Quays, have been presented in terms of a set of local particularities marked by the emergence of a diverse 'urban growth coalition' of city elites spanning the arts, popular culture and the creative industries.[2]

The relationship between culture, class and identity has been a consistent theme linking studies of Manchester's past and present. Just as the opening up of 'high' cultural institutions as the focus of a new public sphere is associated with the articulation of new middle-class identities in the second half of the nineteenth century,[3] so the formal cultural fabric of the present-day urban centre – comprising many of the same institutions – has been invoked as the focal point in a process of symbolic identification with the city through 'elective belonging' among an otherwise diverse array of current middle-class residents.[4] However, the significance of the city's traditional cultural venues to the wider Manchester public is less clear. While theatre and classical music were given as the main reasons for visiting the city centre by the respondents in a study by Mike Savage *et al.*,[5] a contemporaneous survey of local arts attendance showed market penetration at below the national average in almost two-thirds of Manchester and Greater Manchester postcodes, with annual attendance rates at arts venues averaging out at 20 per cent of the population.[6]

Accordingly, what I want to explore in this essay is the apparent disconnect between Manchester's long-established, high-profile cultural institutions and the majority of those who live in the city. In particular, I focus here on the 'non-users' of such institutions, who, in the profiling discourses of audience development in the arts, are deemed to be culturally disengaged. In doing so, I draw on research arising directly from within this discourse, generated as a by-product of a project designed to create a dialogue between academics working on issues of cultural taste and the concerns of the local cultural sector. The findings of this work offer a very different sense of the role of culture in articulating identities – both identification with Manchester and self-identity – among working-class residents of the city, while for those concerned with the arena of cultural policymaking, they highlight the limitations of an official model of participation, the assumptions, processes and technologies of which obscure and so neglect the realm of everyday participation and its significance.

Cultural policy and participation under New Labour

Labour's 1997 election victory was quickly followed by a radical overhaul in the administration of the subsidised cultural sector, which profoundly challenged the preceding 'arm's length' principle of culture governance.[7] This was marked in particular by the creation of the Department of Culture, Media and Sport (DCMS) in place of the Department of National Heritage and by the formation of the Regional Cultural Consortia, as New Labour sought to co-ordinate and integrate cultural policy within its wider political programme.

Alongside this new interventionist structure, the dynamics of cultural policymaking were transformed by the explicit adoption and intensification of a new style of public administration, dubbed the 'New Public Management'.[8] Rooted in the concerns of Conservative governments of the 1980s to expose public spending to market mechanisms and models of accountability based on the private sector, this focused on an instrumentalist, resource accounting approach to cultural investment. Such investment had to be justified in terms of the cultural sector's contribution to the government's wider economic and social objectives. This was established through Public Service Agreements (PSAs) with the Treasury by which funding was performance-dependent and both the DCMS and its sponsored Non-departmental Public Bodies (NDPBs) committed to target-setting to ensure best value.[9]

Participation – expressed in terms of widening access to cultural activities – was at the heart of New Labour's cultural project and accordingly remained a consistent priority for the DCMS after 1997. The party's cultural policy document *Create the Future* had asserted that the arts must be 'for the many not the few' and that 'Access will be the cornerstone of our cultural policy', a position re-confirmed in *Culture and Creativity: The Next Ten Years*,[10] and pursued through initiatives such as free entry to National Museums and Galleries and the setting of precise targets for increasing engagement among socially disadvantaged groups and young people. Following the 2007 Comprehensive Spending Review, the department adopted a set of core strategic objectives, the first of which (DS01) was 'Opportunity: to encourage more widespread enjoyment of culture, media and sport'.[11]

The drive to increase participation was predicated primarily on instrumental concerns with equity and social inclusion.[12] It was conceded that consumption of the largely traditional art forms and cultural assets funded by the DCMS and its NDPBs was the preserve of a small minority, with a large proportion of public funds going to support iconic metropolitan institutions. Democratising access was therefore necessary to justify such spending to the taxpayer and establish value for money. At the same time, it was presented as a way of combating social exclusion by spreading cultural capital and in the process developing a more inclusive 'cultural citizenship'.[13]

Establishing the impact of policies to widen access was a primary concern. The Labour government's embrace of the New Public Management framework had brought issues of evidence, and in particular the requirement for 'measurable outcomes', to the fore. As a report by the DCMS's Quality, Efficiency and Standards Team made clear, 'The [cultural] sector cannot continue to compete with other increasing demands for expenditure of education, health, law, etc. without the essential ammunition that performance measurement offers.'[14] However, while the drive to collect data became pivotal to the department's operations, the quality, consistency and mobilisation of what was produced left much to be desired.[15] Subsequently, in an attempt to address such criticisms, the DCMS commissioned *Taking Part*, a major annual survey of participation in culture and sport, which was designed using National Statistics protocols to ensure 'quality assurance'.[16]

This short account of the development of Labour's core policy narrative on cultural participation paints a picture of the widening access agenda and its prosecution as a seemingly neutral technocratic process. Yet, viewed from beneath the surface, what can be seen to underlie this procedural framework of 'evidence-based' policymaking is a deficit model of participation, which both helps to define and is reinforced by a politics of differentiation and exclusion. In the first place, the 'official' model of participation remains a top-down affair, operationalised as a demarcated set of activities and practices, defined largely by what government has traditionally funded, and informed by middle-class norms and understandings of what counts as 'legitimate' culture.[17] From this perspective, the 'non-users' of culture can, in turn, be construed as a social problem: a passive, isolated and inadequate group morally adrift from the mainstream and therefore in need of mobilisation. Such a formulation casts the DCMS and its NDPBs in the role of cultural engineers. As the 2003 Arts Council England (ACE) manifesto *Ambitions for the Arts* put it:

> We will argue that being involved with the arts can have a lasting and transforming effect on many people's lives. This is true not just for individuals, but also for neighbourhoods, communities and entire generations, whose sense of identity and purpose can be changed through art.[18]

In this way the notion of social inclusion in cultural policy can be reinterpreted as a polarising device, simultaneously allowing for the cajoling of those 'in deficit' while marking them out and marginalising their practices.[19]

Moreover, the technologies and conceptual models that are employed to provide 'robust' evidence of the impact of cultural policy tend to be self-confirming of this narrow and tendentious view of participation and participants. *Taking Part* is a cross-sectional or 'snapshot' survey focused on those traditional and formal activities that are associated with the DCMS's funded sectors and a set of variables that have been selected for the purpose of evaluating performance against targets rather than research into the socio-cultural dynamics of participation.[20] This approach reflects the adherence of government social research to a positivist model of social science, which ranks large-scale quantitative data and variable-led 'causal' analysis at the top of a 'scientific methods scale'.[21] This is a framework that relegates descriptive and qualitative methods, which can reveal the contexts, meanings and significance of participation, to an ancillary status.

Another important factor in the delimiting of the official perspective on participation is the strong influence of market models on policy design and evaluation. Traditionally government has relied on partnerships with market research agencies, much more than academic researchers, to produce, analyse and interpret data on participation. Most recently, this can be seen in the DCMS's CASE (Culture and Sport Evidence) programme, which constructs actual and potential participants as customers in a market for culture and adopts a linear, logic-chain, approach to assessing policy impacts on levels of consumption and the 'drivers of demand'.[22]

Engaging the local cultural sector in participation research

In the sections that follow, evidence from a collection of in-depth qualitative interviews is employed to probe the apparent disengagement and marginali-sation of those labelled as 'non-users' of culture on the basis of quantitative population surveys such as *Taking Part*. These interviews demonstrate that many are in fact positively engaged in forms of interaction and participation that are not usually captured by survey evidence. That is, they make positive choices about not engaging with traditional or high cultural forms, even though they might actually appreciate their wider value. At the same time there is another group of people to which this label is applied who actually do engage with these forms. However, they do so in a personal or private way and therefore don't see themselves as members of an 'arts' community or as cultural participants more broadly.

The interviews arose from a wider study of engagement with the cultural sector in Manchester, designed to explore the value and application of academic research to local institutions.[23] Eleven prominent organisations were contacted and discussions were held with directors and their marketing and outreach staff to scope issues of interest for potential research collaboration.[24] What quickly became evident during the course of these discussions, however, was the way in which policy imperatives defined at the centre held sway, reflecting a strong process of alignment of regional and sub-regional cultural governance with the DCMS's national agenda.[25] Although a range of possibilities was covered, the overwhelming concern for these organisations was to grow whilst broadening their audience. As one marketing manager put it, 'There's a lot of interesting things we'd like to do but basically we are in the business of bums on seats.'

On the basis of this series of consultations, it was therefore decided to focus a research project on those people who didn't attend the kinds of organisations and venues involved in the study, whom the institutions themselves found by their very nature particularly illusive and 'hard-to-reach'. A range of issues – which included the time and availability of personnel, the set up and focus of marketing departments, and data protection limitations – made direct collaboration with the institutions difficult, but contrasting samples of cultural 'users' and 'non-users' were eventually identified with the help of the city's arts development agency, Arts About Manchester.[26]

Interviewees were recruited by means of a questionnaire about leisure practices and engagement, which included a question about willingness to be interviewed in detail. The users were contacted via Arts About Manchester's online e-bulletin. Candidates for interview were then selected by postcode from among the 192 respondents who completed the e-survey. The non-users were contacted via the mailing lists of the national marketing organisation CACI, from which households that have declared a lack of interest in arts attendance and participation in marketing surveys can be identified. A total of 2,000 surveys were sent out – 500 in each area – and 133 people responded.

The final result was a collection of 102 semi-structured, in-depth interviews with users and non-users of Manchester's mainstream cultural institutions, with samples drawn in roughly equal proportions from four area types in and around the city: the largely affluent areas of Sale and Altrincham to the south-west, the ethnically mixed areas of Longsight and Levenshulme on the city's south-eastern fringe, the predominantly white working-class communities of Openshaw and Gorton further out in east Manchester, and both the new and more traditional residential districts of the city centre. Interviewees were asked a range of questions designed to explore their interests and practices in the context of their backgrounds and day-to-day lives as Manchester residents using a topic guide organised under four main headings: 'Home and neighbourhood'; 'Leisure interest and activities'; 'Cultural influences and trajectories'; and 'Manchester as a place'.

Cultural ambiguities: the importance and irrelevance of the arts

While not amounting to a 'scientific' sample survey, the questionnaire responses from which the interviewees were recruited provide an overall, aggregate picture of the differing demographic and attitudinal profiles of those who do and don't take part in formal arts and cultural activities. Confirming what we would expect on the basis of previous studies,[27] Table 1 indicates that these samples of users and non-users of formal cultural sites in Manchester are strongly demarcated by gender, age, income, education and lifestyle. Users tend more often than non-users to be female, younger, wealthy, highly educated and middle class. Particularly striking in this analysis is not just the relative levels of formal economic and cultural capital displayed by these two groups but the absolute disadvantage of non-users, around half of whom had annual incomes of less than £10,000 and a quarter no educational qualifications. This may in part reflect the fact that a moderate incentive was offered to people who returned questionnaires and were subsequently interviewed. Yet it is notable that one in eight of the respondents who subscribed to the Arts About Manchester e-bulletin actually hailed from the most deprived category of households in ACORN's life-style classification of consumers by postcode,[28] and while almost none of the non-users returning survey forms were from the wealthiest households, one in ten were relatively prosperous (ACORN Categories 1–3).

Notwithstanding the contrasts in the aggregate demographic profiles of users and non-users, what is striking about their responses to a series of attitudinal questions about the value and significance of the arts and culture is the broad level of agreement they reveal (Table 2). Whether or not people directly engaged with them, Manchester is recognised by a large majority as being a major centre for the arts and culture, suggesting the city's leading

Table 1: Demographic profiles of users and non-users of formal cultural institutions, per cent (rounded).

Characteristic	Users	Non-users
Women	76	43
Men	24	57
Aged 16-45	69	53
Household income under £10,000	9	45
Household income over £50,000	21	4
No educational qualifications	1	23
With postgraduate degree	31	6
Non-white	8	14
ACORN Cat. 1 ('Wealthy Achievers')	18	1
ACORN Cat. 5 ('Hard Pressed')	13	59
N.*	192	133

* This number refers to the size of the overall sample obtained in each case. The number of cases varies slightly for some analyses due to missing values, where respondents failed, or chose not, to provide information.

cultural institutions have what economists refer to as a high level of 'existence value'. Regardless of their own particular interests, most people also agree that the arts should be more central to mainstream education.

The views of participants and non-participants diverge mainly in two respects, and in one in particular. First, a significant minority of non-users think that arts and cultural opportunities are not very accessible. Secondly, and here the disjunction is stark, there is disagreement about the justification for public investment in the arts. Those who gain most from such funding in terms of use are very largely satisfied that the type of 'high' culture supported by government is of universal benefit, while almost half of those who don't take part feel that such art forms are irrelevant to the lives of the majority. On the face of it, the apparent ambiguity of non-participants who recognise wider value in a set of activities they don't themselves practise seems curious. However, as previous Arts Council research indicates, this is not an isolated finding.[29] Nor is the fact that the main reason given by non-participants in Manchester for not taking part in the arts is that they are just 'not interested' (32%), which was also the top reason for not attending arts events, given by 31% of respondents, in the first wave of the national *Taking Part* survey.[30]

What lies behind such responses? In the remainder of this essay I explore

Table 2: Attitudes towards the arts and culture – users and non-users of formal cultural institutions, per cent (rounded) agreeing with the statements shown.

Agree that:	Users	Non-users
Manchester is a major international centre for the Arts and culture	78	70
Arts and cultural events and venues in Manchester are very accessible	79	62
The Arts should have a larger role in school education	81	71
Arts as funded by government are of little relevance to ordinary people	10	45
One person's taste in drama, literature, music etc. is as good as the next person's	58	58
N.	180	128

non-users' narrative accounts of participation and identity to examine the nature of their estrangement from the formal cultural sphere.[31] What these accounts reveal is two distinct groups: firstly, those for whom the arts are irrelevant because they are already positively engaged in practices and activities that are not captured by standard indicators of participation; and second, a group of people who are not really non-users at all but whose participation in traditional culture is largely hidden from view and which the standard participation survey approach again fails to pick up. Moreover, both of these groups can be seen to actively dis-identify from the cultural city, but in different ways, which in both cases turn prevailing assumptions about the relationship between arts participation and social exclusion on their head.

Everyday participation and ordinary culture

In the context of a cultural policy defined by the twin concerns of social exclusion and audience development, the problem of dealing with non-participation is couched in the language of 'barriers' and their removal. Reflecting on the extensive consultation exercises carried out as part of Arts Council England's 'arts debate', the study's lead author concludes that behind expressions of a lack of interest and supposed practical barriers, the causes of non-participation in the arts are at root psychological.[32] Arts participation is 'risky' for the uninitiated because they don't know what to expect or how to behave and feel out of place, and therefore the solution is to develop strategies and approaches that reassure them.

It is certainly possible to detect this kind of personal insecurity amongst the non-users of Manchester but what is missing from such individual-level interpretations is an appreciation of the relational socio-cultural context that shapes understandings and encourages behavioural norms. Adopting the frame of interpretation developed by Pierre Bourdieu,[33] participation in the arts and other high cultural practices reflects and reinforces a process of social distinction, so that cultural preferences are a defining feature of class 'habitus' and division. For many Manchester interviewees the formal cultural institutions of the city centre and the kinds of practices they represented were alien to or at odds with their own lifestyle and simply not part of their world.

This is reflected in the way the term 'culture' evokes an entirely different set of meanings for people from working-class and minority communities. When asked during their interviews whether they thought Manchester was a 'cultural place', this group, rather than mention theatres, museums or art galleries, invariably talk about the mixed ethnic profile of the city and of culture as a way of life:

> Oh, there's a very diverse cultures, Manchester and you get all walks of life don't you, blacks, Asians, lot of Polish influence now and Czech now, yeah ... yeah, there's quite a lot, like, you know. (Male, 30s, Ancoats)

In terms of their own practices, the detachment of people from the forms and sites of traditional cultural participation rarely implied a state of social exclusion. Indeed, most of the non-users interviewed were not passive and isolated at all but were instead members of vibrant informal cultural networks defined by ordinary, ostensibly mundane, pursuits and centred on relationships with friends and family. Their expression is found in a vast swathe of activities, hobbies and pastimes, such as house visiting, barbecues, meeting friends over coffee, shopping and (just as important for those on low incomes) window shopping, weekend pub meals, driving out to garden centres and other attractions (including the moors, the Lakes and Blackpool), following football, swimming, going to the gym, cooking, gardening, fishing, gambling, listening to music, watching TV and DVDs, reading, drinking and clubbing.

These forms of everyday participation are often highly structured and planned out. Here a young single mother from South Manchester who works part-time describes a typical weekly routine:

> Right. Monday ... go for a mooch into Altrincham ... a bit of browsing, think of what I'm going to buy on Thursday ... Do window shopping first, and then pick my daughter up from nursery, go to the local park, bring her back and watch the telly, do her tea, bed, watch the telly ... And Thursdays, when I get my money [laughs], love it, go to Tesco, do my food shopping, and I go into Altrincham and think, ooh, what shall I ... what shall I treat

myself to this week? I normally go in to every single clothes shop, and then start out at the end and work my way up and then go back to the end again and think I'll have that one. So I do that, go and have a coffee somewhere and then go and pick my daughter up from nursery, go back to Tesco, do a bit more food shopping ... Saturdays, it depends on what my daughter wants to do, park or swimming or whatever ... Sundays ... maybe go up and see my mum and dad.

The intensity of engagement that underpins this apparently prosaic routine then comes through when the interviewee was asked to talk about her favourite activity:

I love going food shopping. I love it. I'd love to go into Tescos and think right I haven't got a budget, boom, boom, boom, boom, boom ... I love going round and thinking, you know ... 'cause I watch Gordon Ramsey, I think ooh what can ... what can I make tonight, you know. I think ooh, ooh I'll have that, I'll have that and I love doing all weird concoctions.

The remoteness of formal cultural institutions from this informal, vernacular culture of the everyday is reinforced by community norms expressed in peer group pressures, as another young woman, living in Levenshulme, explains:

... because, like, none of my other friends are into, like, going to museums and stuff like that, so ... you just wouldn't do it ... Yeah, I think if I told my friends I wanted to go to a museum they'd probably just laugh at me.

This external pressure to fit in creates an internal pressure not to stand out. A slightly older woman from Longsight, who does have an interest in art stemming from a textile degree that she took as a mature student, describes why she feels unable to reveal her interests to people in the neighbourhood:

... there's someone up the road and if I was walking down the road with her I would not be talking about going to an art gallery because she'd just be like, 'You what?' She really would. I don't mean that nastily either, you know, but she'd just be thinking, 'Who do you think you are?' 'cause that's ... there's still a lot of people like that round here unfortunately, you know. And I'm not saying I'm better either, you know, I just try different little things, that's all really. But there is a lot of that.

At another point in the interview, she refers to the way in which her own socialisation in a white working-class family had been antagonistic to the development of broader cultural horizons:

I mean my mum was very much ... my mum's worked probably since she was about 11 years of age, you know and I think early on in life she'd be going on about going to university and then when it coming close to the school end it was like, 'You need to get a job' kind of thing, you know, and she was more encouraging me to work. Because my mum doesn't have that many interests, in all honestly ... she never took us swimming, I don't think she's ever been to a cinema in her life, and things like that ... All I can, kind of, remember is my mum at work all the time, all the time ...

This is a familiar refrain amongst interviewees growing up in such communities, where economic necessity was paramount, and where long working hours and shift patterns imposed parameters on both the amount of spare time available and the ways in which people could – and preferred to – use it.

Hidden participation and ghostly engagements

Alongside the importance of ordinary, everyday pursuits and relationships, the other notable feature to emerge from the narratives of individuals classified as non-participants by marketing questionnaires and standard participation surveys is that a significant number do after all turn out to be, or to have been at some time, engaged with the realm of legitimate culture. This highlights an important issue with the use of standard indicators for cultural engagement, which cannot account for the ways in which people, regardless of what they actually do, decide to identify – or not – as a particular type of participant.

A number of non-users refer to a kind of incidental participation in formal culture, which is presented in largely instrumental terms. Often this type of engagement is life-course related. In particular, it might involve taking children to museums and heritage sites. Here the content and experience of an arts or cultural venue is secondary to its use as a form of distraction and entertainment, 'something to do' at the weekend alongside a range of mundane activities:

Saturday or on Sunday I might take the kids out so ... Normally take them to Parrs Wood [a local entertainment complex] or sometimes we hit the museum ... What we do normally is go to the museum like we did last time, we went to the museum then we went to town, did a bit of shopping, clothes shopping and went to Nandos then just came back home. (Male, 30s, Levenshulme)

However, the interviews also revealed several quite serious cultural participants who are hidden from view because their engagement is personal, private and divorced from any mainstream institutional context. 'Maria', for example, is a single mother of two children in her late 30s who lives in east Manchester, works part-time on the night shift in a local supermarket and is a prolific painter. An advocate for the arts in general, she is also a fan of classical and operatic music, which she follows by reading, watching documentaries and listening to CDs rather than attending concerts. Having failed to get onto a university arts course when younger, Maria feels resentful of what she sees as a socially closed arts establishment:

> I've always done art as a hobby because I never wanted to let go. I've always been ... haven't been able to express my feelings a lot, so I've always done a lot of it in art ... I've actually now considered taking it up full time and doing it as a job but it's just knowing what steps to take and where to turn to and who to talk to ...

Maria does not see herself as part of the arts community but her identity as an artist is central to the way in which she presents her role and relationships in her neighbourhood:

> I had an old boy on the street, it was his birthday ... and I'm trying to do a painting now of him ... it's the character that has to shine through the paint and people don't understand it ...
> ... there's like Ray and Carol across the road ... He has a lot of interest in art which he didn't realise that he had and so it's good because we can sit ... we sit down outside sometimes ... and ... he'll say, 'Oh, I went into so and so gallery down London.' And I'm like, 'Oh great, did you like it?' 'Yeah.' And then we have a discussion ...

Although examples of such concealed or 'ghostly' participation spanned a range of forms, painting and visual arts were the most commonly practised. A strong theme running through these accounts is the ambivalence of the practitioners to the sites and venues of the official arts world. 'Richard', a young financial services adviser who paints three times a week, wants to turn his interest into a business but is going about this independently, by getting leaflets printed and setting a website up 'so I can do loads of art when I want'. He has little time for art in formal settings:

> to be honest I wouldn't really go out of my way to go to museums but if I'm with my girlfriend and we've got time to kill then we'll go in and have a look around and like just like be amazed at how some things can be perceived as art ...

Similarly 'Michael', who paints watercolours which his father-in-law thinks are good enough to sell, was originally inspired by the Sky Arts channel on TV and, as his account of a recent trip to The Lowry indicates, has no wider interest in galleries:

> There was some artist on, we didn't go specially for that, it was just that we went down there ... Catherine, my daughter, was there doing a thing

for school and … while we were there, there was an exhibition on for some artists so I went around and took a look at them. Couldn't tell you who it was …

These stories of private participation in social and cultural isolation from the arts establishment tend to have a strong spatial dimension, as narratives of dislocation and disorientation. With the exception of some younger non-users, for whom it was a place to hang out and go shopping – or more often window shopping – in by day and for drinking and clubbing by night, Manchester city centre was commonly viewed as a remote place, infrequently visited, providing little by way of a reference point in people's lives. This was a feeling shared even by some centrally located residents, one of whom remarked, 'although I'm like spitting distance from the city centre, I feel a bit detached from it'. However, it was a sentiment expressed most frequently by those interviewees living in south and east Manchester, with the latter more often than not facing the other way entirely, towards Ashton-under-Lyne, for services and amenities.

Several non-users with an interest in the arts identified the regeneration of Manchester as having negative effects on local cultural resources. Although Maria was enthusiastic about the city's cultural institutions, particularly its museums, she had reservations about the regeneration process for its neglect of the urban periphery:

> I think the problem is that there's so much regeneration going on in the centre, because that's where the money is, that they're tending to forget about the ones in the outer sites. You know, I mean something like, a little … just a tiny gallery opened up round here, how many eyes would that wake up, you know, how many people would come?

Older residents pointed to the displacement of cultural amenities, with the loss of institutions that used to provide a focal point for the local community, and the reallocation of such resources towards the city centre. Along with the constant flux of population churn caused by council-sponsored growth of the private letting sector to accommodate the need for social housing in such outlying areas, this had resulted in a sense of disorientation. This is well expressed by 'Frank', a retired former council transport worker:

> Well some of the people living here now, some are a bit rough. Because they pulled houses down, they're just housing them here, there and everywhere … But the general area has gone down … We've got a park over there, yeah, well I go in there because I play bowls … But other than that we've got nothing. No picture houses. We used to have two picture houses just across the road. They're both gone. We had one a bit lower down … And then we had one,

two, three, four more lower down towards Manchester. All within five, ten minutes from here …

Frank also expresses a widely held distaste among people of his age for the way Manchester's cityscape has been transformed in recent years. An evident pride in the city's history and profile is mixed with a feeling of a loss of ownership and control over what has been done to it, which he communicates in a scathing critique of the regeneration aesthetic. When asked if he thinks the city is changing, he replies:

> It's completely completely changed … In every way, shape and form … all of the new buildings they're putting up, I don't like them. I don't think there's anything nice about them … Too many clubs, far too many clubs now. I wouldn't go down there at night. I'll stay away from it … They're supposed to be modernising it, but I think they're ruining it. And that … what's the other building? That one on Corporation Street. Bit of a museum it's supposed to be … Urbis. I think that's an eyesore …

Conclusion: (dis)identification with the cultural city

The non-users of Manchester's cultural institutions have an uneasy and ambivalent relationship to the city. Unlike the middle-class residents in the 2005 study by Savage *et al.*, they actively dis-identify with it, and their relationship to the formal realm of legitimate cultural practices plays a central role in this process. Non-participants from white working-class communities around the city tend to understand culture primarily in ethnic terms and as a way of life rather than something to do with 'the arts'. There is recognition of the symbolic value of the high cultural institutions in the city centre but these are felt to be of no relevance and little interest to them. Here the narratives confirm the conclusion of Bennett *et al.* that such communities are detached from legitimate culture but are not thereby excluded.[34] This is because the people in them maintain a rich vernacular culture of everyday practices based around ostensibly mundane activities and social networks. There is, however, another group of people labelled as non-users in the official statistics who do in fact participate in legitimate culture but are missed by the standard data-gathering methods employed by government and consumer research agencies. These are people who participate largely in isolation from the sites and institutions of the arts establishment. For some members of this group, particularly older people and those living in outlying areas, their dis-identification from the cultural city is bound up with a sense not of irrelevance but of remoteness and loss caused by the centripetal effects of the regeneration process.

This last observation draws attention to the role of spatiality and territorialisation in mediating the relationship between culture, participation and identity[35] and the ways in which the re-centring of culture in Manchester is actually an important dynamic in the broader distribution and decentring of urban life.[36] In relation to the policy context that informed the research project on which this essay is based, the participation narratives of the non-users of traditional cultural institutions highlight the shortcomings of a model of evidence-based policymaking rooted in the assumptions and technologies of market research and the New Public Management. The effect of the emphasis on indicators and measures in this approach is to decontextualise participation by abstracting from place, space and social relations. By obscuring and discounting the practices and significance of the everyday realm, the outcome of this process is to re-affirm the official model of participation and the domination of the middle-class norms that underpin it.

Notes

1 Simon Gunn, 'The sublime and the vulgar: the Hallé concerts and the constitution of "high culture" in Manchester, c.1850–1880'; Jamie Peck and Kevin Ward, 'Placing Manchester', pp. 4–5.

2 J. O'Connor and X. Gu, 'Developing a creative cluster in a post-industrial city: CIDS and Manchester', pp. 125, 129–30.

3 Gunn, 'The sublime and the vulgar'.

4 Mike Savage *et al.*, *Globalization and Belonging*.

5 *Ibid.*, p. 119.

6 Arts About Manchester, *Manchester 1998–2003. Report on Arts Attendance within Greater Manchester District Boundaries.*

7 Sara Selwood, 'A part to play?', pp. 35–8.

8 Christopher Hood, 'A public management for all seasons?'; Eleonora Belfiore, 'Auditing culture. The subsidised cultural sector in the New Public Management'.

9 Selwood, 'A part to play?', pp. 37–8.

10 Quoted in Robert Hewison and John Holden, *The Right to Art. Making Aspirations Reality*, pp. 4–5.

11 DCMS, *Annual Report & Accounts 2009*, p. 31.

12 Eleonora Belfiore, 'Art as a means towards alleviating social exclusion: does it really work? A critique of instrumental cultural policies and social impact studies in the UK'.

13 Tony Bennett and Mike Savage, 'Introduction: cultural capital and cultural policy', p. 9.

14 Quoted in Belfiore, 'Auditing culture', p. 189.

15 Sara Selwood, 'The politics of data collection: gathering, analysing and using data in the subsidised cultural sector in England'.

16 The first sweep of *Taking Part: The National Survey of Culture, Leisure and*

Sport took place in 2005. It was originally based on a representative sample of 29,000 people (aged 16 and above) but numbers were subsequently reduced to 14,000.

17 Pierre Bourdieu, *Distinction. A Social Critique of the Judgement of Taste*; Ross McKibbin, *Classes and Cultures: England 1918–1951.*

18 Arts Council England, *Ambitions for the Arts 2003–2006*, p. 3.

19 Ruth Levitas, 'Let's hear it for Humpty: social exclusion, the third way and cultural capital'.

20 Andrew Miles and Alice Sullivan, 'Understanding participation in culture and sport: mixing methods, reordering knowledges'.

21 For a general critique, see Ray Pawson, 'Assessing the quality of evidence in evidence based policy: why, how and when?'.

22 DCMS, 'Understanding the drivers, impact and value of engagement in culture and sport. An over-arching summary of the research'.

23 The project was funded by the Higher Education Funding Council for England and the Northwest Regional Development Agency as part of the second round of the Higher Education Innovation Fund.

24 These institutions were the Manchester City Art Gallery, Royal Exchange Theatre, Museum of Science and Industry, Opera House, Contact Theatre, Palace Theatre, People's History Museum, The Lowry, Urbis, Green Room and Comedy Store.

25 Deborah Stevenson *et al.*, 'Tracing British cultural policy domains: contexts, collaborations and constituencies'.

26 Arts About Manchester subsequently had its remit expanded and was re-branded as All About Audiences, the audience development agency for the North West. Recently it merged with Audiences London Plus to become The Audience Agency, the national audience development agency for England.

27 For example, Ken Roberts, 'Leisure inequalities, class divisions and social exclusion in present-day Britain'; Tony Bennett *et al.*, *Culture, Class, Distinction*.

28 CACI, *ACORN User Guide*.

29 Adrienne Skelton *et al.*, *Arts in England: Attendance, Participation and Attitudes in 2001*.

30 Emily Keaney, 'Understanding arts audiences: existing data and what it tells us', p. 107.

31 All personal names mentioned in these accounts have been changed in order to preserve the anonymity of interviewees. Some of the material cited here was previously used in Miles and Sullivan, 'Understanding participation in culture and sport'.

32 Keaney, 'Understanding arts audiences', p. 109.

33 Bourdieu, *Distinction*.

34 Bennett *et al.*, *Culture, Class, Distinction*, p. 212.

35 See Talja Blokland and Mike Savage (eds), *Networked Urbanism: Social Capital in the City*.

36 Ash Amin and Nigel Thrift, *Cities: Reimagining the Urban*.

Bibliography

Amin, Ash and Nigel Thrift, *Cities: Reimagining the Urban* (Cambridge: Polity Press, 2002).

Arts About Manchester, *Manchester 1998–2003. Report on Arts Attendance within Greater Manchester District Boundaries* (Manchester: Arts About Manchester, 2005).

Arts Council England, *Ambitions for the Arts 2003–2006* (London: ACE, 2003).

Belfiore, Eleonora, 'Art as a means towards alleviating social exclusion: does it really work? A critique of instrumental cultural policies and social impact studies in the UK', *International Journal of Cultural Policy*, 8:1 (2002), pp. 91–106.

Belfiore, Eleonora, 'Auditing culture. The subsidised cultural sector in the New Public Management', *International Journal of Cultural Policy*, 10:2 (2004), pp. 183–202.

Bennett, Tony and Mike Savage, 'Introduction: cultural capital and cultural policy', *Cultural Trends*, 13:2 (2004), pp. 7–14.

Bennett, Tony, Mike Savage, Elizabeth Silva, Alan Warde, Modesto Gayo-Cal and David Wright, *Culture, Class, Distinction* (London: Routledge, 2009).

Blokland, Talja and Mike Savage (eds), *Networked Urbanism: Social Capital in the City* (Aldershot: Ashgate, 2008).

Bourdieu, Pierre, *Distinction. A Social Critique of the Judgement of Taste* (Cambridge, Mass.: Harvard University Press, 1984).

CACI, *ACORN User Guide* (London: CACI, 2004).

DCMS, *Annual Report & Accounts 2009* (London: DCMS, 2009).

DCMS, 'Understanding the drivers, impact and value of engagement in culture and sport. An over-arching summary of the research', Cultural and Sport Evidence Programme (London: DCMS, 2010).

Gunn, Simon, 'The sublime and the vulgar: the Hallé concerts and the constitution of "high culture" in Manchester, c.1850–1880', *Journal of Victorian Culture*, 2:2 (1997), pp. 208–28.

Hewison, Robert and John Holden, *The Right to Art. Making Aspirations Reality* (London: Demos, 2004).

Hood, Christopher, 'A public management for all seasons?', *Public Administration*, 69:1 (March 1991), pp. 3–19.

Keaney, Emily, 'Understanding arts audiences: existing data and what it tells us', *Cultural Trends*, 17:2 (2008), pp. 97–113.

Levitas, Ruth, 'Let's hear it for Humpty: social exclusion, the third way and cultural capital', *Cultural Trends*, 13:2 (2004), pp. 41–56.

McKibbin, Ross, *Classes and Cultures: England 1918–1951* (Oxford: Oxford University Press, 1998).

Miles, Andrew and Alice Sullivan, 'Understanding participation in culture and sport: mixing methods, reordering knowledges', *Cultural Trends*, 21:4 (2012), pp. 311–24.

O'Connor, J. and X. Gu, 'Developing a creative cluster in a post-industrial city: CIDS and Manchester', *The Information Society*, 26:2 (2010), pp. 124–36.

Pawson, Ray, 'Assessing the quality of evidence in evidence based policy: why, how and when?', Working Paper No. 1 (2003), ESRC Research Methods Programme.

Peck, Jamie and Kevin Ward, 'Placing Manchester', in Jamie Peck and Kevin Ward (eds), *City of Revolution: Restructuring Manchester* (Manchester: Manchester University Press, 2002).

Roberts, Ken, 'Leisure inequalities, class divisions and social exclusion in present-day Britain', *Cultural Trends*, 13:2 (2004), pp. 57–71.

Savage, Mike, Gaynor Bagnall and Brian Longhurst, *Globalization and Belonging*, (London: Sage, 2005).

Selwood, Sara, 'The politics of data collection: gathering, analysing and using data in the subsidised cultural sector in England', *Cultural Trends*, 12:47 (2002), pp. 13–84.

Selwood, Sara, 'A part to play?', *International Journal of Cultural Policy*, 12:1 (2006), pp. 35–53.

Skelton, Adrienne, Ann Bridgwood, Kathryn Duckworth, Lucy Hutton, Claire Fenn, Claire Creaser and Adrian Babbidge, *Arts in England: Attendance, Participation and Attitudes in 2001* (London: Arts Council of England, 2002).

Stevenson, Deborah, Kieryn McKay and David Rowe, 'Tracing British cultural policy domains: contexts, collaborations and constituencies', *International Journal of Cultural Policy*, 16:2 (2010), pp. 159–72.

Class conflict and the myth of cultural 'inclusion' in modern Manchester

Selina Todd

In August 2009, a theatre group from north Manchester enjoyed an incredible box-office success. MaD theatre company's production, *Angels with Manky Faces*, was a dramatic exploration of nineteenth-century gang violence, adapted from historian Andrew Davies's book *The Gangs of Manchester*.[1] MaD's cast of twenty-one staged seven sell-out performances at the Library Theatre in Manchester city centre, and three at the Dancehouse on the city's Oxford Road. After completing the run of *Angels*, MaD's founders and scriptwriters, Rob Lees and Jill Hughes, set about planning a more ambitious production for 2010, which they wanted to perform in a larger city centre venue. But *Angels* did not lead to the lasting success for which Lees and Hughes hoped. By 2011, MaD was performing to small audiences in north Manchester community centres.

In this essay, I examine MaD's experience and argue that policymakers and middle-class cultural practitioners marginalise working-class cultural production. The cultural and social 'inclusion' of working-class people has been an objective of social policy for more than a decade. But this strategy is based on a myth: that culture and class can be divorced from one another. Manchester City Council describes culture as 'the unique characteristics that make [Manchester] different from any other city'.[2] This definition of culture as formed by and in a particular place fits with a widely accepted scholarly definition of culture as 'a system of shared meanings, attitudes and values, and the symbolic forms (performances, artifacts) in which they are embodied.'[3] Against this emphasis on geographic community, I suggest that capitalist societies are unable to foster 'classless' cultural products. Culture is produced by – in the words of the historian E.P. Thompson – 'a particular equilibrium of social relations, a working environment of exploitation and resistance to exploitation, of relations of power'.[4]

While many studies of working-class culture, and of cultural 'inclusion', have focused on participation, I argue that we need to pay closer attention to cultural production.[5] Although politicians and arts agencies promote working-class participation in cultural institutions, I show that they challenged MaD's role as a cultural producer. The first section of the essay outlines MaD's history, activities and aspirations. I then discuss my methodology, and explain the centrality of class to my analysis. The third section places MaD into a historical context. Although a superficial understanding of Manchester's radical past provides a shared referent for the city's policymakers and cultural practitioners, working-class cultural producers are able to use a history of class struggle to assert the value of their own work. I then examine today's cultural and political context, arguing that aesthetic judgements of 'taste' are used to marginalise working-class cultural participation. From here I explore MaD's relationships with specific arts agencies to show how cultural 'inclusion' is interpreted as very specific forms of limited participation, and certainly does not offer working-class practitioners any role as *producers* of culture. However, the final section of the essay demonstrates that working-class groups are forging cultural networks of resistance which promise a 'regeneration' of working-class culture outside the institutions – such as trade unions or labour history museums – in which scholars generally expect to find it.

MaD: an overview

MaD is a self-identified 'working-class community theatre company' based in Moston, a working-class district of north Manchester.[6] Rob Lees and Jill Hughes founded the company in 1996, and initially called it Moston Active Drama. MaD's new, abbreviated name testifies to the company's expansion since 2000: MaD's activities stretch beyond Moston, across the north of the city and into Rochdale and Bury. Running MaD is a full-time job for Lees and Hughes. Their working life is spent leading weekly drama workshops for over 200 young people and adults with learning disabilities; scriptwriting; applying for funding; and organising the company's annual production.

Between 2005 and 2009 MaD's membership and audiences increased. A grant from Children in Need funded some of the company's weekly workshops. This allowed Lees and Hughes to dedicate more time to writing and helped them to build a strong core membership of about thirty young people and adults, who were willing to dedicate time to rehearsing the company's annual production. Between 2005 and 2009 MaD performed an original play each year at the city's Library Theatre. MaD could confidently expect to sell out three or more performances, meaning that almost 1,000 people were attending each production. The company was one of the Library Theatre's biggest box-office draws.

MaD aims to bring those whom Lees and Hughes call 'ordinary working-class people' into the theatre. Their productions clearly attracted and enthused a large cross-section of Mancunians. A questionnaire-based audience survey conducted at two of the performances of *Angels with Manky Faces* suggested that 60 per cent of the audience came from north Manchester, Bury or Rochdale. They worked as manual and clerical workers, were unemployed or were in full-time secondary or tertiary education. Over 80 per cent of these respondents had not visited a theatre within the past year. The remaining 40 per cent of the audiences came from more middle-class districts of south Manchester and Cheshire.[7]

In defining MaD as a working-class theatre company, Lees and Hughes defined themselves and their intended audiences against the cultural tastes of middle-class theatregoers. Far from worrying that their intended constituency might be 'hard to reach' – a common concern among policymakers seeking to interest working-class people in the arts – Lees and Hughes believed that working-class people were likely to be culturally omnivorous. In his press interviews, Lees recalls his own youth, when as a member of Oldham Theatre Workshop he performed in Manchester's theatres:

> I was performing in this play, and the FA Cup Final was on, and we were doing this matinee. And so every time I came off stage I was asking, 'What's the score, what's the score?', and no one in the cast had a clue – 'Er, the score of what?'. So I was going backstage to the crew, asking the scene shifters and that. They knew. And it brought home to me how narrow some of these people were, like their city's team is playing in the FA Cup and they just didn't have a clue.[8]

Of course football fans are not exclusively working-class people. As we shall see, MaD had strong links with FC United, a football club established by and for people who could no longer afford to regularly watch Manchester United, and who regard the club as having lost its regional and working-class roots.[9] FC's founders and fans share Lees' belief that many working-class people are culturally omnivorous because they don't worry about conforming to accepted notions of superior taste.[10] For Lees, who identifies as working class, MaD provides 'a space for people like me, who want to watch football and enjoy drama'.[11]

In 2009, Lees' philosophy was apparently paying off. MaD had drawn a large audience into a city centre theatre. And as the run of *Angels* came to an end, MaD learned that their application for a large National Lottery grant had been successful. They were now guaranteed core funding for five years. However, the future direction of MaD was uncertain, because the city's Library Theatre – which had staged the company's annual productions – had closed for renovation for five years. It was at this stage that I began to work with MaD.

Methodology

I undertook a case study of MaD in order to understand more about the role of cultural production in creating working-class Mancunian identity. Lees and Hughes were very positive about my working alongside them for one day each week between September 2009 and June 2010. I provided practical assistance, advising on funding applications and helping with administration. I observed Lees and Hughes as they wrote, produced and sought to perform their new play, *Thai Brides and Teacakes*. This production addressed the impact of immigration and the threat of far-right political activism in north Manchester. Lees and Hughes were ambitious for the production, and hoped that my involvement would help them to forge stronger links with the city's universities, which they saw as important given Manchester City Council's commitment to establishing an 'educational corridor' along Oxford Road – the major thoroughfare that connects the universities to the city centre. In particular, Lees and Hughes hoped that our relationship might help them to secure performance space at one of the city centre or university theatres.

I drew on my training as a historian to undertake this research. I was trained in contemporary history, the philosophy of which is that present policy and popular understandings of Britain often reflect 'unexamined historical assumptions and cliches' and that 'historians can shed light on the causes of current problems and even suggest innovative solutions ... to current issues' – in this case cultural exclusion.[12] My research encompassed observing Lees and Hughes at work, conducting thirty semi-structured interviews with them – individually and jointly – and more structured interviews with representatives from other agencies, as well as reading relevant policy documents. I recognise that the situations in which I found myself were mediated by my presence, but the many times that Lees and Hughes openly contradicted my assumptions supports a conclusion reached by other scholars: that while we influence our subjects, they still exercise agency.[13]

During the course of my research my objectives changed. My initial aim was to study class as a collective identity forged through shared experiences of specific communities. However, during my months with MaD, I came to understand class in a Thompsonian sense: that is a relationship rather than an identity, one forged through the tensions between groups that possess unequal amounts of power.[14] Pierre Bourdieu's understanding of culture as a field within which people seek distinction and accrue 'cultural capital' proved useful.[15] However, this allows little scope for working-class resistance, which in MaD's case took the form of seeking to create an alternative and oppositional cultural space. As we shall see later in this essay, MaD's actions support Jacques Rancière's conclusion that working-class actors can exercise a degree of autonomy and resistance within the cultural sphere, albeit within strict limits.[16]

I came to understand that any class analysis must interrogate those who hold power as well as those who lack it. Unfortunately, time constraints prevented me from undertaking in-depth case studies of the agencies that influenced MaD's work. Nevertheless, I do not believe this significantly weakens my study. I was able to draw on abundant sources to analyse the perspectives of these powerful actors: the policy documents, artistic programmes, websites and funding criteria they produce; the many sociological studies of contemporary middle-class identity; and anthropological and sociological research on arts institutions and governance.[17] We know a great deal about today's middle class. We know far less about working-class cultural practitioners' needs and perspectives, of which both policymakers and scholars appear woefully ignorant. This essay is a contribution towards a deeper understanding.

While this is a local case study, we can only make sense of its actors in the broader context of neoliberal global capitalism. Working-class cultural participation is limited in Manchester because this reinforces the privileges of a small elite. However, I suggest that the actions of policymakers, funding agencies and theatre managers were shaped not by a calculated and coherent strategy, but by the broader neoliberal context within which they operated. Cultural and educational participation are limited, the role of the state is minimal, and securing recognition for cultural ventures depends on finding recognition within a global marketplace. Both middle- and working-class people have to grapple with these constraints. Nevertheless, 'middle-class people's attempts to sustain their limited privileges are responsible for reproducing social inequality'.[18]

Manchester and culture: the historical perspective

Angels with Manky Faces, like MaD's preceding productions, was firmly rooted in a shared understanding of Mancunian identity. The actors used dialect and slang; reference was made to the city's football teams; and the film scenes were shot in north Manchester's pubs and parks. Even the most critical press review concluded that the play was 'authentic but flawed'.[19] Authenticity is often cited as intrinsic to MaD's appeal, and tends to mean the portrayal of the urban north as socially 'gritty' and emotionally down-to-earth. *City Life* praised MaD's 2007 production, *She's Just Nipped Out for Fags*, as 'another gritty, likeable and hilarious slice of contemporary Mancunian life'.[20] In 2010, Becky Want, a presenter on BBC Radio Manchester, described Rob Lees as one of the city's 'quality writers', whose 'plays are gritty, topical, and, above all, Northern'.[21]

MaD is a self-proclaimed 'working-class' theatre company. MaD's productions adopt a form which Ngugi wa Thiong'o argues 'reflects that centrality of people in history', where the 'community of ordinary men and women and children is the principal actor'. Equal space is given to multiple voices, emphasising the equality of children, women and men. But the perspective is always that of working-class people. The central dramatic device is the characters' transformation from 'a people in themselves, with lives governed by ... local allegiance, to a people *for* themselves, governed by a vision that goes well beyond [these] boundaries.'[22] Usually this transformation results from an encounter with the powerful, whether entrepreneurs bent on regenerating the neighbourhood – and pricing the residents out – as in *Les Puddings Noir*; or lawmakers, as in *ASBO*, which explores the implications of an antisocial behaviour order.

The alignment between 'northern' and working-class culture has never been straightforward. Indeed, during the first half of the twentieth century many northern writers and playwrights were from middle-class backgrounds and wrote from their experience.[23] More recently, Manchester City Council has promoted the city's past as a foundation for Manchester's 'radical history', but ascribes this to northernness rather than to a specific working-class experience of exploitation.[24]

Working-class cultural practitioners, including MaD's founders, draw on a different understanding of the past, one that emphasises class conflict. Mancunian writers and artists made a significant contribution to forging a connection between northern identity and working-class culture. As the world's first industrial city, Manchester moved its workforce into large factories and shops far more quickly than was true in other industrialised areas of the north, such as the textile towns of Lancashire or the West Riding where small workshops remained the norm well into the nineteenth century. As a large conurbation surrounded by small towns with high levels of trade union activity, Manchester became the centre for political conflict, from Peterloo in 1819 to the suffrage rallies of the early twentieth century. The labour movement influenced the city's working-class culture, whether through the Co-operative Movement's guilds and youth movement, the Clarion cycling club or the theatre and reading groups of the Communist Party.[25]

Only a minority of people participated in the labour movement's cultural activities. However, working-class Mancunians were unusually conspicuous as leisure consumers. The city's range of industries and trades meant that workers earned, on average, higher wages than their counterparts in other northern towns and cities, and were less likely to be unemployed.[26] As Davies has shown, the city's large number of music halls, dance halls and cinemas testified to the city's relative prosperity.[27] Young women, recalled Robert Roberts, the son of a Salford shopkeeper, were '[c]reamed, perfumed and powdered … young men in their ever widening "bags" and double-breasted jackets … "jazzed" with the shameless females in those dance halls'.[28] Their leisure activities provided Manchester's workers with the material to craft aspirations that transcended the reality of their workaday world; while these were often more nebulous (or materialistic) than the socialist vision offered by the labour movement – focusing on romance and glamour – they nonetheless provided an alternative world vision to that offered by employers and politicians.[29]

Although the labour movement's cultural influence diminished after the Second World War, the cultural conspicuousness of Manchester's working class grew. Communist agit-prop gave birth to Theatre Workshop, led by Joan Littlewood and the working-class Salfordian folk singer Ewan MacColl. This group found a home in Manchester's Library Theatre during the 1940s before Littlewood moved it to East London in the 1950s. Theatre Workshop was distinguished by its desire to stage scenes from working-class life, and to make use of working-class talent. Among its hits was *A Taste of Honey*, a play written by eighteen-year-old Shelagh Delaney, an office worker from Salford. Delaney's play portrayed the life of a young working-class woman in contemporary Salford and made the point that poverty hadn't gone away, but also that working-class life was culturally rich and vibrant. When Theatre Workshop staged *A Taste of Honey* in 1958, Delaney's play found a niche in the new wave of 'kitchen sink' drama and fiction being produced by writers like John Braine and Alan Sillitoe.[30] At the same time, Manchester's new Granada television studio broadcast programmes about northern – and especially Mancunian – life to a national audience. The station's greatest success was Tony Warren's working-class soap opera, *Coronation Street*, first aired in 1961.

While cultural representations of the post-war working class were not confined to Manchester,[31] the city's artists and writers took a distinctively different approach to many of their contemporaries. Their productions were more overtly oppositional to established, middle-class entertainment. Delaney was provoked to write to challenge 'plays where factory workers come cap in hand and call the boss "Sir"'.[32] The team behind *Coronation Street* was determined to challenge what Derek Granger, one of the programme's first producers, called 'the stock figures in a stock formula – Mr and Mrs Everyman from a sweetly, antiseptic, dehydrated no-class land'.[33] Their protagonists were not the upwardly mobile young men of much kitchen sink drama – many of them were women and few of them wished to escape their working-class background. Characters like Jo in *A Taste of Honey* wanted to rise with their class, not from it. The reasons for these regional distinctions still require analysis, but the high level of women's employment in Manchester, and the labour movement's influence on the city (Delaney's father, like MacColl's, was an active trade unionist) are partially responsible. This historical trajectory is an important legacy on which MaD's founders draw. Lees and Hughes regularly cited Delaney and Warren as role models.

Yet if Manchester offers a proud history of working-class culture on which MaD can draw, this has been shaped by a tension that continues to the present: whether to seek inclusion in existing cultural institutions, or to establish an oppositional culture. As Stephen Yeo has shown, the Edwardian labour movement never fully resolved which approach to take.[34] In the 1950s, Ewan MacColl broke with Theatre Workshop because he feared it was compromising its working-class 'authenticity' to win larger audiences, while Joan Littlewood argued that this was necessary in order to influence, and change, British cultural life.[35] For many northern artists, this debate has become intertwined with geography. As Dave Russell points out, northern England has long been understood as occupying a distinctive space within British culture – but as being distinctly inferior to London.[36] Achieving wide recognition has meant moving to the capital. In the late 1950s, A.J.P. Taylor lamented the loss of a distinctive, northern, radical culture: 'The *Manchester Guardian*,' he wrote in 1957, 'now speaks for the enlightened everywhere, not for Manchester.' Taylor perceptively concluded that 'sooner or later (and I would guess sooner) the *Manchester Guardian* will be printed in London'.[37] Four years later, in 1961, he was proved correct. By that time, Delaney had settled in London. In an interview that reflected an ambivalence shared by many northern writers, she told Ken Russell that Salford was 'like a horrible drug' from which she wanted 'to get away'. At the same time, she 'loved' the 'street life' of the inner city; 'it takes years to build up all those friendships and talking to your neighbours', she said; when one moved away 'it is all lost'.[38]

We shall see that this tension between regional and national recognition continues today. It is at the heart of Manchester Council's cultural policy, which celebrates the local, but only in so far as it helps to establish Manchester within a global network of culturally significant cities. Working-class culture is treated as parochial, while cultural agencies that move around the globe, or can attract global players to them, are celebrated for their cosmopolitanism. While this tension has historical antecedents, it has in fact grown in recent years, because cultural products, just like all other products, increasingly have to compete in a global marketplace. Artistic brilliance has become defined as the rejection of class or regional identity.

Manchester and culture: the current situation

In the late 1980s, after fifteen years of economic decline, Manchester began a redevelopment process centred on the entertainment and leisure industries. In the 1990s these became major employers and attracted students and visitors to the region. In the late 1990s, the city council's ambitions for cultural regeneration grew: cultural participation became a means of overcoming social deprivation. This reflected New Labour policy. In 1997, Tony Blair's Labour government launched New Deal for Communities, which promised a 'holistic set of interventions' within a single neighbourhood, designed to reduce crime rates, enhance the physical environment, increase educational participation, improve health and reduce unemployment. Cultural participation was among the most important of these interventions.[39]

Manchester City Council's ruling Labour Group embraced New Labour's approach. In 1998, Manchester became one of the first local authorities to sign up to New Deal for Communities. In 2002, the council employed private consultants to put together a regeneration plan for north Manchester, which stressed the need to obtain 'private investment' to bring jobs into the area.[40] While economic development was left to the private sector, the public sector focused on increasing social inclusion. In 2002 the council launched its first comprehensive cultural strategy.[41] Manchester's policymakers have repeatedly guaranteed 'to ensure that culture makes the fullest possible contribution to the health, wealth and cohesion of Manchester's many communities'.[42]

This approach has been sustained despite robust challenges to its logic. In 1999, for example, the Department of Culture, Media and Sport commissioned a review of the impact that the arts had on social inclusion. The authors concluded that 'relative to the volume of arts activity taking place in the country's poorest neighbourhoods, the evidence of the contribution it makes to neighbourhood renewal is paltry'.[43] In other words, the impact of cultural participation was negligible, a conclusion also reached by Mark Jayne's examination of Stoke on Trent.[44] Lisa McKenzie's study of Nottingham points out that the neighbourhood-oriented approach of civic regeneration excludes working-class people from fully participating in the life of their city centre. It also removes any incentive for civic cultural institutions to welcome working-class visitors.[45] The assumption that inclusive participation can be confined to deprived districts means that the presence of working-class people in increasingly privatised city centres can become suspect; as Anna Minton points out, working-class Mancunians are routinely surveilled and stopped by police and security officers in the city. Manchester's council has the dubious honour of having implemented more anti-social behaviour orders (ASBOs) than any other local authority. Although most of these are issued as a result of incidents occurring within the recipient's neighbourhood, one of the most common sanctions is to prohibit a recipient from entering Manchester city centre.[46] Cultural 'inclusion', whether at neighbourhood or city level, cannot overcome the problems of economic inequality and may even reinforce them.

The council's cultural strategy distinguished between 'community' and 'global' cultural production in a manner that subtly divided artistic work into two camps. While the city centre was assumed to be the appropriate home for cultural innovators offering 'global excellence',[47] the strategy suggested that 'debates about culture and community become locked into the important but tired story about how to "reach" more people with the city centre's cultural offer'. Instead of bringing its working-class inhabitants into the centre, Manchester would provide their 'communities with real opportunities to develop the cultural offer and build an enhanced sense of neighbourhood identity and pride'.[48] In other words, writers and artists who aimed their work at working-class audiences would need to meet social objectives, such as increased cultural and social inclusion. Meanwhile, cultural entrepreneurs in the city centre would showcase artistic excellence, as in Manchester's biennial International Festival, which was launched in 2007.

The council's distinction between 'community' and 'global' cultural production is based on a highly elitist understanding of cultural excellence. Rarity is intrinsic to this understanding of brilliance; mass participation cannot result in artistic excellence because excellence can intrinsically only belong to a few. As Eleonora Belfiore points out, this assumption shapes the objectives of many arts agencies and arts sponsors as well as civic 'inclusion' strategies. Yet, as she argues, this understanding of artistic excellence excludes many working-class practitioners. It is a socially elite notion of what constitutes 'good' taste.[49] Inherent in cultural policy is the assumption that community or working-class theatre groups will provide social benefits for their participants, but not necessarily aesthetic value.

MaD and cultural conflict: class, city and nation

Like many cultural practitioners, MaD's founders were engaged in a struggle between their desire to produce original, high-quality work, and the pressures imposed by sponsors, policymakers and host institutions.[50] MaD's aspirations conflicted with those of the City Council. Lees and Hughes wished MaD to remain a working-class theatre company but they also wanted to find a central role in their city's cultural life. This included staging their work in a city centre venue. They wanted to encourage working-class cultural participation (as both producers and consumers) but also to attain artistic excellence. It quickly became clear, however, that most of the agencies with whom they dealt shared the assumptions and approach of Manchester Council. Here I outline just three encounters that emphasise how strategies of cultural 'inclusion' actually marginalise working-class cultural production.

In order to secure funding, MaD consistently had to present its objectives as primarily social rather than artistic, and its work as of secondary importance to its social objectives. Manchester's cultural strategy is committed to supporting 'innovation', 'original, new work', and 'creativity'.[51] These aims are shared by the organisers of the city's flagship cultural event, Manchester International Festival.[52] These were also words that Lees and Hughes would use to describe their work. However, they were careful not to use them when applying for funding or sponsorship. Hughes wrote most of the company's funding applications. In 2009, she applied for a grant from the O2 Community Foundation. As Hughes explained to me, 'they want to think they are giving money to poor kiddies – "aaah, the poor children" sort of thing. I'd die if they saw our lot.'[53] In her application, she took care to emphasise the role MaD plays in encouraging the cultural participation of young people in 'areas of high socio-economic deprivation'. The accuracy of Hughes's observation was borne out by 'Anthea' at the O2 Community Foundation, who explained to me why MaD's application had been successful:

> We funded a group like this down in Kent … and it's marvellous, because they get these children and some of them have nothing and they give them a work ethic, a sense of purpose … the plays they put on, well, they aren't very good; some of them are pretty bad; but that's not what matters, really, is it?[54]

Perhaps some community theatre groups would agree – MaD did not. Lees and Hughes felt pressured to invest in a discourse of social exclusion that downplayed the very rich cultural assets of the communities in which they work and glossed over the aesthetic appeal that their work seemed to have for large audiences.

Allocating funds to groups on the basis of 'disadvantage' is a questionable means of encouraging participation. The stigma attached to poverty is powerful: it helps explain why not everyone eligible for means-tested benefits takes them up.[55] This stigma affects children as well as adults. After hearing that Children in Need had awarded MaD a large grant, thirteen-year-old James said, 'I think it's great, because whenever I give money to Children in Need, I'll know I'm really giving it to us.'[56] Like other members of MaD, James was ambivalent about identifying himself with the grateful recipients who appear on the charity's annual televised appeal. He preferred to associate himself with the 'givers', rather than the 'excluded'. Many of MaD's young participants shared Lees and Hughes's knowing attitude towards funders, who they depicted as a naive but necessary group whose priorities had to be respected but not allowed to thwart MaD's ambitions. This proved a very difficult balance to maintain.

This treatment of working-class theatre subtly undermines MaD's claim to be serious cultural producers. The emphasis that policymakers and arts agencies place on cultural 'inclusion' implies that working-class people should step into a cultural framework constructed by powerful others. The Manchester International Festival, for example, promotes local involvement– but the form this takes is dictated by MIF Creative, the Festival's 'creative learning programme'. Local people are invited to participate in a cultural programme which is designed by 'international performers' and practitioners allocated 'artist residencies'. There is no scope for local working-class theatre groups to set the cultural agenda in this top-down model of participation.

The difficulty of producing working-class theatre became even clearer when Lees and Hughes sought to find a venue for their 2010 play, *Thai Brides and Teacakes*. In December 2009, having tried and failed to secure a more central venue, Lees and Hughes asked the management of the Contact Theatre – affiliated to the University of Manchester, on whose campus it is situated – for a meeting to discuss the possibility of performing there. Three months later, none of MaD's emails or phone calls had been returned. Eventually, the Contact offered one date, rather than the five nights MaD proposed – only to withdraw this the following day when an 'international booking' was confirmed. A member of the Contact's staff told me that 'we have this international festival now, you see, we're getting a lot more international artists wanting to come here, and we want to welcome them'.[57] The Contact had invested time and energy into expanding its international profile, in line with the objectives of Manchester Cultural Partnership – the network which delivers the city's cultural strategy and in which the University of Manchester is a key player. The Contact's stated values included the 'development of new artists, audiences and practitioners reaching under served or excluded young people', but this didn't allow for the fact that Manchester's 'excluded young people' might already be cultural producers, requiring a platform for their work.[58] Talent was something that was located outside Manchester.

The Contact was one of several theatres that proved reluctant to host MaD's production. Lees and Hughes were convinced that this reluctance stemmed from the middle-class bias inherent within Manchester's cultural scene. They gave this somewhat abstract class analysis a specific context by focusing their bitterness on the middle-class residents of Chorlton, an area of urban gentrification in south Manchester. A recent sociological survey of Manchester conducted by Mike Savage and others found that Chorlton's residents self-identified as 'bohemian' and 'arty'. They are particularly active in the city's cultural scene, as both producers and consumers.[59] Hughes resented what she interpreted as this group's sense of social superiority, explaining, 'I feel that they look down on you, because if it isn't performed in Chorlton, or it doesn't include them, well, they don't want to know.'[60]

Why didn't these cultural producers and consumers 'want to know' about working-class culture? Although not all of them lived in Chorlton, the dispro-portionately large number who did mean that Mike Savage et al.'s study of the neighbourhood provides valuable insights into their attitudes. This research found that Chorlton's residents valued 'diversity' more than most of Manchester's middle-class inhabitants. However, this commitment to 'diversity' celebrated the global at the expense of the local. Savage et al. identified 'the symbolic importance of London ... as an imagined cosmopolitan space' among many of Manchester's middle-class inhabitants.[61] Celebrations of ethnic and racial diversity sustain middle-class Mancunians' sense of belonging to a global, cosmopolitan city, but social diversity has no such appeal.[62]

The valuing of the global over the local was reflected in the arts world. Local knowledge was not considered important; global identities were. For example, the official Manchester tourist website profiled Contact Theatre's former Artistic Director, Baba Israel, as 'a beatboxing, theatrical New Yorker'.[63] As Savage et al. suggest, 'global cosmopolitan identities [are] asserted on the basis of specific imaginary connections with a leading world city'.[64] MaD's self-declared Mancunian and working-class identity clearly threatened this vision of Manchester as a global player.

There is another, connected reason why middle-class cultural producers did not find MaD appealing. Recent scholarship highlights that the commitment to diversity shown by a fragment of the contemporary middle class does not extend to social mixing.[65] 'It's quite a mixed place', one Chorlton resident told Savage et al.; 'next door he's first violin with the Hallé; over there is a cartographer and a writer ... next door down to that a Hare Krishna and a solicitor.'[66] MaD's own work knowingly played on the limits of this middle-class cosmopolitanism. In Angels with Manky Faces, a talking monkey predicts the future to characters living in Ancoats (a working-class inner-city district) in the 1890s. 'What's that, monkey?' one character asks. 'In one hundred years our dirty slums will be converted into trendy apartments for the up and coming urban creative? Some with Juliet balcony?'[67] At each performance this generated knowing laughter and loud applause: the urban regeneration company Urban Splash had recently used similar wording to advertise apartments in gentrified Ancoats (now called 'New Islington'). MaD presented bohemianism as consumer conformity, and claims to cosmopolitanism as parochial investments in a Londoncentric identity. By contrast, the cast and audiences' shared local knowledge was presented as a valuable asset in a critique of global capitalism: they knew that New Islington was an overpriced former slum.

Underpinning MaD's riffs on middle-class diversity was a more serious message: that such a shared identity could exclude the less economically powerful. 'And what's going to happen to people like us?' one of the characters asks the talking monkey in *Angels*. 'He says we'll be out on our ear!' responds her father, and they kick the invisible prophet off the stage.[68] But in reality, MaD's founders and participants were powerless to silence or displace the city's middle class. Chorlton's bohemians were just as likely as other middle-class residents of Manchester to use what Diane Reay calls 'middle-class practices' to secure and reproduce privilege, for example by seeking to get places for their children at schools they viewed as 'good', or by using their capital to buy homes in districts from which working-class residents were priced out.[69] The result of such practices is not simply to acquire a certain resource, but to exclude others from having that resource; indeed, in neoliberal societies, resources become prized ('valuable', aesthetically 'excellent', or 'good' schools) because they are scarce and have to be competed for.[70]

MaD's experience highlights the danger of social policies that prize diversity over equality. Celebrating diversity does not only fail to resolve economic and social inequality, but can actually legitimate it. As Walter Benn Michaels argues, a 'society in which white people were proportionately represented in the bottom quintile (and black people proportionately represented in the top quintile) would not be more equal', he points out; 'it would be exactly as unequal'.[71] Celebrating difference may offer some, very limited, gains for those discriminated against on the grounds of gender, race or sexuality. But it makes no sense for those at the bottom of the economic pile (who are dispro-portionately female and black). They do not require celebration; they need political and economic change. Groups like MaD are not asking for respect, or for celebration of their difference; they are demanding that the injustices that are meted out to working-class people are recognised and struggled against. Instead, they were marginalised by a cultural sector intent on constraining working-class cultural involvement to participation in localised activities, outside the city centre, which do not question the expertise and authority of policymakers and arts agencies.

Eventually, MaD managed to find a city centre venue: they returned to Oxford Road's Dancehouse. The venue is primarily home to a ballet school and lacks the marketing and publicity machine from which MaD had benefited at the Library Theatre. Nevertheless, MaD performed to packed houses in this 420-seat theatre for two nights, and enjoyed a sell-out performance at Bury's Met Theatre. But the experience of preparing for *Thai Brides and Teacakes* had not been a positive one for either Lees or Hughes. In the summer of 2010 they decided on a policy of what Lees called 'retrenchment'.[72] Having fruitlessly tried to be culturally 'included', they decided that in future MaD would stage its productions at Moston's Simpson Memorial Hall.

New networks

The conclusion to MaD's story offers some hope. MaD's founders and participants were not left without any room for manoeuvre. When Lees and Hughes decided to relinquish their ambition for a city centre presence, they did so in the knowledge that they are part of a Mancunian network of working-class and radical cultural agencies. Most prominent among these was FC United of Manchester.

FC United, like MaD, situates itself in a longer, radical, working-class Mancunian history of collective protest. FC United's social club – Course You Can Malcolm – offers a platform for local bands, poets, writers and actors – including members of MaD. Successive MaD productions have included an 'FC United night' at which fans are offered discounts on theatre tickets; minor alterations to the script allow the inclusion of jokes or anecdotes recognisable to the fans. It was through one of these events that Andrew Davies – himself an FC United fan – initiated the collaboration with MaD that led to *Angels with Manky Faces*.

MaD shares with FC United an understanding of cultural excellence that is different from that of Manchester's policymakers and arts agencies. They value the local over the global, and do not see excellence as existing in tension with mass participation. Both organisations value 'authenticity': the connection of culture to everyday working life. This enables them to critique the economic and political developments in the wider city, and to connect this to a broader critique of capitalism. As Adam Brown points out, FC United's fans explicitly reject the role of consumer, and thus the dominance of the global marketplace, in favour of being active participants in their club. While Manchester United's players may be technically more proficient than FC United's team, the value of this is questioned by fans who place greater value on connections between players and fans than on global repute.[73]

MaD also valued authenticity. Lees used this to criticise the artistic standards of Manchester's middle-class cultural practitioners:

> I used to go to these parties in Chorlton and I couldn't believe it, because every other person would be saying, 'Oh, I'm a poet', 'I'm a potter', 'I'm a photographer'. And I thought, bloody hell, maybe I should move here, there must be a lot of creative people about. But then I went to this one art show – it was crap. And then the woman that's doing it, it turns out, she's like

'I'm an artist, I'm an artist', but they weren't really, they worked in cafés or something.[74]

For Lees and Hughes, much middle-class cultural production was 'rubbish' because it did not derive from the shared, social experience of everyday life. Lees critiqued the 'Chorltonians' for suggesting art was divorced from, and superior to, café work, recognising that in doing so these artists claimed the social and cultural 'distinction' that separates the middle from the working class.[75] While claiming distinction could reinforce their social superiority, however, Lees suggested that it also undermined the aesthetic value of their art, which simply became a statement of their wealth and privilege – albeit a wealth that was deferred while they played at being café workers. By contrast, MaD could lay claim to authenticity – to the ability to imagine a different kind of world in a manner that made sense to very large audiences precisely because it arose from widely shared circumstances. MaD and FC United thus foster a Rancièrian 'politics of aesthetics' that treats culture as being intimately connected to everyday life, yet simultaneously providing a space within which to reimagine that life – 'at once material and symbolic, of a specific space-time, of a suspension with respect to the ordinary forms of sensory experience'.[76]

In September 2011 FC United received planning permission to develop a football ground in Moston, just minutes away from the Simpson Memorial Hall. During the months leading up to this decision, a group of north Manchester artists formed a co-operative and re-opened a former miners' bath house in Moston as an art gallery and community centre. By the time FC United's planning application was approved by Manchester City Council, MaD had established a group at the new Miners' Club, which was attracting interest and support from the local council estate. Lees and Hughes were in talks with FC United about a planned programme of cabaret and drama events at the club and a potentially permanent presence at the new football ground. Within the constraints imposed upon them, they forged a new kind of cultural production and participation.

Conclusion

MaD's story, told here in the context of a longer history of working-class culture, indicates the fallacy of cultural 'inclusion'. Social and cultural 'participation' cannot overcome economic inequality. Indeed they are not meant to: for 'inclusion' and 'participation' are based on a neoliberal 'respect' for 'diversity' which celebrates difference rather than challenging inequality. Culture and class are intimate relations. Working-class culture is a response to exclusion and exploitation, but that response can be hopeful and warm, for the artist can imagine a world different from the present. In doing so, some practitioners draw on a shared understanding of Manchester's history as forged by the resistance of ordinary people to capitalism. Excellence is built on mass participation, which in turn springs from the acknowledgement of shared experience.

Manchester's significance as a historic centre of the labour movement is distinctive in this regard. However, the kinds of working-class organisation identified here are not inevitably limited to Manchester, for they are sustained by the class conflicts that exist across the neoliberal world. Rather than looking for such networks in their 'traditional' home – the labour movement – we may need to scrutinise other sites, including sporting events and community centres, to identify them.

Notes

1 Andrew Davies, *The Gangs of Manchester. The Story of the Scuttlers, Britain's First Youth Cult*.
2 Manchester City Council, *Cultural Strategy*, p. 1.
3 Alfred L. Kroeber and Clyde Kluckhohn approvingly quoted in Peter Burke, *Popular Culture in Early Modern Europe*, p. iv.
4 E.P. Thompson, *Customs in Common*, p. 7.
5 Excellent historical studies of cultural participation include Angela Bartie, 'Culture in the everyday: art and society in twentieth century Scotland' and Claire Langhamer, *Women's Leisure in England, 1920–60*. On cultural inclusion, see Kevin Coffee, 'Cultural inclusion, exclusion and the formative roles of museums' and Mark Jayne, 'Culture that works? Creative industries development in a working-class city'.
6 MaD Theatre Company, 'Our Method.'
7 One hundred questionnaires were distributed and there was an 80 per cent response rate. The numbers are not statistically significant but my conclusions on audience composition are supported by unstructured interviews with three staff at the Manchester Library Theatre.
8 Interview with Rob Lees (13 December 2009). I carried out all interviews. Fieldnotes are in my possession and may be consulted on request.
9 Adam Brown, '"Our club, our rules": fan communities at FC United of Manchester'.
10 George Poulton, 'Cultural participation, the making of distinction and the case of fans of FC United of Manchester', pp. 4–5.
11 Interview with Lees (5 October 2009).
12 History and Policy (website), 'Our philosophy'.
13 Robert Perks and Alistair Thomson (eds), *The Oral History Reader*; Alessandro Portelli, *The Death of Luigi Trastulli and Other Stories*.
14 E.P. Thompson, *The Making of the English Working Class*, p. 8.

15 Pierre Bourdieu, *Distinction: A Social Critique of the Judgement of Taste*, pp. 7–15.
16 Jacques Rancière, *The Politics of Aesthetics*, pp. 23–4, 62.
17 Diane Reay, *Class Work: Mothers' Involvement in their Children's Primary Schooling*; Mike Savage *et al.*, *Globalization and Belonging*; Bourdieu, *Distinction* and Tony Bennett, *Critical Trajectories: Culture, Society, Intellectuals*.
18 Reay, *Class Work*, pp. 30–4.
19 Natalie Anglesey, 'Ambitious Angels is ambitious but flawed'.
20 Kevin Bourke, 'She's Just Nipped Out for Fags @ Library Theatre'.
21 Becky Want, 'Manchester's MaD theatre company'.
22 Ngugi wa Thiong'o, 'Freeing the imagination', pp. 164–5.
23 For example Winifred Holtby, *South Riding: An English Landscape*.
24 Cultural Ambition Steering Group, 'Reframing Manchester's cultural strategy', p. 2.
25 Denis Pye, *Fellowship is Life: The Story of the Clarion Cycling Club*; Declan McHugh, 'A "mass" party frustrated? The development of the Labour Party in Manchester, 1918–31'.
26 Andrew Davies, *Leisure, Gender and Poverty: Working-class Culture in Manchester and Salford, 1900–1939*, pp. 14–17.
27 *Ibid.*, pp. 82–4.
28 Robert Roberts, *The Classic Slum: Salford Life in the First Quarter of the Twentieth Century*, p. 224.
29 Langhamer, *Women's Leisure*, pp. 98–100; Selina Todd, *Young Women, Work, and Family in England, 1918–1950*, pp. 115–17.
30 Shelagh Delaney, *A Taste of Honey*.
31 Stuart Laing, *Representations of Working-class Life, 1957–1964*; Dave Russell, *Looking North: Northern England and the National Imagination*, pp. 1–14.
32 Quoted in Laurence Kitchin, *Mid-century Drama*, p. 168.
33 Quoted in Laing, *Representations of Working-class Life*, p. 51.
34 Stephen Yeo, 'A new life: the religion of socialism in Britain, 1883–1896'.
35 Ewan MacColl, *Journeyman: An Autobiography*, p. 266.
36 Russell, *Looking North*, p. 8.
37 A.J.P. Taylor, 'Manchester', p. 322.
38 Ken Russell, *Shelagh Delaney's Salford*.
39 Geoff Fordham, *New Deal for Communities National Evaluation*, p. 8.
40 Kitty Lymperopoulou and Brian Robson, *New Deal for Communities: National Evaluation Main Phase Report on the Beswick and Openshaw Partnership*, pp. 3 and 8.
41 Manchester City Council, *Cultural Strategy*, p. 2.
42 Cultural Ambition Steering Group, 'Reframing Manchester's cultural strategy', p. 18.
43 Department of Culture, Media and Sport, *Research Report: Arts and Neighbourhood Renewal*, p. 6.

44 Jayne, 'Culture that works?'.

45 Lisa McKenzie, 'The Sociology/Social History of Class' symposium.

46 Anna Minton, *Ground Control: Fear and Happiness in the Twenty-First Century City*, pp. 43, 50–6; Decca Aitkenhead, 'When home's a prison', p. 6.

47 Manchester City Council, *Cultural Strategy*, p. 20.

48 *Ibid.*

49 Eleonora Belfiore, 'Art as a means towards alleviating social exclusion: does it really work? A critique of instrumental cultural policies and social impact studies in the UK', p. 101.

50 Jenny Hughes, 'Ethical cleansing? The process of obtaining "ethical approval" for a new research project exploring performance in place of war', p. 231.

51 Cultural Ambition Steering Group, 'Reframing Manchester's cultural strategy', p. 18.

52 Manchester International Festival (website), 'About us'.

53 Interview with Jill Hughes (2 December 2009).

54 Telephone interview with 'Anthea' (pseudonym) (20 December 2010).

55 McKenzie, 'Sociology/Social History of Class'; Ruth Lister, *Moving Back to the Means Test: A Memorandum to the Chancellor of the Exchequer from the Child Poverty Action Group*.

56 Interview with James Creer (10 June 2010).

57 Telephone conversation with 'Becky' (pseudonym) (10 April 2010).

58 Contact Theatre (website), 'What we do: values'.

59 Savage *et al.*, *Globalization*, p. 120.

60 Interview with Hughes (2 May 2010).

61 Savage *et al.*, *Globalization*, pp. 94–5.

62 Jon Binnie and Beverley Skeggs, 'Cosmopolitan knowledge and the production and consumption of sexualized space: Manchester's gay village'.

63 Visit Manchester (website), 'Meet Contact Theatre's Baba Israel'.

64 Savage *et al.*, *Globalization*, p. 95.

65 *Ibid.*, pp. 42–3; Diane Reay *et al.*, 'Re-invigorating democracy? White middle class identities and comprehensive schooling'.

66 Quoted in Savage *et al.*, *Globalization*, p. 42.

67 Rob Lees and Jill Hughes, *Angels with Manky Faces*.

68 *Ibid.*

69 Savage *et al.*, *Globalization*, pp. 62–4.

70 Reay, *Class Work*, pp. 5–10; Reay *et al.*, 'Re-invigorating democracy?', pp. 248–51.

71 Walter Benn Michaels, 'What matters', p. 11.

72 Interview with Lees (14 June 2010).

73 Brown, '"Our Club, our rules"', pp. 346–7.

74 Interview with Lees (14 June 2010).

75 Bourdieu, *Distinction*.

76 Rancière, *Politics of Aesthetics*, p. 23; see also Thompson, *Customs*, p. 12.

Bibliography

Aitkenhead, Decca, 'When home's a prison', *Guardian*, 24 July 2004, p. 6.

Anglesey, Natalie, 'Ambitious Angels is authentic but flawed', *City Life*, 19 August 2009.

Bartie, Angela, 'Culture in the everyday: art and society in twentieth century Scotland', in Lynn Abrams and Callum G. Brown (eds), *A History of Everyday Life in Twentieth-Century Scotland* (Edinburgh: Edinburgh University Press, 2010).

Belfiore, Eleonora, 'Art as a means towards alleviating social exclusion: does it really work? A critique of instrumental cultural policies and social impact studies in the UK', *International Journal of Cultural Policy*, 8:1 (2002), pp. 91–106.

Bennett, Tony, *Critical Trajectories: Culture, Society, Intellectuals* (Oxford: Blackwell Publishing, 2007).

Binnie, Jon and Beverley Skeggs, 'Cosmopolitan knowledge and the production and consumption of sexualized space: Manchester's gay village', *Sociological Review*, 52:1 (February 2004), pp. 39–61.

Bourdieu, Pierre, *Distinction: A Social Critique of the Judgement of Taste* (London: Routledge, 1986).

Bourke, Kevin, 'She's Just Nipped Out for Fags @ Library Theatre', *City Life* (24 August 2007): http://www.citylife.co.uk/news_and_reviews/news/10010672_she_s_just_nipped_out_for_fags___library_theatre (accessed 19 August 2012).

Brown, Adam, '"Our club, our rules": fan communities at FC United of Manchester', *Soccer and Society*, 9:3 (2008), pp. 346–58.

Burke, Peter, *Popular Culture in Early Modern Europe* (New York: Harper and Row, 1978).

Coffee, Kevin, 'Cultural inclusion, exclusion and the formative roles of museums', *Museum Management and Curatorship*, 23:3 (2008), pp. 261–79.

Contact Theatre (website), 'What we do: values': http://contactmcr.com/about/what-we-do/values/ (accessed 19 August 2012).

Cultural Ambition Steering Group, 'Reframing Manchester's cultural strategy' (2010): http://john-knell.com/resources/Reframing%20Manchester's%20Cultural%20Strategy%20-%20John%20Knell.pdf (accessed 1 June 2011).

Davies, Andrew, *Leisure, Gender and Poverty: Working-class Culture in Manchester and Salford, 1900–1939* (Buckingham: Open University Press, 1992).

Davies, Andrew, *The Gangs of Manchester. The Story of the Scuttlers, Britain's First Youth Cult* (Preston: Milo Books, 2007).

Delaney, Shelagh, *A Taste of Honey* (London: Methuen, 1982).

Department of Culture, Media and Sport, *Research Report: Arts and Neighbourhood Renewal* (London: HMSO, 1999).

Fordham, Geoff, *New Deal for Communities National Evaluation* (London: HMSO, 2010).

History and Policy (website), 'Our philosophy': www.historyandpolicy.org/philosophy.html (accessed 20 May 2011).

Holtby, Winifred, *South Riding: An English Landscape* (London: Collins, 1936).

Hughes, Jenny, 'Ethical cleansing? The process of obtaining "ethical approval" for a new research project exploring performance in place of war', *Research in Drama Education*, 10:2 (2005), pp. 229–32.

Jayne, Mark, 'Culture that works? Creative industries development in a working-class city', *Capital and Class*, 28 (Winter 2004), pp. 199–210.

Kitchin, Laurence, *Mid-century Drama* (London: Collins, 1960).

Laing, Stuart, *Representations of Working-class Life, 1957–1964* (Basingstoke: Macmillan, 1986).

Langhamer, Claire, *Women's Leisure in England, 1920–60* (Manchester: Manchester University Press, 2000).

Lees, Rob and Jill Hughes, *Angels with Manky Faces* (currently unpublished).

Lister, Ruth, *Moving Back to the Means Test: A Memorandum to the Chancellor of the Exchequer from the Child Poverty Action Group* (London: Child Poverty Action Group, 1980).

Lymperopoulou, Kitty and Brian Robson, *New Deal for Communities: National Evaluation Main Phase Report on the Beswick and Openshaw Partnership* (London: OPDM, 2004).

MacColl, Ewan, *Journeyman: An Autobiography* (London: Sidgwick and Jackson, 1990).

McHugh, Declan, 'A "mass" party frustrated? The development of the Labour Party in Manchester, 1918–31', PhD dissertation, University of Salford, 2001.

McKenzie, Lisa, 'The Sociology/Social History of Class' symposium, *Putting Bourdieu to Work on a Council Estate in Nottingham Conference*, University of Manchester, May 2010.

MaD Theatre Company (website), 'Our method': http://www.madtheatrecompany.co.uk/our-method-2/ (accessed 24 July 2012).

Manchester City Council, *Cultural Strategy* (Manchester: Manchester City Council, 2002).

Manchester City Council, *Prosperity for All: The Greater Manchester Strategy* (Manchester: Manchester City Council, 2009).

Manchester City Council, *Manchester's Cultural Ambition: Report for Resolution* (10 March 2010): www.manchester.gov.uk/egov_downloads/CulturalAmbition.pdf (accessed 23 July 2012).

Manchester International Festival (website), 'About us': http://mif.co.uk/about-us/ (accessed 24 July 2012).

Michaels, Walter Benn, 'What matters', *London Review of Books*, 31:16 (27 August 2009), pp. 11–13.

Minton, Anna, *Ground Control: Fear and Happiness in the Twenty-First Century City* (London: Penguin, 2009).

Perks, Robert and Alistair Thomson (eds), *The Oral History Reader* (London: Routledge, 1996).

Portelli, Alessandro, *The Death of Luigi Trastulli and Other Stories* (Albany: State University of New York Press, 1991).

Poulton, George, 'Cultural participation, the making of distinction and the case of fans of FC United of Manchester', *CRESC Working Paper*, 73 (2009).

Pye, Denis, *Fellowship is Life: The Story of the Clarion Cycling Club* (Bolton: Clarion, 1995).

Rancière, Jacques, *The Politics of Aesthetics* (London: Continuum, 2006).

Reay, Diane, *Class Work: Mothers' Involvement in their Children's Primary Schooling* (London: UCL Press, 1998).

Reay, Diane *et al.*, 'Re-invigorating democracy? White middle class identities and comprehensive schooling', *Sociological Review*, 56:2 (2008), pp. 238–55.

Roberts, Robert, *The Classic Slum: Salford Life in the First Quarter of the Twentieth Century* (Harmondsworth: Penguin, 1973).

Russell, Dave, *Looking North: Northern England and the National Imagination* (Manchester: Manchester University Press, 2004).

Russell, Ken, *Shelagh Delaney's Salford* (London: BBC, 1960).

Savage, Mike, Gaynor Bagnall and Brian Longhurst, *Globalization and Belonging* (London: Sage, 2005).

Taylor, A.J.P., 'Manchester', in *Essays in English History* (Harmondsworth: Penguin, 1976).

Thiong'o, Ngugi wa, 'Freeing the imagination', *Transitions*, 100 (1998), pp. 164–5.

Thompson, E.P., *The Making of the English Working Class* (Harmondsworth: Penguin, 1968).

Thompson, E.P., *Customs in Common* (London: Merlin Press, 1991).

Todd, Selina, *Young Women, Work, and Family in England, 1918–1950* (Oxford: Oxford University Press, 2005).

Visit Manchester (website), 'Meet Contact Theatre's Baba Israel': www.visitmanchester.com/articles/video/contact-theatre's-baba-israel/ (accessed 11 April 2011).

Want, Becky, 'Manchester's MaD theatre company': www.bbc.co.uk/blogs/beckywant/2010/09/manchesters_mad_theatre_compan.html (accessed 20 May 2011).

Yeo, Stephen, 'A new life: the religion of socialism in Britain, 1883–1896', *History Workshop Journal*, 4:1 (1977), pp. 5–56.

Index

EU authorised representative for GPSR:
Easy Access System Europe, Mustamäe tee 50,
10621 Tallinn, Estonia
gpsr.requests@easproject.com